Sounds Fascinating

How do you pronounce *biopic, synod*, and *Breughel*? – and why? Do our cake and archaic sound the same? Where does the stress go in *stalagmite*? What's odd about the word *epergne*? *Pontcysyllte* is obviously Welsh, but *Penge* is Welsh too! How cool is *Caol* in the Highlands of Scotland? What can Wesley's hymns tell us about sound change in English? How do people pronounce *Wrocław* in Poland? How can anyone manage to say *Gdynia* as just two syllables? Why is the village of *Frith* in the island of Montserrat usually pronounced as if spelt *Frits*? What embarrassing faux pas in English did a Russian conglomerate make? Should I *bild* a *cubbard* instead of building a cupboard? How should we capitalize an exclamation mark, and why might we need to? What's a depressor consonant? As a finale, the author writes a letter to his 16-year-old self.

J. C. WELLS is Emeritus Professor of Phonetics in the University of London and a Fellow of the British Academy. His interests centre on the phonetic and phonological description of languages but also extend to lexicography and language teaching. For seven years he wrote a daily phonetic blog. Based in Britain at UCL throughout his career, he has lectured in many countries around the world. He enjoys walking, speaking different languages (including Esperanto), singing, and playing the melodeon.

Sounds Fascinating
Further Observations on English Phonetics and Phonology

J. C. WELLS

Emeritus Professor of Phonetics, University College London

Illustrations by Lhinton Davidson

CAMBRIDGE
UNIVERSITY PRESS

CAMBRIDGE
UNIVERSITY PRESS

University Printing House, Cambridge CB2 8BS, United Kingdom

Cambridge University Press is part of the University of Cambridge.

It furthers the University's mission by disseminating knowledge in the pursuit of education, learning, and research at the highest international levels of excellence.

www.cambridge.org
Information on this title: www.cambridge.org/9781107157798

© J. C. Wells 2016

This publication is in copyright. Subject to statutory exception and to the provisions of relevant collective licensing agreements, no reproduction of any part may take place without the written permission of Cambridge University Press.

First published 2016

Printed in the United Kingdom by Clays, St Ives plc

A catalogue record for this publication is available from the British Library.

ISBN 978-1-107-15779-8 Hardback
ISBN 978-1-316-61036-7 Paperback

Cambridge University Press has no responsibility for the persistence or accuracy of URLs for external or third-party Internet Web sites referred to in this publication, and does not guarantee that any content on such Web sites is, or will remain, accurate or appropriate.

Contents

Preface   *page* xi

PART I   WORDS, NAMES, PEOPLE, AND PLACES   1

1 Unusual Words   3
   1.1   Ask Your Gardener   3
   1.2   Zhoosh It Up   3
   1.3   Speleothems   4
   1.4   Netsuke   5
   1.5   Abseiling   7
   1.6   Mayoral Elections   8
   1.7   Keirin   9
   1.8   Biopic   10

2 Food and Drink Words   11
   2.1   Flummery   11
   2.2   Conchology   11
   2.3   Kumquat   12
   2.4   Lychee   13
   2.5   Physalis   15

3 Interesting Words   16
   3.1   Obstruent   16
   3.2   Rowlocking Fun   16
   3.3   Jewellery, Jewelry   17
   3.4   Synod   17
   3.5   Algebraic Ordinals   18
   3.6   Remuneration and Anemones   18
   3.7   Sojourn   19
   3.8   Seismic   19
   3.9   Mandragora   20
   3.10   Quasi-   20
   3.11   Allegedly Aged   21
   3.12   Than   22
   3.13   Ha'p'orth   23
   3.14   Diamond   24
   3.15   Epergne   25

3.16	Antimony	25
3.17	Canine	27
3.18	Met a What?	27
3.19	Stress Changes	28
3.20	Sainthood	29

4 Names — 31
4.1	Israel	31
4.2	Laocoön	31
4.3	Bombardier	32
4.4	Ulysses	33
4.5	Mysterious Derived Forms	34

5 People — 36
5.1	Boris and His Great-Grandfather	36
5.2	Poets and Archangels	36
5.3	Joe Mc-What?	37
5.4	Eugenie	38
5.5	An Archiepiscopal Mnemonic	38
5.6	Coetzee	39
5.7	Breughel	40
5.8	Kim Jong-Un	40
5.9	Voldemort	41

6 Places — 43
6.1	Liverpool Suburbs	43
6.2	An Unwritten Possessive	43
6.3	Pontcysyllte	44
6.4	Bessacarr	45
6.5	Slaugham	45
6.6	Arnos Grove	46
6.7	Caol	46
6.8	English Places	46
6.9	Where Was That Again?	48
6.10	Penge	49
6.11	Machynlleth	50
6.12	Acres	50
6.13	Beguildy	51

7 Abroad — 52
7.1	Sichuan	52
7.2	L'Aquila	52
7.3	Rock Law	53
7.4	Duisburg	53

8 Home from Abroad — 55
8.1	Agrément	55
8.2	An Italian Wine	55

	8.3	Ginkgo	56
	8.4	Liebestod	57
	8.5	Women's Tennis	58
	8.6	Raw Fish	59
	8.7	A Heavenly Haven	60
	8.8	Muchas Gratsias	60
	8.9	The Letter *z*	60
	8.10	Greek Politics	62
PART II	SOUNDS AND LETTERS		63
9	**Allophones**	65
	9.1	Mysteries of Existence	65
	9.2	ʔ ≠ 0	66
	9.3	Is Our Cake Archaic?	66
	9.4	Bedroom Wardrobe	67
	9.5	Incomplete? Unreleased?	69
10	**Phonetic Processes**	73
	10.1	But...	73
	10.2	Spinach Sandwiches	73
	10.3	Corn Beef and Fry Rice	75
	10.4	The Irish Sea	76
	10.5	Aitches	77
	10.6	Nonfinal Syllabic Consonants	77
	10.7	Classical Elision	80
	10.8	Initial Clusters	82
	10.9	I Must Haplologize	83
11	**Spelling**	85
	11.1	Phrasebooks	85
	11.2	Spanish Phonetics for the Layman	86
	11.3	Going Awry	87
	11.4	Yoo-Hoo	88
	11.5	Habeas Corpus	89
	11.6	Curly or Kicking?	89
	11.7	A Spelling-Based Faux Pas	90
	11.8	Sh!	90
	11.9	*rh* and *rrh*	91
	11.10	Prusiking Around	92
	11.11	The Digraph *zh*	93
	11.12	Speech and Writing	94
	11.13	Pronunciation and Spelling	95
	11.14	Latin Double Velars	96
	11.15	Bilding a Cubbard	97
	11.16	Stenotypy	98
	11.17	Final *mb* and *mn*	99

	11.18	Keeping Shtoom	100
	11.19	Faustian	101
	11.20	Digraphs in the Alphabet	102
	11.21	English Spelling: What Should We Do?	103
	11.22	Romeo Papa	104
	11.23	Going Up	105
	11.24	Family Words	106
	11.25	Casing Clicks	107
12	**Transcription**		**108**
	12.1	Explicitness in Transcription	108
	12.2	Syllabic Plosives	109
	12.3	happY Again	109
	12.4	False Alarm	111
	12.5	Ram's Horn and Gamma	114
	12.6	Constraints on Diacritics	115
	12.7	Ban Legacy Fonts!	116
	12.8	What [a] Means	118
	12.9	Old Nonsense	120

PART III APPLYING PHONETICS 123

13	**Classification**		**125**
	13.1	Fricative or Approximant?	125
	13.2	VOT Is That?	126
	13.3	Labiodentals	128
	13.4	Unreleased	128
	13.5	Implosives and Ejectives	130
	13.6	Guttural	133
	13.7	Trilling	134
	13.8	Ooh!	135
	13.9	A Multiplicity of Schwas	136
	13.10	A Controlled Rolling Grunt	137
	13.11	Initial ŋ	138
	13.12	The Palatal Nasal	139
	13.13	Lateral Fricatives	140
	13.14	Russian ж	142
	13.15	Depressors	143
	13.16	Gdynia Unmasked	145
	13.17	Breathiness	147
	13.18	Tap, Tap	147
	13.19	Voicing Basics	149
14	**EFL**		**151**
	14.1	Institutionalized Mispronunciations	151
	14.2	English **r**	151
	14.3	Ask Your Favour	152
	14.4	Buttressing?	152

			Contents	ix

	14.5	English 3	153
	14.6	French/English Interference	154
	14.7	Southern Country	155

15	**Accents**		157
	15.1	Shadow of Death	157
	15.2	An Epiphany	157
	15.3	Kerry, Carrie, and Carey	158
	15.4	*-ing*	159
	15.5	Fronted GOOSE	160
	15.6	The Quality of SQUARE	161
	15.7	The Poet and the Phonetician	162
	15.8	Fair's Fur	163
	15.9	Going on Twur	164
	15.10	Double Affricates	164
	15.11	EE RIP	165
	15.12	A Four-Letter Word	168
	15.13	Bajans	168
	15.14	A Jamaican Allophone	169
	15.15	He Nar Get None	170
	15.16	*Bawl* and *Ball*	171

16	**Lexical Stress**		173
	16.1	Prevalence	173
	16.2	Europeans and Shakespeareans	174
	16.3	Tautonyms	175

17	**Connected Speech**		177
	17.1	Accenting the Unaccentable	177
	17.2	Irritating Hamburgers	179
	17.3	Impressed?	180
	17.4	You Would Say That!	181
	17.5	Open Wide, Please	182

18	**Texts in Transcription**		184
	18.1	ə bɔːltɪk kruːz	184
	18.2	ædɪŋ ˈstres	184
	18.3	ɪn ðə pʌb	186
	18.4	kænədər ən əlæskə	187
	18.5	strəʊk	188

PART IV	ROUNDUP		189

19	**Rhetoric**		191
	19.1	Presentation Techniques	191
	19.2	I Can't Help It: It's Just the Way I Am	192
	19.3	Sound Advice	192

20	**Language Mosaic**		194
	20.1 Ndjuka		194
	20.2 As We Were		194
	20.3 Miscellanea		199
	20.4 Vowel Colour		200
	20.5 False Friends		201
	20.6 Polish Spoken Here		202
21	**Postscript**		204
	21.1 Skills Now Useless		204
	21.2 Memory		205
	21.3 Letter to My 16-Year-Old Self		206

Index of Words 208
General Index 210

Preface

The success of my book *Sounds Interesting* (Cambridge University Press 2014) encourages me to offer a further similar volume. Like its predecessor, *Sounds Fascinating* is mainly a compilation from the phonetic blog I wrote over the years following my retirement.

I've assumed that the reader is familiar with basic phonetic concepts and with the International Phonetic Alphabet. If you're not quite up to speed on the IPA, please consult the *IPA Handbook* (Cambridge University Press 1999) and the IPA chart (www.internationalphoneticassociation.org). To brush up on theory, there are various textbooks available. I particularly recommend *Practical Phonetics and Phonology* by Beverley S. Collins and Inger M. Mees (Routledge 2013, 3rd edition). Wikipedia is a useful and generally reliable guide, particularly since Peter Roach took the phonetics entries in hand. You may wish to refer to my own works: *Accents of English* (Cambridge University Press 1982, three volumes), *Longman Pronunciation Dictionary* (Pearson Education 2008, 3rd edition – referenced below as LPD) and *English Intonation: an Introduction* (Cambridge University Press 2006).

In this book I put phonetic symbols in **bold**, without slashes or brackets unless it is relevant at that point to distinguish phonemes (in slashes //) from allophones or general-phonetic sound-types (in square brackets []). Note that in my IPA transcription of English I use the symbol **e** for the DRESS vowel, **aʊ** for the MOUTH vowel, and **eə** for the SQUARE vowel.

To indicate letters as opposed to sounds, I use italics.

The prosodic conventions I use are a vertical stroke (|) to show an intonation phrase boundary, underlining to show the location of the nuclear (tonic) syllable, and the marks \, /, and V to show a fall, a rise, and a fall-rise, respectively. For fuller discussion see *Sounds Interesting*, 4.1–2.

Words written in capitals, e.g. DRESS, are keywords standing for the entire lexical set of words containing the vowel in question: see my *Accents of English*, chapter 2.2, or the Wikipedia article on 'lexical set'.

I hope this further collection inspires readers to explore traditional general phonetics and make their own observations on how both English and other languages are pronounced. There's always something new to be heard.

PART I

Words, Names, People, and Places

1 Unusual Words

1.1 Ask Your Gardener

In my garden I have a *choisya* – an attractive low-maintenance flowering shrub of Mexican origin. Following my parents' example, I have always called it a ˈtʃɔɪsiə. Apparently most people call it a Mexican orange.

Its botanic name *Choisya* is not in any of our pronunciation dictionaries. The OED, however, gives it as either ˈtʃɔɪziə or (don't laugh) ˈʃwɑːziə, the latter recalling the name of the Swiss botanist after whom it is named, Jacques Denys Choisy ʃwazi (1799–1859).

Uncertainty and variability seem to be the norm for many botanical names in English. Their spelling is fixed (on the whole), but their pronunciation is either arbitrary or variable.

We all call a *fuchsia* plant a ˈfjuːʃə, even though it is named after the German botanist Leonhard Fuchs fʊks and might well therefore have been ˈfʊksiə (but isn't). The *dahlia* is named after the Swedish botanist Anders Dahl dɑːl, but we Brits call it a ˈdeɪliə and the Americans a ˈdæljə (or ˈdɑːljə, the swots).

I grew up calling *weigela* wɪˈdʒiːliə, and wrongly imagined it to be spelt correspondingly as *wigelia*. In fact it is named after Christian Ehrenfried Weigel ˈvaɪɡl̩; in LPD I now recommend waɪˈdʒiːlə, while also mentioning several other possibilities.

Most florists seem to call *gypsophila* ˌdʒɪpsəˈfɪliə, though it 'ought' to be dʒɪpˈsɒfɪlə.

Let's not even think about *eschscholzia*.

1.2 Zhoosh It Up

There's a word we can agree neither how to spell nor how to pronounce: but let's list it as ʒʊʒ *zhoozh*, as in *to zhoozh something up*, meaning to make more attractive, smarter, more exciting, to jazz it up.

The OED gives only the pronunciations ʒʊʃ and ʒuːʃ and the spellings *zhoosh* and *zhush*. But I think that many, perhaps most, of the people who use this word pronounce it with a final voiced consonant, ʒ. And I am not sure that I have ever heard it pronounced with uː rather than ʊ. I think the usual pronunciation is indeed ʒʊʒ, which twice violates the usual phonotactic constraints on ʒ, a consonant usually confined in English to intervocalic position, as in *pleasure* ˈpleʒə – the phoneme ʒ doesn't normally appear at the beginning of a word, or indeed at the end of a word after a short vowel. The Wikipedia article on Polari confirms my opinion, saying that 'the word begins and ends with the same phoneme, the "zh" sound as in the word "measure"'.

Although I have heard other people use this word, it is not one I would actively use myself. Stylistically it strikes me as not just slang but camp slang (and I may be gay but I have never been camp). Indeed, the OED's first citation (1977) is from *Gay News*, from a sentence which is written entirely in Polari, and which reads like a quote from Julian and Sandy in *Round the Horne*.

> As feely homies ... we would zhoosh our riahs, powder our eeks, climb into our bona new drag, don our batts and troll off to some bona bijou bar.

In 2003, W. Stephen Gilbert commented that:

> you might zhush up a tired salad by adding some garnish, or stick some zhush in an article for the Guardian by adding a couple of dubious jokes.

Sorry I didn't pick this word up in time to make it into the third edition of LPD.

1.3 Speleothems

On a visit to Barbados I learnt a new word, *speleothem* ˈspiːliəʊθem. It refers to any underground rock formation, more precisely to 'secondary mineral deposits formed from water in caves'. Examples include stalactites and stalagmites. According to the OED, this word was coined (from Greek) as recently as 1952.

On the island we visited an impressive series of limestone caverns, Harrison's Cave, which has only recently been developed as a tourist attraction. You are driven around underground in a 'tram' (a train of wagons pulled by a tractor) through tunnels and caverns full of stalactites, stalagmites, and other, um, speleothems. It was somewhat reminiscent of Postojna in Slovenia, and is well worth a visit.

I was struck by the fact that our guide, presumably a native Barbadian, pronounced stəˈlæktaɪt and stəˈlægmaɪt (or with stæ-). The usual British pronunciations, I think, are ˈstæləktaɪt and ˈstæləgmaɪt. I don't think I have ever heard penultimate stress in these words in BrE (British English), though apparently that is the stressing that some Americans use.

My correspondents have come up with various mnemonics to help remember which is which, stalactite or stalagmite. Stalac*tites* cling *tight*ly to the ceiling, while stalag*mites might* one day reach it. Or stalagmites, with a G, grow from the ground. And a stalac*t*ite has the shape of a capital T.

I do wonder, by the way, why the last syllable of name of the island, bɑːˈbeɪdɒs (or the like), is usually pronounced in BrE with a short vowel and voiceless fricative, like *doss*. In comparable words such as *tornado, desperado, avocado, torpedo* we pluralize in the usual way with z and retain long əʊ, like *doze*. But we Brits treat *Barbados* like *chaos* and *ethos*.

1.4 Netsuke

     A correspondent asked why *netsuke* is conventionally pronounced as if spelt *netski*. Why is a vowel that is present in the Japanese-derived spelling completely elided (even in careful speech) in English?

    If you're not sure what a netsuke (根付) is, there's a helpful explanation in Wikipedia.

    The LPD entry for *netsuke* reads

  ˈ**net ski** -skeɪ; ˈnets ʊk i, -eɪ – *Jp* [ne ˌtsu̥ ke]

    My decision to prioritize ˈ**net ski** was based on what I have heard antiques experts say on television. I see that the Cambridge English Pronouncing

Dictionary (CEPD) prioritizes the **-skeɪ** variant, but its authors and I agree that the most common pronunciation in English has only two syllables.

Why is this? It's because of the way the Japanese pronounce the word. The vowel is not 'present' in the phonetic sense in Japanese, even though it may be there phonologically. High vowels in Japanese are normally elided between voiceless consonants.

So this is an instance of the English spelling being a transcription of the Japanese orthography/phonology, while the pronunciation reflects a surprisingly sophisticated awareness of the Japanese pronunciation – a situation which is unusual. After all we don't write *a certain je ne sais quoi* while making a point of saying ʒən sɛ kwa *je n' sais quoi* as the French do. Possibly the snobbery surrounding antiques helps to reinforce this counter-intuitive pronunciation as a kind of shibboleth, as with stereotypically aristocratic names like *Cholmondeley* and *Althorp*.

It's not clear how we should best transcribe these elidable Japanese vowels. Which is best, **ne ˌtsɯ ke, ne ˌtsu̥ ke,** or **ne ts ke**? There's a certain amount of regional and gender variation, but as I understand it, the first represents a theoretical pronunciation that you might get if you asked a Japanese speaker to say the word very slowly and carefully, indicating the identity of each mora in turn. The second is still slow and careful. The third is the ordinary pronunciation.

Where an **i** or an **ɯ** is devoiced/elided in this way it may still leave a trace in the form of a secondary articulation on the preceding consonant, making /k/ [kʲ] in /ki/ and [kᵚ] in /ku/. (See Section 12.2.)

In the simple Japanese question これはなんですか *kore wa nan desu ka* 'what's this?' the last two words are typically pronounced not **desɯka**, not **desu̥ka**, but (to my ear at least) just **deska**.

Anyhow, the antiques dealers have clearly based their English pronunciation on the Japanese spoken form, not on the written romaji.

1.5 Abseiling

My uncle Gilbert was not only a marathoner but also a keen climber, and I suppose it is from him that I must have learnt the verb *abseil* (OED: 'to descend a rock face or other near-vertical surface using a rope fixed at a higher point and coiled round the body or passed through a descendeur, the speed of descent being controlled by the rope's friction'.)

He pronounced this word ˈæbseɪl; so do I, and so do most of the people I have heard use the term. It stopped being a mountaineers' technical term and entered general usage when people started abseiling not only down mountains but also down the outside of buildings, for charity, for fun, or in protest.

The etymology of the word is straightforwardly German: the neuter noun *Seil* means 'rope' or 'cable', and its derivative *abseilen* means 'to lower (something, or oneself) on a rope', hence 'to abseil (down)', and also, figuratively, 'to skedaddle'. No doubt it was borrowed into English by the early pioneers of mountain climbing in the Swiss Alps.

The German pronunciation is **zail,** ˈ**apzailən**. The German spelling *ei* regularly corresponds to the sound **ai** (or however you choose to write this German diphthong).

So why, despite this, does our prevailing pronunciation have **eɪ**? It could easily be accounted for as a spelling pronunciation – compare *eight, rein, veil, vein*, etc. On the other hand, in native English words the spelling *ei* can correspond not only to **eɪ** but also to **aɪ** (*eider, height, kaleidoscope*) and **iː** (*ceiling, deceive, Keith, seize*). As we all know, *either* and *neither* can go either way.

All other German loanwords with *ei*, as far as I can see, have English **aɪ**, as *Eiger, eigenvalue, Einstein, Freiburg, Geiger, gneiss, Holbein, Leipzig, Weimar, Zeiss, zeitgeist*. What is special about *abseil*?

I think the explanation must be contamination from *sail*, even though abseiling has nothing to do with sails. (It seems improbable that its long obsolete homophone *sale* 'rope for tying up cattle' could have had any influence.)

According to LDOCE, *abseil* is BrE only, the AmE (American English) equivalent being *rappel* **ræˈpel, rə-**. The OED, on the other hand, defines the two terms slightly differently, rappelling involving a doubled rope but abseiling just 'a rope'.

1.6 Mayoral Elections

A well-known British television presenter introduced an item on the topic of London's meɪˈɔːrəl election, only to segue immediately into calling it the ˈmeərəl election.

There's a well-known disagreement about how we pronounce the stem from which the adjective *mayoral* is derived, namely the noun *mayor*. In the United Kingdom (or in England, at least), we generally pronounce it as a homophone of *mare*. This makes it monosyllabic, with the SQUARE vowel, thus **meə** (or some might prefer to write **mɛː**). In the United States, on the other hand, *mayor* is commonly disyllabic and rhymes with *player*, thus ˈmeɪɚ; though you do also get a monosyllabic variant **mer** (i.e. a homophone of *mare*), particularly when immediately followed by a proper name.

The OED offers a lengthy historical discussion of the pronunciation of the word. The nub is that:

> A disyllabic pronunciation existed in Middle English, where it was a variant of a more common monosyllabic one … The disyllabic pronunciation survived in Britain at least into the 17th cent. … as one possible

pronunciation, but other sources of similar date show that this was by then highly conservative in British usage. In North America, however, disyllabic pronunciations appear to have remained current in all periods.

I've sometimes wondered whether *Mare* Street in Hackney in northeast London ought really to be spelt *Mayor* Street. Disappointingly, though, it appears that the name has a quite different origin, and comes from an old word *mere* or *meer* meaning 'boundary'.

Back to *mayoral*.

- In LPD I give the main BrE pronunciation as ˈmeərəl, with an alterative meɪˈɔːrəl. For AmE I give just ˈmeɪərəl. (With hindsight, I ought to have included AmE meɪˈɔːrəl too, perhaps even as the main AmE form.)
- CPD/EPD, 18th edition, gives BrE ˈmeərəl, AmE ˈmeɪɔːrəl. The editor tells me that both ˈmeɪɔːrəl and meɪˈɔːrəl ought to be included as AmE possibilities.
- OPD and the online OED give BrE ˈmɛːrəl, AmE meɪˈɔːrəl, ˈmeɪərəl.
- My main American reference dictionary, Webster's Collegiate, 11th edition, gives three pronunciations, the equivalent in IPA of ˈmeɪərəl, ˈmerəl, meɪˈɔːrəl.
- The online resource Forvo has BrE ˈmeərəl, AmE meɪˈɔːrəl.

Time for a survey, perhaps; but even a preference poll isn't going to reveal inconsistent usage like that of the newscaster who sparked my curiosity.

1.7 Keirin

A new word I learnt from the London Olympics was *keirin*, one of the forms of cycle racing. Everyone on British TV seems to call it ˈkeɪrɪn (though one correspondent told me 'the *keiren* event was usually pronounced ˈkɪərən in my experience'). This is phonetically interesting, because in BrE we normally get the sequence **eɪr** only across a morpheme boundary, as in *play#room, hay#ride, day-release, way round*. Within a morpheme, historical FACE plus **r** plus a vowel normally develops into **eər**, as in *Mary, various, sharing*. The only similar case I can think of is *Beirut*, which sometimes has **eə**. sometimes **eɪ**. Anyhow, we pronounce *keirin* as if it were spelt *kay-rin* or *K-rin*.

I find that the word is actually borrowed from Japanese 競輪, or in kana ケイリン, *keirin, keerin*. (In Japanese the diphthong *ei* and the long monophthong *ee* are not distinct.) The OED, which dates the word to as long ago as 1957, gives an alternative pronunciation with final stress, keɪˈrɪn. In Japanese the word is accentless.

My correspondent's version looks as if it could have been influenced by the Irish-derived man's name *Ciarán* or *Kieran*, which is regularly ˈkɪərən.

1.8 Biopic

I noticed an interesting misinterpretation of spelling from a television quizmaster. He referred to a certain film (movie) as a **baɪˈɒpɪk**, that is a *biopic*, a film about someone's life, a filmed biography. It is, of course, normally called a **ˈbaɪə(ʊ)pɪk**, being composed of *bio-* plus *-pic(ture)*.

Given *bionic* **baɪˈɒnɪk** and *myopic* **maɪˈɒpɪk** 'short-sighted', you can understand how he came to pronounce the word this way. After all, *biopic* looks as if it contains the suffix *-ic*, which regularly throws the word stress onto the preceding syllable.

This word thus joins a list that includes being *misled* (**ˈmɪzld** instead of **ˌmɪsˈled**) and items such as the *seabed* **siːbd** at the bottom of the ocean, *infrared* **ɪnˈfreəd** rays, *inclement* **ˈɪŋklmənt** weather, and (my favourite) *sundried* **ˈsʌndrɪd** tomatoes (see Section 11.3).

2 Food and Drink Words

2.1 Flummery

The cartoonist Steve Bell had a strip in the Guardian in which he shows the Queen saying, 'One does so enjoy a spot of flummery, does one not?'.

Flummery ˈflʌm(ə)ri is one of the very few words which English has borrowed from Welsh. It comes from *llymru* ˈɬəmri and originally, both in Welsh and English, denoted a kind of porridge. Its earlier etymology is unknown. In English it acquired in time its present meaning 'flattery, humbug, meaningless trappings'. It's interesting that *flummery* diversified in this way, while *porridge* has widened its meaning quite differently, coming to mean 'jail time, period of imprisonment'.

The initial consonant in Welsh *llymru* is of course ɬ, the voiceless alveolar lateral fricative, a sound we don't have in English (*Sounds Interesting*, Section 7.4). As with the name of Shakespeare's stereotypical Welshman *Fluellen* (Llewelyn) and in the *Floyd* variant of *Lloyd* (Welsh *llwyd* 'grey'), the English **fl** captures the distinctive phonetic components of ɬ, while spreading them out over two separate successive segments, the first voiceless and fricative, the second alveolar and lateral. Our modern lame English attempts at ɬ, namely xl and θl, and the ʃl that South Africans sometimes use in *Hluhluwe* (Zulu ɬuˈɬuːwe) all exemplify the same tactic.

2.2 Conchology

As I'm sure you know, a conch is a mollusc, namely a kind of large saltwater snail or its shell. Not only is it edible, its shell can be used as a sort of trumpet (as blown by Triton).

In William Golding's *Lord of the Flies*, a conch shell is used to call the boys together, and at meetings is held by whoever is speaking, as a symbol of democracy and order.

Anyhow, when I was at school we called it a **kɒŋk**. Pronouncing it with final **k** marks the word as being of Greek origin: its immediate Latin source *concha* is taken from Greek κόγχη *kongkhē*. (In Greek and Latin it seems to have referred primarily to a mussel rather than to anything larger, but no matter.)

However, some people pronounce the word **kɒn(t)ʃ**, which presumably originated as a spelling pronunciation (though the OED thinks it may be the earlier form, having come in via French).

In words spelt with final *ch* there is an interesting interaction between pronunciation and spelling. If the sound is **tʃ**, we form the plural by adding *-es*, as in *churches, touches, inches*. But if it is **k** we add just *-s*, as in *monarchs, epochs, matriarchs, triptychs*.

So those of us who say **kɒŋk, kɒŋks** logically spell the plural *conchs*. Those who say **kɒn(t)ʃ, ˈkɒn(t)ʃɪz** spell it *conches*.

West Indians, for many of whom *conch* is an everyday word, pronounce it with final **k** (though in some islands the conch is known instead by the alternative name *lambie*).

On a Caribbean recipe webpage I found a recipe for CURRIED LAMBIE/CONCHS. The spelling tells you how the author of the recipe pronounces the name of the main ingredient.

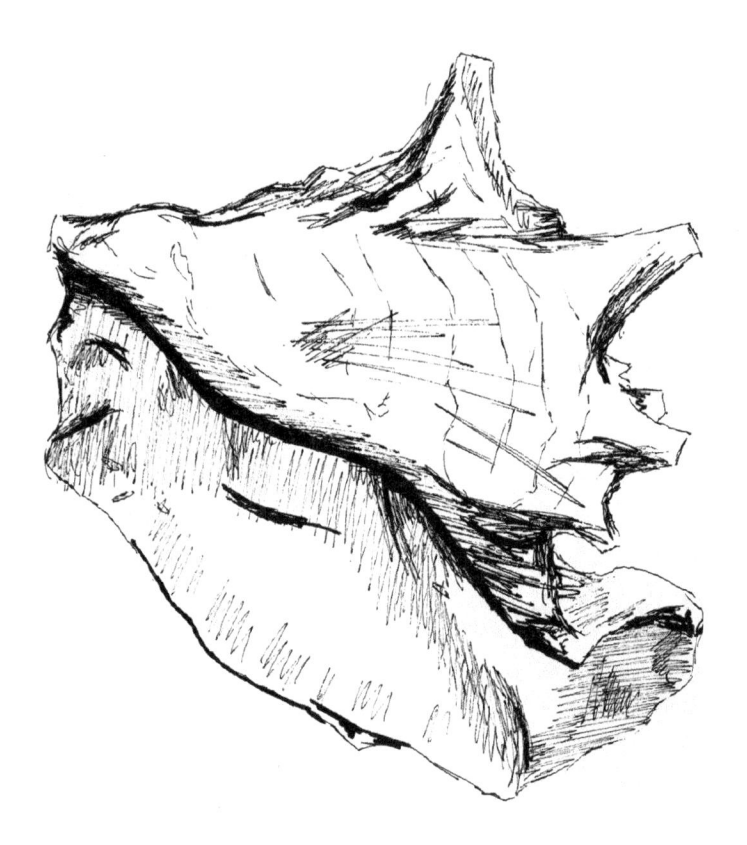

2.3 Kumquat

My local supermarket now sells kumquats. I like to slice these tiny citrus fruits whole and add them to salads.

But how do we pronounce the name? Personally, I say **ˈkʌmkwɒt**. Probably most speakers of English do the same. The word comes to us from Cantonese, where it is pronounced **k⁼ɐm k⁼wɐt** (with tone 1, high level, on each syllable).

Cantonese ɐ sounds like English ʌ, so it makes sense to map it accordingly, giving the English word a first syllable **kʌm**, which we logically spell *kum* or *cum*.

I've heard one or two people, though, pronounce the first syllable **kʊm** instead of **kʌm**. This must be a kind of spelling pronunciation, springing from the false idea that short *u* in foreign words ought to be pronounced ʊ. We tend to get the same thing in *Punjab, feng shui*, and *Cymru* (*Sounds Interesting*, Section 1.21).

I'm sticking with a first syllable that sounds identical to *come*.

2.4 Lychee

When I was a child the range of fruit and vegetables available in the shops was very limited compared with what is on offer today. Mostly, they were just those that grow in Britain – apples, pears, raspberries, redcurrants, blackcurrants, plums, cherries, blackberries, gooseberries; carrots, peas, cabbage, marrows, onions, leeks, turnips, and broad and runner beans. I think the only exotics ordinary people were familiar with were oranges, lemons, bananas and melons, and during the war and the post-war austerity even they were not to be had.

It wasn't until I was studying for my master's in London that I first tasted a green pepper or discovered that marrows picked early can be eaten as courgettes (AmE zucchini). I didn't discover aubergines (AmE eggplant) until 1960 when

I first visited Greece. I think I first ate a mango in 1966 when I visited Jamaica for my PhD fieldwork.

In the late fifties, when I was an undergraduate in Cambridge, we sometimes had a meal in an Indian restaurant. So I had probably eaten cooked aubergine, under the name brinjal, but without knowing what it looked like as a raw vegetable.

As undergrads we also sometimes ate in Chinese restaurants. There, for dessert, we often chose lychees. These were certainly tinned; the actual fruits wouldn't have become available in British supermarkets until thirty or forty years later.

We called this fruit a ˌlaɪˈtʃiː, or perhaps ˈlaɪtʃiː. It was written on the menu as *lychee*. This spelling, and the pronunciation with **aɪ** in the first syllable, are also what you find in Daniel Jones's EPD. When the time came to compile LPD, I recorded this word in line with my own usage and DJ's, with the spelling *lychee* and a main pronunciation ˌlaɪˈtʃiː. I'm aware, though, that some people pronounce the first syllable with **i:** rather than **aɪ**, and some people spell it *litchi*.

What about AmE? I note that Webster's Collegiate prefers the spelling *lychee*, and gives both ˈliː- and ˈlaɪ- as possible pronunciations.

The OED, however, spells the word *litchi* and gives only the pronunciation ˈliːtʃiː. This corresponds well to the Linnaean name of the tree that bears the fruit, *Litchi chinensis*. The French name, too, is indeed *litchi*, and the German name *Litschi*.

The OED doesn't make much of an effort about the word's etymology, saying just:

> Etymology: < Chinese *li-chi*. First used as a generic name in P. Sonnerat *Voyage aux Indes Orientales* (1782) III. 255.

Research shows that the Mandarin name is 荔枝, which would nowadays be written (in Pinyin) as *lìzhī*.

So where does the prevailing, or at least widespread, British pronunciation with **aɪ** come from? Is it just a spelling pronunciation, an English misinterpretation of the ambiguous *y* or *i* of the spelling?

Not necessarily. Further research reveals the interesting fact that the Japanese name of the fruit is not the **riichi* that you might expect, but *reishi*.

Apparently the Japanese name comes not from Mandarin but from Cantonese, where the pronunciation would be romanized as *lai⁶ji¹*. Here is a ready explanation of our English pronunciation ˌlaɪˈtʃiː. Our forebears must have become acquainted with the fruit, and its local name, through contacts with the Cantonese-speaking former British colony of Hong Kong. Chinese restaurants established in the United Kingdom by immigrants from Hong Kong would have introduced us to the fruit together with its Cantonese name.

Perhaps our colonial contacts with Malaya (now Malaysia) also played a role: the name of the fruit in Malay is *laici* ˈlaɪtʃi.

2.5 Physalis

As I wander round the fruit-and-veg aisles in my local supermarket, I know how to pronounce most of the stuff on offer. I know about *mooli* (a word we have borrowed from Hindi; I even know that in AmE this sort of big white radish is called by its Japanese name *daikon*), I know about *kumquats*.

One of the fruit I buy from time to time is *physalis* (aka Cape Gooseberry, I'm told). But I really don't know how people pronounce it. I say it to myself as **faɪˈseɪlɪs**, and that's what I put in LPD.

One correspondent tells me he makes it rhyme with the comparably spelt *chrysalis* ˈ**krɪsəlɪs**, which seems reasonable. The OED gives us a whole range of possibilities: ˈ**faɪs-,** ˈ**fɪs-, faɪˈseɪl-** or **faɪˈsæl-**.

So it's one of those scientific terms on whose spelling we agree, but on whose pronunciation there is no agreement. (See *Sounds Interesting*, Section 1.17.)

For what it's worth, the Greek etymon, φυσαλλίς 'bladder', has a long upsilon. But you only have to consider *dynamo, dynamic*, and *hyper-* (all with short upsilon) to see that Greek vowel length is no predictor of the English vowel length.

Interestingly, the Greek word also has double lambda, so that the word 'ought' to be *physallis*, which would no doubt have penultimate stress and **æ**.

I wonder what the supermarket produce buyers call it. Or, for that matter, the farmers who grow it, who according to the label are Colombian. When I visited Ecuador I noticed that there it was labelled *uvilla*, but I am told that in Colombia it is called *uchuva*.

3 Interesting Words

3.1 Obstruent

A correspondent asked about the place of the main stress in the word *obstruent*, the phonetic cover term for plosives, fricatives, and affricates. He had a colleague who pronounced it with stress on the penultimate, thus əbˈstruːənt. I share his surprise. I have never heard anything but initial stress for this word, thus ˈɒbstruənt.

All other English words ending in *-uent* have antepenultimate stress for most speakers: *affluent, effluent, congruent, constituent*. However, some Americans do say *conˈgruent* with penultimate stress, and a few do the same with *affluent* and *effluent*, But I don't think anyone ever says *constiˈtuent*.

Words with other vowel stems plus *-ant* or *-ent* include *brilliant, radiant, valiant, variant, gradient, lenient, prurient*. They all have initial stress. On the other hand *compliant* and *defiant* have penultimate stress, no doubt because of the final-stressed verbs *comply* and *defy*.

A word I don't think I've ever encountered outside early nineteenth century poetry is *reboant* 'resounding, echoing'. The OED used to give it initial stress, but now, in the third edition, 2009, opts for penultimate-stressed rɪˈbəʊənt. I've never heard this word actually spoken.

3.2 Rowlocking Fun

What is the AmE pron of *rowlock*? In a sense there isn't one, because the Americans call the object in question an *oarlock*.

In BrE, where we do use the word *rowlock*, those who are familiar with rowing and oarsmanship call it a ˈrɒlək (or possibly ˈrʌlək). Those who are not may instead use a spelling pronunciation ˈrəʊlɒk (compare *forehead*, where the spelling pronunciation has by now largely displaced the traditional ˈfɒrɪd).

One might assume that any American who actually needs to use the British term would use a BrE-style pronunciation. In a trivial way, the same sort of question arises if we ask what the BrE pronunciation of *rowboat* is. In a sense there isn't one, because in BrE a boat you can row is called not a rowboat but a rowing boat.

But we have to draw a line somewhere: no one wants to say that in AmE *trousers* is pronounced **pænts**. Nor is a *lift* to carry you up a building pronounced ˈɛləveɪdɚ.

3.3 Jewellery, Jewelry

Being British, I spell the -*ery* form of *jewel* as *jewellery*. But I pronounce it ˈdʒuːəlri. (Or I can smooth the vowels, giving ˈdʒʊəlri.) Some Brits, though, pronounce it ˈdʒuːləri, which I have labelled in LPD as 'non-RP': it certainly triggers in me adverse prejudicial reactions as strong as those triggered by prəˌnaʊnsiˈeɪʃn̩.

Americans spell the word *jewelry*, which fits my pronunciation and presumably theirs too.

The *-(e)ry* suffix normally appears as *-ery* (potentially disyllabic) when attached to a stem that is monosyllabic or final-stressed, but as *-ry* (monosyllabic) when attached to a stem ending in an unstressed syllable. Thus on the one hand we have *bakery, fishery, slavery, buffoonery, machinery*, but on the other *mimicry, rivalry, devilry, archdeaconry, weaponry*.

So if *jewel* is pronounced as two syllables, ˈdʒuː əl, we would expect *jewelry* ˈdʒuːəlri. If on the other hand it is pronounced as one syllable, dʒuːl (as in popular London speech), or as the derived dʒʊəl, we would expect *jewellery* ˈdʒuːləri, ˈdʒʊələri.

3.4 Synod

The word *synod* has often been in the news in Britain, particularly when the Anglican General Synod was agonizing over such issues as women bishops.

In LPD I prioritize the traditional pronunciation with a weakened second vowel, ˈsɪnəd. This was the only pronunciation recognized in EPD during Daniel Jones's editorship. But nowadays one often hears this word said with a strong vowel in the unstressed syllable, ˈsɪnɒd.

Classicists will recognize that *synod* is parallel in its morphology with *method* and *period*, words whose final syllable is unquestionably always weakened to -əd. All three consist etymologically of a Greek prepositional prefix plus the stem of ὁδός *hodos* 'way, travel' (cognate with Russian ходить 'go'). Etymologically, a synod is a 'way together', a method is a 'way with', and a period is a 'way round'.

We have other words in English that have this structure. The book of *Exodus* ˈeksədəs in the Old Testament is an account of the 'way out', with the Latin nominative ending *-us* replacing Greek *-os*. *Anode* (etymologically 'way up') and *cathode* ('way down') were coined in 1834 by William Whewell, master of Trinity College, Cambridge, at the request of his friend Michael Faraday. Another friend, one Dr Nicholl, coined *electrode* ('amber/electric way'). Strange, then, that Whewell and Nicholl chose to write them with a final unetymological (or French-style) *e* and to say them with the corresponding strong pronunciation -əʊd. This was then also applied to the later coinings *diode, triode, pentode*, etc.

3.5 Algebraic Ordinals

What is the ordinal numeral corresponding to the cardinal numeral (n+1)?

The ordinal numeral corresponding to 1 is *first*, so we write *1st*. The ordinal corresponding to 2 is *second*, so we write *2nd*. The ordinal corresponding to 3 is *third*, so we write *3rd*. The ordinal numerals corresponding to 4 and upwards are formed with the suffix *th*, so we write *4th, 5th, 6th, 7th*, and so on. But after *20th* come *21st, 22nd*, and *23rd*.

When we use algebraic expressions instead of ordinary numerals, the ordinal corresponding to n is *nth*, pronounced **enθ**. That corresponding to x is *xth*, pronounced **eksθ**. The physics teacher at the secondary school I attended had the nickname **kjuː θ**, i.e. *qth*.

But it is not clear how to form ordinals for expressions such as x^2, (x+1), and (x–2).

I was quite taken aback when, in the course of reading *Seeing Further* (ed. Bill Bryson, London: HarperPress for the Royal Society, 2010), I came across the sentence (p. 379)

> [May, Oster and Yorke] identified simple features displayed by wide classes of difference equation relating the *(n+1)*st to the *n*th state of a system as it made the transition from order to chaos.

Do we really say **en plʌs fɜːst**? It feels wrong to me. If pushed, I think I'd go for saying **en plʌs wʌnθ**, and writing *(n+1)*th. Similarly, I'd write *(n+2)*th and say **en plʌs tuː θ**.

Enquiries among mathematical colleagues reveal that usage is indeed divided. Some go for one solution, others for the other.

3.6 Remuneration and Anemones

There seems to be something particularly difficult about VCVCV strings involving nasals at different places of articulation. We can manage *enemy* ˈ**enəmi**, but *an enemy* **ən ˈenəmi** can start to feel slightly like a tongue-twister. By the time we get to the flower *anemone* **əˈnemən**i and give it an indefinite article, *an anemone* **ən əˈnemən**i, we may have to monitor ourselves carefully as we pronounce it.

I remember as a child being shown some *wood anemones* by my mother and thinking they were *wooden enemies*.

What started me on this line of thought was an email in which someone was discussing an employee's 'renumeration'. This should of course be *remuneration*. But the **m – n** pronunciation problem in **riˌmjuːnəˈreɪʃn** is reinforced by an evident etymological/semantic confusion involving words such as *numeral* (count the salary!).

The prevalence of the spoken form (mispronunciation) with -ˈnjuːm- instead of -ˈmjuːn- leads often enough to the written form (misspelling) with *-num-* instead of *-mun-*.

Etymologically, *remuneration* has nothing to do with numbers. The *-mun-* part is the same as in *munificent* 'generous', and goes back to the Latin *mūnus, mūneris*, a word with several meanings, one of which is 'gift'. Cicero used the term *remūnerātio, -ōnis* in the sense of 'recompense, repayment', and the word has been in use in English since around 1400.

To remember the correct order of nasals in *remunerate*, think of *money*.

You might like to practise the difference between *antinomy* (logical contradiction, paradox) and *antimony* (chemical element, Sb: see 3.16).

3.7 Sojourn

Being the son of an Anglican priest, I have always been familiar with the word *sojourn*, the biblical term for making an overnight or temporary stay in a place.

> And there was a famine in the land: and Abram went down into Egypt to sojourn there; for the famine was grievous in the land.

> Israel also came into Egypt; and Jacob sojourned in the land of Ham.

Since it's a word I've always known, I don't hesitate about its pronunciation, which for me is ˈsɒdʒən (automatically implying ˈsɒdʒn̩ as an alternative).

Daniel Jones, while recognizing ˈsɒdʒən as a possibility, nevertheless preferred ˈsɒdʒɜːn, with a strong vowel in the second syllable. He also allows ˈsʌdʒ- for the first syllable. Meanwhile AmE tends to prefer soʊˈdʒɜːn, ˈsoʊdʒɜːn, sometimes with a stress difference between noun and verb.

For many people this is no doubt a word which – if they know it at all – they know only or mainly in its written form, so it is not surprising that the pronunciation is nowadays rather uncertain.

I wonder if anyone has **r** in the first syllable. Probably not. According to the OED, in Middle English this word was sometimes spelt with *r*, as *surgerun*. This may reflect the second of the two possible Latin sources, *subdiurnāre* and *superdiurnāre*.

3.8 Seismic

The English spelling *ei* is particularly opaque. In LPD I said that usually the pronunciation corresponding to this spelling is eɪ, as in *veil*, or less frequently iː, as in *receive*, aɪ, as in *height*, or e, as in *heifer*; while before *r* we can have BrE eə, as in *their*, or ɪə, as in *weird*. We all know about the uncertainty in *either* and *neither*; there are also words such as *atheism* in which *ei* is not a digraph.

Other examples with the pronunciation eɪ, I continued, include *beige, deign, feint, rein, surveillance, vein*. Others with iː include *codeine, protein, seize, Keith, Leith, Neil(l), Reid*. Others with aɪ include *eider, kaleidoscope, Eileen, Brunei* and German-derived words or names such as *zeitgeist, Einstein*. There is also the Greek-derived *seismic*.

... At least, that's the way I assumed everyone pronounces *seismic*: ˈsaɪzmɪk. But then I heard someone speak of a ˈseɪzmɪk shift in something or other.

Ancient Greek σεισμός *seismós* 'a shaking, shock' had eː during the classical period, yielding i in Modern Greek **siz'mos**. The regular development of Greek ει in post-GVS English is aɪ, which we also see, for example, in *dinosaur* ˈdaɪn-, based on δεινός *deinós* 'terrible' (though *dinosaur* is of course a relatively recent coinage, dating just from 1841). Within the same discipline of geology and paleontology we also have *Pleistocene* **ˈplaɪstə(ʊ)siːn** (Greek πλεῖστος *pleîstos* 'most'). There is also *paradise* **ˈpærədaɪs**, borrowed from Iranian via Greek παράδεισος *parádeisos*.

As can be seen from these examples, the English spelling of words with Greek ει is sometimes *ei* and sometimes simple *i*. At *seismic* the OED comments that 'the normal form would be *sismic'.

English is unusual among languages in that there are a large number of words whose spelling is firmly fixed, but whose pronunciation is not.

3.9 Mandragora

In the film *Harry Potter and the Chamber of Secrets*, Hermione is asked by a teacher at Hogwarts to tell the class about the plant called *mandrake*, a specimen of which they are about to repot (an alarming procedure). 'The mandrake or ˌmændrəˈgɔːrə ... ' Hermione begins, and immediately captures my attention. Because I call a *mandragora* mænˈdrægərə.

The OED gives antepenultimately-stressed **mænˈdræg(ə)rə** as the British pronunciation, but the penultimately-stressed **mændrəˈgɔːrə** as the preferred American version.

In fact my own pronunciation (with penultimate stress) is what one would expect from the etymology, which comes via Latin from Ancient Greek *μανδραγόρας*. As you can tell from the omicron used to spell the penultimate vowel, this was a short vowel (if it were long, it would have been written with an omega). The Latin stress rule (see *Sounds Interesting*, Section 2.12) accordingly puts the word stress on the preceding syllable, giving English -ˈdræg-.

3.10 Quasi-

Speaking in the House of Commons, the Prime Minister David Cameron used the word *quasi-judicial*. He pronounced the prefix *quasi-* as ˈkwɑːzaɪ.

This pronunciation, while by no means unusual, is interesting in that it combines in the same morpheme two different ways of treating Latin words taken into English.

One is to follow the usual English reading rules (spelling-to-sound rules), which treat long vowels as having undergone the Great Vowel Shift. This is what is done for Latin words that are well integrated into English. Thus we have for example *creator* and *major* with **-eɪ-**, and *aquarium* with **-eə-** deriving from an earlier **-eɪ-**. Likewise, we have for example *appendicitis* and *minor* with **-aɪ-**.

The other is to give the long vowels 'continental' values, rendering Latin *ā* as **ɑː** and *ī* as **iː**. This is what we do with words perceived as being less thoroughly integrated. We usually pronounce *errata* with **-ɑː-** nowadays, though that was not always the case. Similarly, *in vivo* usually has **-iː-**. (But *viva* meaning 'oral exam' is ˈ**vaɪvə**.)

The word *quasi* 'as if, as it were' actually has short vowels in Latin, *quăsĭ*. Latin stressed short *ă* is normally mapped onto English **æ**, as in the examples *aquifer* and *per capita*, so this prefix might be expected to be ˈ**kwæsi**. But English speakers are often pretty cavalier with Latin vowel quantities in English, and even those who have studied Latin (such as Mr Cameron, who must have done it at Eton) often get them wrong. If, as is usual, the vowels in this prefix are treated as long, we should get either GV-shifted ˈ**kweɪzaɪ** or 'continental' ˈ**kwɑːsi(ː)**. Dave's ˈ**kwɑːzaɪ** is a combination of the two.

A complicating factor in this word is that the stressed vowel has a preceding **w**. As we know from words such as *wattle, wash, water, war, swan, quantity, quarter*, **w** has historically triggered a backing of a following open vowel, from TRAP to LOT, or from START to NORTH. Hence for *quasi-* we can further expect possible **kwɒ-** or **kwɔː-**. We get the first sometimes in *Quasimodo*, though I don't think I have ever heard the second.

Given the further uncertainty over whether or not to voice the intervocalic *s* – is it **s** or **z**? – we end up with quite a combinatorial explosion of possibilities for this humble prefix.

3.11 Allegedly Aged

How do you pronounce *aged*?

It depends on where it stands in the sentence. If it is used attributively, before a noun, meaning 'old, very old', then it has two syllables, ˈ**eɪdʒɪd** (or, for some, ˈ**eɪdʒəd**). This is what you say in *an aged woman* or *my aged parents*. It is also the pronunciation we use in, for example, *care of the aged*, where you could argue that it is used attributively before a deleted (understood) noun *people*.

But when it is used predicatively, meaning 'having a specific age', then it is pronounced as a monosyllable, **eɪdʒd**. This is what you say in *children aged 5 or over* or *a man aged between 30 and 35*.

There are one or two other *-ed* words that vary in the same fashion, notably *blessed*. Attributively, disyllabic: *a moment of blessed silence; where's my blessed notebook?* Predicatively, monosyllabic: *we're both blessed with good health; the couple had their marriage blessed (by the vicar)*. Against this rule, however, in the hymn *Our blessed redeemer, ere he breathed | his tender last farewell* the word has to be pronounced as a monosyllable despite being attributive.

There's also *accursed*, which for me is always əˈkɜːsɪd. But others always say əˈkɜːst. Others again may vary, as with *aged* and *blessed*. In modern English, though, the word is really only used attributively: we can say *all this accursed mud*, but not ?*all this mud is accursed*.

As we all know, there are a few adjectives in *-ed* in which the ending is irregularly pronounced as a separate syllable. The general rule is that this pronunciation belongs only after stems ending in **t** or **d**. Examples are *crooked, learned, naked, rugged, wicked, wretched*, all disyllabic. (As verb forms, however, *crooked* and *learned* are monosyllabic: *she crooked* **krʊkt** *her finger, he learned* **lɜːnd** *what had happened*.)

Derived forms in *-edly* and *-edness* seem mostly to have the syllabic pronunciation. So *markedly* and *markedness* have three syllables each, while *supposedly* and *allegedly* have four. But there are also those that have a nonsyllabic *ed: determinedly, ill-favouredness, good-naturedness*. I think *shamefacedly* can go either way.

Alleged is an interesting case. Would you speak of someone's əˈledʒɪd crime, or their əˈledʒd crime? I think I'd normally say əˈledʒd, though others (particularly Americans?) may go for the three-syllable version. On the other hand I'd certainly include the extra syllable in *allegedly*.

3.12 Than

A headline in the Liverpool Echo newspaper read 'I'm feeling better then ever, says Liverpool FC skipper'.

Do you notice anything wrong here? Yes, *then* ought to be *than*.

I was quite surprised the first time I came across this misspelling, which was a few years ago. But the explosion of material published on the internet without the attention of a copy editor (and sometimes even with such attention, as presumably here, the *Echo* being a reputable newspaper) has made me realize how very widespread it is. (Since there is also a perfectly good word *then*, it would not be trapped by a simple spellchecker.)

There are plenty of examples to be found on the web. And yet I don't think people commonly misspell *ran* as *(w)ren*, or *tan* as *ten*. In all core native accents of English the words of the TRAP set are consistently distinguished from those of the DRESS set. So what's going on?

In speech, the word *than* is almost always pronounced in its weak form, ðən.

ˈbetə ðən ˈevə
ˈmɔː ðən ju kʊd biˈliːv

It is difficult to envisage a context in which one would want to accent it, thereby triggering the strong form. I exclude the obvious one of naming the word rather than using it, as in *'How do you spell "than"?'*.

The only way to trigger an obligatory strong form in ordinary conversation seems to be by resorting to stranding (*Sounds Interesting*, p. 58)

A mouse is something that an elephant is bigger than.

The syntax here involves the fronting of *a mouse*, with the consequence that *than* is stranded, deprived of the noun phrase it governs. As with prepositions and indeed all other function words, such stranding in English calls for the use of the strong form of the stranded item. The word normally remains unaccented.

I would say

ə ˈmaʊs ɪz sʌmθɪŋ ðət ən ˈelɪfənt ɪz ˈbɪgə ðæn

I wonder if anyone actually pronounces the strong form as **ðen** (to rhyme with *ten*). That is not inconceivable, given the extreme rarity of strong *than* and therefore the extreme rarity of opportunities for the language-acquiring child to hear how it is pronounced. (After all, the usual **ðən** might result from the weakening of any of putative **ðen, ðæn, ðʌn, ðɑːn, ðɒn** – compare the strong and weak forms of *them, at, us, are, from*.)

You'd think, though, that most children would have been exposed somewhere along the line to such utterances as *Who are you bigger than? Who is Mary younger than? Which of your brothers are you older than?*

Nine is one fewer **ðən** ten. Ten is what nine is one fewer **ðæn**.

No, the most probable explanation is that many speakers (unlike me) have **ðən** as a weak form of *then*. That means that *than* and *then* are distinct in their strong forms, but identical in their weak forms (like *had* and *would*, or *of* and *have*). This makes the explanation of *better then* the same as the explanation of *could of*.

3.13 Ha'p'orth

If you hear a word spoken, but then want to write it down, you may be in some uncertainty how to spell it.

At least in English, that is. If we had a thoroughly transparent spelling system, you might think, it wouldn't be such a problem.

Years ago, when I was working as a pronunciation consultant on a dictionary project, there was a young lexicographer who suggested that we ought to add the missing word *apeth*, since it was in general use in expressions such as 'a daft apeth'. (She may have thought that it literally meant some kind of baby monkey.) We had to tell her, gently, that the established spelling of this word is *ha'p'orth*, or in full *halfpennyworth*, with the pronunciation **ˈheɪpəθ**, and that it refers to the

British predecimal coinage, superseded before she was born. (Another saying, not yet I think entirely obsolete, involves losing the ship for a ha'p'orth of tar. Apparently it was originally a *sheep* that was lost, not a *ship*.)

It's also clear that if you hear an unfamiliar word spoken you may not hear it in exactly the same way as the person who said it intended. That could lead to spelling it wrong (or differently) even in the most perfectly phonemic orthography. It is the source of 'mondegreens' (think of *Gladly, the cross-eyed bear*, or *Olive, the other reindeer* who used to laugh at Rudolph and call him names; and there's *her hairy tongue over her shoulder*, along with the black velvet band).

The *feck* in *feckless* is, according to the OED, 'apparently aphetic < *effeck*, variant of EFFECT n.'. Rather than ɪˈfekt, someone must have heard *effect* just as **fek**. They then spelt it correspondingly as *feck*, which subsequently was adopted by everyone in *feckless*.

I suspect there was a similar process in the development of *flimsy* from *film(s)* + *-y* (which the OED strangely labels an 'onomatopoeic' formation). In fact *film* is regularly pronounced **flɪm** in Jamaican Creole (as well as ˈfɪləm in Irish English, which is a different matter).

3.14 Diamond

When the Queen's Diamond Jubilee was being celebrated in 2012, I was struck by the number of commentators on British television whom I noticed pronouncing *diamond* as ˈdaɪmənd rather than ˈdaɪəmənd (or the smoothed variants of the latter ˈdaəmənd, ˈdaːmənd).

In LPD I mark ˈdaɪmənd with the sign §, indicating that as far as BrE is concerned I considered this 'non-RP'. For AmE, on the other hand, I perhaps went too far in giving only this possibility.

I was wondering, has ˈdaɪmənd always been around, though presumably always considered incorrect (since it does not correspond to the spelling)? Or is it a recent import from AmE? Anyhow, why do Americans tend to use this pronunciation, given that it does not accord with the spelling?

On consulting the OED, I was somewhat surprised to find that ˈdaɪmənd has a considerable history in BrE. The word itself appears to be etymologically cognate with *adamant*, via late Latin *diamas, diamant-* from the Greek ἀδάμας, ἀδάμαντ- *adámas, adámant-* 'untamed, unalterable, unbreakable'.

> The a of the middle syllable has tended to disappear since the 16th cent., as shown by the spelling *di'mond, dimond*. Sheridan and other early orthoepists recognize the dissyllabic pronunciation, but most recent authorities reckon three syllables. In Shakespeare the word is more frequently a trisyllable; but it is very generally dissyllabic in Pope, Thomson, Young, Cowper, Keats, and Tennyson.

So perhaps I'd better remove the § mark. And this word will be a good candidate for inclusion in the next pronunciation preference poll I conduct.

The only other *dia-* word I can find with a similar pronunciation is *diaper*. In AmE it seems usually to be ˈdaɪpɚ, to rhyme with *wiper*, though Webster's Collegiate adds ˈdaɪəpɚ as an 'also' pronunciation. Since this word is not used in modern BrE (though it is found in Shakespeare), it is difficult to say whether there is any established BrE pronunciation of it.

Other candidates? As far as I know, no one says *ˈdaɪdem for *diadem* or *ˈdaɪgræm for *diagram*. Words where the aɪ(ə) is followed by a liquid, such as *diary*, are a special case, since schwa frequently comes and goes in that environment. Though I'm not sure how many people would say ˈdaɪlekt for *dialect*, rather than the usual ˈdaɪəlekt.

3.15 Epergne

Not for the first time, I heard an antiques expert on TV tell us that a silver-plated object being shown to us was an *epergne*. 'It's a – a French word, it's an eɪˈpeən – a French word for a table-centre display.'

Fair enough, except that the name of the object in question, *epergne*, is not a French word at all. Despite its spelling, which looks more or less French (though if it were really French it would probably have an acute accent on the first vowel, so *épergne*), and despite the more or less French pronunciation that the expert used (as if in French it were epɛʁɲ(ə) – despite this, there is no such word in French. The nearest French word that does exist is *épargne* epaʁɲ(ə); but that means 'savings', and has nothing whatsoever to do with table decorations.

In LPD I followed EPD in giving the main pronunciation as ɪˈpɜːn, with variants e-, -ˈpeən. I did add a note, 'not actually a French word', and for that reason gave no French pronunciation. Perhaps I ought to have given one, though, so as to cater for those, like the TV expert, who pronounce it as if it were.

3.16 Antimony

In my first year at secondary school, which I entered at age 12½, we were given taster classes in science: an hour a week each of chemistry, biology, and physics.

I remember that when the physics teacher had explained to us how an electric bell worked I asked him what determined the frequency of the beats in the ringing. But instead of giving me a serious answer, perhaps involving either the dimensions and elasticity of the vibrating clapper or the characteristics of the current applied, he sarcastically replied, 'Why don't you count them?'. This rather put me off physics.

The chemistry teacher, on the other hand, showed us sodium, magnesium, potassium, and other elements, and did experiments involving explosions and brightly coloured flames. He even showed us a Geiger counter and sources of alpha, beta, and gamma rays.

When I let slip that I knew that the lead (Pb) resulting from the radioactive decay of thorium has a different atomic weight from that of ordinary lead, he was so excited that he made a serious effort to recruit me to study science. But I had just started classical Greek, and I decided to stick with that, while continuing (as I do to this day) to read popular science books in my spare time and try to be reasonably well-informed about scientific subjects.

So you will understand that when I came to make a dictionary I took it as obvious that the headword list should include, for example, the names of all the chemical elements. I noticed with amusement that Daniel Jones's EPD had *ytterbium* and *yttrium*, but not the other two elements named after the ore mines at Ytterby in Sweden, namely *erbium* and *terbium*. Naturally, LPD has all four (as does the current Cambridge EPD).

This brings me to the question of element number 51, Sb, *antimony*. At school I acquired the pronunciation æn'tɪməni for this element, with antepenultimate stress. This is also the pronunciation recorded in Daniel Jones's EPD, at least up to and including the twelfth edition (1963). However, when Gimson took over the editorship for the fourteenth edition (1977), he added (and prioritized) the initial-stressed 'æntɪməni. The on-line OED gives only this latter; whether this is the pronunciation recorded in 1885 or one reflecting a more recent editorial decision I do not know. After informally consulting colleagues in the chemistry department at my university, I also decided to go with this in LPD. Merriam-Webster shows the same initial stress, but with a strong ('stressed') penultimate vowel, 'æntə‚moʊni, so bringing it into line with such words as *testimony, alimony, ceremony*. For what it's worth, the *-mony* part of *antimony* does not seem to derive from the classical Latin *-mōnium* that we see in these words (nor from the 'anti-monk' origin given by Dr Johnson, which the OED calls an 'idle tale'). The OED thinks it is 'probably, like other terms of alchemy, a corruption of some Arabic word, refashioned so as to wear a Greek or Latin aspect'.

Nor is this chemical term to be confused with the philosophers' *antinomy* (though it sometimes is).

When I was young, relatively few transuranic elements had been named. As Tom Lehrer sang in 1959, the 102 elements then known were 'the only ones of which the news has come to Ha'vard | and there may be many others, but they haven't been discavard'.

So in LPD I've got *lawrencium, rutherfordium* and *dubnium*, but not *seaborgium, bohrium, hassium, meitnerium*, or *darmstadtium*, still less such exotic newcomers as *roentgenium* and *ununtrium*. According to Hugh Aldersey-Williams in his *Periodic Tales* (Penguin 2012), the International Union of Pure and Applied

Chemistry, the organization in charge of ratifying chemical nomenclature, requires each new element to have a name 'that is easily pronounced'. It's not clear to me what that means in the last three cases I have mentioned, in each of which there is more than one possibility in English that could be supported by the spelling.

3.17 Canine

I was about to have one of my front teeth crowned, and my dentist asked me to visit the dental technician for him to determine the appropriate colour match. I did so, and was impressed by his evident mastery of his subject. He took a whole series of photos of my face and teeth, first taking me into the natural daylight outside the building in which he worked, and explaining to me how the replacement would be built up from multiple layers of porcelain of different translucencies and shades.

What struck me, however, was that he pronounced the word *canine* as kəˈnaɪn. For this word I'm only familiar with ˈ**keɪnaɪn** and ˈ**kænaɪn** (the former, I think, predominating; think of Dr Who's robotic dog *K9*); so his version was new to me. Yet for him this is an everyday technical term of his professional speciality.

I see the OED gives all three pronunciations without comment, so perhaps he's not alone. (Merriam-Webster Collegiate gives ˈkeɪ-, adding ˈkæ- for BrE only.)

This word is one of several that we have taken from Latin, all meaning 'X-related', where X is the name of an animal: *aquiline, feline, asinine, vulpine*, and so on. Canine teeth are 'dog-like' teeth (Latin *canis* 'dog'). It is regular in these adjectives for the suffix to be pronounced **aɪn** and for the stress to go on the stem. In some cases the Latin vowel length in the stem is preserved: ˈ**ækwɪlaɪn** (Latin *ăquĭla* 'eagle'), ˈ**fiːlaɪn** (*fēles, felis* 'cat'), ˈ**æsɪnaɪn** (*ăsĭnus* 'donkey, ass'), ˈ**vʌlpaɪn** (*vŭlpes* 'fox'), and so on – but in other cases, not: *bovine* ˈ**bəʊvaɪn** (*bōs*, but stem *bŏv-* 'ox, cow'), *ovine* ˈ**əʊvaɪn** (*ŏvis* 'sheep'). (Middle English open-syllable lengthening accounts for the latter.) Hence the hesitation in *canine* ˈkeɪ- ~ ˈkæ-, which we also see in *equine* ˈiːk- ~ ˈek- (*ĕquus* 'horse').

The only cases I can think of in which a Latin adjective in *-īnus* gives an English adjective with final stress do not have a stem designating an animal: *divine* dɪˈvaɪn and *marine* məˈriːn (*măre* 'sea'). The latter is also the only one in which the suffix is pronounced **iːn** rather than **aɪn**.

3.18 Met a What?

I saw an interesting BBC television programme entitled *Metamorphoses*. It was about animals that change their shape and/or lifestyle dramatically in the course of their lives: caterpillars turning into butterflies, tadpoles becoming frogs, and so on.

Metamorphosis, the singular form of *metamorphoses*, is one of those classical-derived words in which English speakers may hesitate about stress placement. In LPD, following Daniel Jones's EPD, I give the main pron ˌmetəˈmɔːfəsɪs, with a secondary pron ˌmetəmɔːˈfəʊsɪs. American dictionaries give only the first-mentioned (antepenultimate) stressing, as does ODP. The Concise Oxford gives both, as does the OED (2001, for BrE; just the first for AmE).

On the TV programme all the scientists who took part, with just a single exception, gave this word antepenultimate stress.

So why do some Brits, at least, want to stress the penultimate? Mainly, no doubt, because of other scientific words in -*osis* such as *psychosis, neurosis, osteoporosis, cirrhosis, symbiosis, meiosis, tuberculosis, osmosis, hypnosis, sclerosis*, all of which have penultimate stress, -ˈəʊsɪs.

Those few of us familiar with Classical Greek will know the etymon μεταμόρφωσις *metamórphōsis*, and in English will know as usual to ignore the classical Greek accentuation in favour of the Latin stress rule. In the Greek spelling the omega (ω, ō) in the penultimate syllable shows that the vowel is long and therefore, by the Latin stress rule, stressed.

Classicists and grammarians, though, may know the word *apodosis* əˈpɒdəsɪs (Greek ἀπόδοσις *apódōsis*) 'then-clause', paired with *protasis* 'if-clause' and having an omicron (o, ŏ) followed by a single consonant in the penultimate syllable, giving a Latin and English antepenultimate stress. But then they'll also know *apotheosis* (Greek ἀποθέωσις *apothéōsis*), which has an omega and therefore penultimate stress like the scientific words. Nowadays those of us who do know it say əˌpɒθiːˈəʊsɪs (or at least the classics teachers who taught me did); but apparently that was not always the case in English.

Under -*osis* the OED comments:

> The older pronunciation of at least some of these words had the stress on the syllable preceding the suffix: see, e.g., the etymological note at *apotheosis* n.

Under *apotheosis* we read (in a note written in 1885):

> The great majority of orthoepists, from Bailey and Johnson downward, give the first pronunciation (sc. æpəʊˈθiːəsɪs), but the second (sc. əˌpɒθiːˈəʊsɪs) is now more usual.

I think I'm becoming a god.

3.19 Stress Changes

I've written about eighteenth-century hymnody before (*Sounds Interesting*, pp. 41–43). In addition to their other merits, these hymns often bear witness to changes in English pronunciation.

I haven't conducted any preference polls for the noun *perfume*, but I am sure that pretty well all Brits today, and some Americans, stress it on the first syllable,

ˈpɜːfjuːm. Yet in Isaac Watts's hymn *Jesus shall reign where'er the sun* it has to be stressed on the second syllable.

> To Him shall endless prayer be made,
> And praises throng to crown His head;
> His Name like sweet perfume shall rise
> With every morning sacrifice.

I think that those of us who know the verb *ascertain* always nowadays pronounce it with final stress, ˌæsəˈteɪn. But in Charles Wesley's great *O for a thousand tongues to sing* it has to be stressed on the penultimate syllable:

> I found and owned His promise true,
> Ascertained of my part,
> My pardon passed in heaven I knew
> When written on my heart.

The two hymns were both originally very long, and nowadays we leave out these particular verses, along with many others, not just because of stress changes and to shorten things, but often because of modern sensibilities.

Some of the original words of Isaac Watts were inspired not by multiculturalism but by Christian triumphalism:

> There Persia, glorious to behold,
> There India shines in eastern gold;
> And barb'rous nations at His word
> Submit, and bow, and own their Lord.

... while Wesley has the casually racist verse:

> Awake from guilty nature's sleep,
> And Christ shall give you light,
> Cast all your sins into the deep,
> And wash the Æthiop white.

No wonder we don't sing those verses nowadays.

3.20 Sainthood

I'm aware of the danger of the 'recency fallacy' that leads commentators on pronunciation to claim that a pronunciation is getting more common when it really isn't.

But I do feel tempted to claim, though admittedly without proper evidence, that the strong form of *Saint* is becoming commoner, where I would expect the weak. I would never use the strong form in names of saints or in names of places, churches or hospitals based on them. For me *St Matthew, St John, St Agatha*, and likewise *St Albans, St Helens, St Leonards-on-Sea* all have **sənt**, or forms still further reduced such as **sn̩t, sn̩**. It's **sn̩** *Thomas's Hospital* and **sm̩** *Paul's Cathedral*.

My impression is that since about 1980 people I am exposed to have started pronouncing these with the strong form **seɪnt**. OK, I know Americans regularly do this. But I'm talking about Brits. (Americans also put what they call a period, and we call a full stop, after the abbreviation. But that's a different issue.)

My late father used to like to recite a verse referring to pairs of apostles who share the same saint's day in the calendar of the Anglican church (1 May and 28 October respectively, since you ask.)

> *Let us emulate the aims*
> *of St Philip and St James*
> *and be very very good*
> *like St Simon and St Jude.*

And when he recited this, all the *St*s were reduced. (His mispronunciation of *good* as **guːd** instead of **gʊd**, to make it rhyme with *Jude*, was intentional.)

There is a London-based TV newsreader who pronounces *St Paul's Cathedral* as ˈseɪnt pɔːlz kəˈθiːdrəl. What I would say myself, of course, is sənt ˈpɔːlz kə ˈθiːdrəl. (The first word, *St*, could also undergo one or more of syllabic consonant formation, glottalling, elision and assimilation, to give sn̩ʔ, sn̩, sm̩p, sm̩ʔ, sm̩.)

I've heard *Seɪnt Albans*, *Seɪnt-Leonards-on-Sea*, and *Seɪnt George's Hospital*, though never yet as far as I am aware *Seɪnt Helens* (the town in Lancashire). Perhaps there is something special about Lancashire: I don't think I've heard *Lytham St Annes* with strong **seɪnt**, either.

Personally, I weaken *saint* not only in all the names just cited but also in the names of West Indian islands, too, though I know the locals don't: *St Martin, St Thomas, St Barts, St Kitts, St Croix, St Lucia, St Vincent*. And when spelling them, since I'm British, I don't put a full stop (period) after the *St*, either.

The only saintly island I can think of in which I wouldn't use the weak form is *St Helena*, in the south Atlantic. But it traditionally has the idiosyncratic pronunciation ˌsentɪˈliːnə (or variants thereof). On the other hand I'd call the saint herself sənt ˈhelənə, and I believe the place in California is ˌseɪnt (h)ɪˈliːnə.

You'll know about the idiosyncrasies of the surnames *St Clair/Sinclair* ˈsɪŋkleə or sɪŋˈkleə, *St John* ˈsɪndʒən, and *St Leger* ˈselɪndʒə, as well as of Gilbert and Sullivan's reference to the London street *St Mary Axe* ˌsɪməriˈæks in the song about someone with a name very similar to my own.

So do we blame this apparent change on the decline of religion, inasmuch as we don't talk about saints very much any more? Or on American influence? Or what? Correction: we're phoneticians. We don't blame anything or anyone; we observe and seek a reason.

There's another word that has a weak form in BrE but not in AmE: *sir*. When stressed, it's sɜː(r) everywhere. But when it precedes a name, in BrE it normally has the weak form sə(r).

So we say sə *Humphrey*, sə *Galahad*, Professor sə *Howard Fergus*. With a possible linking **r**, we have sə(r) *Alexander Fleming* and sə(r) *Alan Sugar*. The only circumstance where *sir* would be strong in this position is if accented for emphasis or contrast.

4 Names

4.1 Israel

Have you noticed how some people pronounce *Israel* as ˈɪzraɪel when singing? I'm struck by how they sing it in the Advent hymn:

> O come, O come, Emmanuel
> And ransom captive Israel!

with its refrain:

> Rejoice! Rejoice! Emmanuel
> shall come to thee, O Israel.

In LPD I said that *Israel*, in speech normally ˈɪzreɪl or ˈɪzriəl, is 'in singing usually ˈɪzreɪel'. But on reflection I certainly ought to have mentioned this further possibility with -aɪ-.

Where on earth could this treatment of the second vowel have come from? It's not straightforwardly based on the spelling; there are all sorts of vowel sounds that correspond to the spelling *a*, but aɪ is not one of them.

On reflection I think that we have a tendency (perhaps 'rule' would be to put it too strongly) to change ɑː to aɪ before a following front vowel (a position from which it is usually shielded by a linking or intrusive r). It's a kind of anticipatory articulation.

We see this in the word *naïve*. On the basis of the French it ought to be nɑːˈiːv. In practice people mostly say naɪˈiːv.

If for *Israel* we assume a starting point ˈɪzrɑːel, based on the spelling or the Latin or Hebrew pronunciation (real or assumed), then my proposed near-rule would make it ˈɪzraɪel. QED.

There are two further Biblical names that are relevant here: *Canaan* and *Sinai*. For foreign words of this vintage, long *a* would be expected to be read as eɪ (as in *Amos, Salem, Jacob, Emmaus*), not as ɑː. But in this unstressed prevocalic position the vowel typically either weakens to i or disappears entirely: ˈkeɪn(i)ən, ˈsaɪn(i)aɪ.

4.2 Laocoön

I hope it's not going to be too boring if I again mention people's increasing ignorance of how to pronounce classical names. A BBC television programme I watched – one which targets an intellectual rather than a popular audience – involved an odd-man-out question in which one of the candidates was *Laocoön*. Classicists and, I imagine, art historians know that this name is traditionally pronounced in English as **leɪˈɒkəʊɒn**. Everyone involved in the TV programme called it **læˈkəʊən**. This does not even correspond to the spelling, since it ignores the *o* of *Lao*-. But they all said it, so I suppose the producer must have told them to.

The reason that the cognoscenti say **leɪˈɒkəʊɒn** is the usual boring one involving historical developments to do with Greek vowel length and the Latin stress rule, feeding into the English Great Vowel Shift. The Greek Λαοκόων *laokóōn* has a short penultimate vowel (accordingly written as an omicron, not an omega), making a light penultimate syllable, causing the Latin stress to fall on the antepenultimate and the English stress likewise. As in *chaos*, Greek χάος *kháos*, English lengthens the prevocalic short *a*, which duly emerges from the GVS as **eɪ**. Same with the penultimate short *o*, which turns into **əʊ**. As we say nowadays, simples.

If you know the 'rules', i.e. the historical principles underlying the traditional English pronunciation of classical names, **leɪˈɒkəʊɒn** is absolutely predictable and unremarkable. However, while knowledge of these rules is certainly useful for the author of a pronunciation dictionary, I can see the force of the argument that not everyone needs to know them.

Knowledge is a tricky thing. I spent my working life in a university environment where people generally felt an obligation to know the correct pronunciation not only of classical names but also of anything from French, German, Italian, or Spanish. This doesn't necessarily apply elsewhere.

On the tube I overheard a couple discussing buying a new washing machine. One of the brands they were considering was *Miele*. They called it **miːɫ**.

But I can't escape from the fact that I know German and therefore think of this brand as **ˈmiːlə**.

Furthermore, I know that *vice versa* has four syllables, not three. I know that *Giotto* has two syllables, not three. And I know that the letter *z* in the Brothers *Karamazov* is not like the *z* in *Mozart*. Millions don't. Rant over.

4.3   Bombardier

While other branches of the British army have corporals and lance-corporals among their non-commissioned officers, artillery units have *bombardiers* and *lance-bombardiers*. As an NCO rank, *bombardier* is pronounced ˌbɒmbəˈdɪə.

A company called *Bombardier* has been in the news, bidding for contracts to build new trains. Referring to this company, the newsreaders use a different pronunciation. They call it **bɒmˈbɑːdieɪ** or something similar. They are correct to do so.

The reason is that – despite its supposed Britishness and its manufacturing works in Derby – Bombardier Inc. is actually a Canadian conglomerate, named after its founder Joseph-Armand Bombardier, a Québécois. He was the inventor of the snowmobile. In French his name is pronounced **bɔ̃baʁdje**, so the English name of the company is an anglicized version of this.

One correspondent who read the above commented that he had always said ˌbɒməˈdɪə, although he had never actually heard the word said. This is understandable, given that *bombardier* is derived from *bomb*, one of the English words that end in a silent *b*. See further in Section 11.17.

4.4 Ulysses

A correspondent referred to his 'life-long puzzlement' over the pronunciation of *Ulysses*. He had always stressed the second syllable, 'but initial stress seems to be the norm'.

Indeed: on the centenary of James Joyce's novel *Ulysses* everyone I heard on BBC Radio Four called it ˈjuːlɪsiːz.

Not me. I've always called it **juˈlɪsiːz**, like the eponymous hero of the Odyssey, Greek *Odysseus* əˈdɪsjuːs and Latin *Ulysses* or (less usually) *Ulixes* (apparently via Sicilian Greek Οὐλίξης). In accordance with the Latin stress rule (stress the penultimate if it is a heavy syllable), all three forms of the name are traditionally stressed on the penultimate. The double *s* of *Odysseus* and *Ulysses*, like the *x* of *Ulixes*, makes the syllable heavy.

In the 12th edition of EPD (1963), the last to be edited by Jones himself, the pronunciation of *Ulysses* is given as

    juˈlɪsiːz (*rarely* ˈjuːlɪsiːz)

(I've modernized the phonetic notation.)

By the 14th edition (ed. Gimson and Ramsaran 1977) the word 'rarely' has been removed, but priority is still given to **juˈlɪsiːz**. It was only when Peter Roach took over as editor that the priority was changed, placing the initial-stressed version first. Judging by what I heard on the radio, Peter was right to make this change.

Perhaps I ought to do the same for LPD. Or at least conduct a preference poll.

The Merriam-Webster Collegiate and other dictionaries suggest that Americans still retain the traditional penultimate stressing. Perhaps it's only the Brits (and only some of them) who have abandoned it.

The influence of my schooldays in the Classical Sixth is still strong. I don't think I'm going to change my own pronunciation. I'll stick with **juˈlɪsiːz**.

4.5 Mysterious Derived Forms

A correspondent asked me why *Harrow* gives us the derived form *Harrovian* while *Congo* gives us *Congolese*.

The brief answer is that I don't know, and I can't find any answer in reference books or on the web.

Harrovian may well be modelled on *Peruvian* (from *Peru*). The OED says that *Peruvia* (1566) was a Latinized form of *Peru*. In classical Latin the two letters *u* and *v* were not distinguished, and the corresponding sound was **u** or **w** depending on whether it was vocalic or consonantal. You can see how a **w** glide would be natural between **u** and a following vowel. But by the fifth century AD, consonantal *u* had become fricative. So a further thousand years after that, when *Peruvia* was coined, there was no phonetic reason to epenthesize **v**. And in Spanish the adjective is just *peruano*; but the French have *péruvien*.

The OED dates *Harrovian* to 1864. Harrow School, like other great public schools, taught Latin to all its pupils and must have invented the Latin name *Harrovia* for itself.

Another interesting formation, and forty years older, is *Monrovia*, capital of Liberia, named in 1824 after the American President James *Monroe*. Unlike with *Harrow*, there is no letter *w* here to provoke a Latinizing letter *v*.

Shavian ˈʃeɪviən, for the writer George Bernard *Shaw*, is more recent (OED 1905). And *Fitzrovia*, for the area around Fitzroy Square near Euston, is a mere half-century old (OED 1958).

Fans of *Doctor Who* are sometimes referred to as *Whovians*. During the 1980s, the Doctor Who Fan Club of America published the Whovian Times as its newsletter.

(Do you think anyone would give *Waugh* an adjective *Wavian*? No? Neither do I.)

Congolese must come from French *congolais*, but where the French took the epenthesized lateral from I cannot imagine. Compare the dwellers in Idaho, who are straightforwardly *Idahoans*.

Next question: why is someone from St Kitts in the Caribbean known as a *Kittitian* kɪˈtɪʃn̩? Answer: I don't know, and I suspect the OED doesn't really know either, though it suggests that *Kittitian* is modelled on *Haitian*. (But *Kitts: Kittitian* is not really like *Haiti: Haitian*.) Richard Allsopp's Dictionary of Caribbean English Usage (OUP 1996) thinks it probably comes from a form *Kittsian*, with 'insertion [-tiš-] by dissimilation or epenthesis'.

And why are purveyors of tobacco known as *tobacconists*? Or for that matter people from Toronto as *Torontonians*? Yet members of LASSO, the Linguistic Association of the Southwest (US), according to Ryan Denzer-King, are addressed as *Lassovians*, and old boys of Stowe (public school) are simply known as *Stoics*.

Shanghainese, from Shanghai, is presumably by analogy with *Chinese* (although the base form *China* contains an *n*, whereas *Shanghai* doesn't, or at least not in the right place). In the east Asia area there are also *Java – Javanese, Sunda – Sundanese*, and *Bali – Balinese*, all with an *n* of no obvious origin unless indeed *China – Chinese* is somehow responsible.

The OED speculates that *tobacconist*, with *-n-* inserted between *tobacco* and *-ist*, is 'perh. suggested by such words as Platonist, with etymological n'. For *Torontonian* it merely says 'f. Toronto, capital of the province of Ontario in Canada + -n- + -IAN'. For the mysterious *Glaswegian* (from Glasgow) it surmises some distant analogy with *Norwegian* (from Norway), via a rare *Galwegian*, more usually *Gallovidian* (from Galloway). Yeah, right (the phrase that proves that two positives make a rather negative evaluation).

5 People

5.1 Boris and His Great-Grandfather

'Who Do You Think You Are?' is a BBC television programme in which well-known personalities trace their ancestry. When Boris Johnson, the mayor of London, appeared on it, we heard how his great-grandfather, who was Turkish, was stoned by a mob and stabbed to death. Boris also found that he is descended from King George II and is therefore related to all the royalty of Europe.

In digging up these facts he took us on visits to both Turkey and Germany. Being an educated chap, he can speak some German. Well, sort of. Searching through the state archives in Augsburg (just before three minutes into the clip) he exclaims:

> ...Natürlich Vater war Prinz Paul von Württemberg...aha!...ich habe der Mystery gecrackt!

I'm not going to comment on his dodgy command of German word order or the mixed English/German vocabulary (in real German the last phrase would probably be something like *ich hab's enträtselt!*). What struck me was the baneful influence on him of German spelling. Boris interprets the letter *V* in the English way, as voiced **v**, instead of in the German way, as voiceless **f**. He pronounces *Vater* as ˈvɑːtə and *von* as vɒn. In real German they are ˈfaːtɐ and fɔn.

Boris can never have heard any German speaker pronounce those words with a voiced fricative. He is probably familiar with them only in their written form. It is the different spelling-to-sound conventions of English and German that are to blame for his mispronunciation.

Actually, though, the situation is slightly more complicated. Although German *v* stands for **f** in most words (*Vater, von, verstehen, Vogel, Bevölkerung*), there are a few words of foreign origin in which it stands for **v**. They include, in Germany at least, *aktive* akˈtiːvə, *nervös* nɛrˈvøːs and, importantly for phoneticians, *Vokal* voˈkaːl, the word for 'vowel'.

5.2 Poets and Archangels

On BBC R4 I heard the middle name of the poet Dante Gabriel Rossetti pronounced as ˌgæbriˈel.

My partner's name is Gabriel, and it is not unusual for people who do not know him personally to ring up and ask for ˌgæbriˈel.

Yet I have never heard the archangel Gabriel called anything other than ˈgeɪbriəl. And that of course is how my partner and very probably all English-speaking men bearing the name pronounce it: with the FACE vowel and initial stress. (OK, minor quibble: in my Gabriel's native island of Montserrat it is usually just ˈgeːbrɪl.)

So why should people have abandoned the old English way of saying this name, supported as it is by biblical and literary tradition?

I think it must be contamination from the woman's name *Gabrielle*, which is indeed pronounced French-style as ˌgæbriˈel. The popularity of the woman's name has risen over recent years while that of the man's name has declined.

Despite his Italian-looking first and last names, the Victorian-era English-born, English-educated poet Rossetti's second name (actually, originally his first) was unquestionably ˈgeɪbriəl.

5.3 Joe Mc-What?

The pronunciation of surnames in *Mc-* or *Mac-* is sometimes quite difficult to predict from the spelling. These thoughts are prompted by the name *McElderry*, which I give in LPD as ˈmæk ᵊl ˌder i or ˌ••ˈ••.

But the winner of a 2009 television talent show, Joe McElderry, calls himself məˈkeld(ə)ri.

As we all know, the prefix *M(a)c-* means 'son of' in Irish and Scottish Gaelic. The general rule is that:

- before a stressed syllable it is pronounced **mək**, or in a more formal style perhaps **mæk**; thus *McBride, McDonald, McEwan, McPherson*
- before an unstressed syllable it is **mæk**, and is itself stressed; thus *McAnulty* ˌmækəˈnʌlti, *McAvoy* ˈmækəvɔɪ, *McEnroe, McIntosh, McNamara*
- but before **k** or **g** it is reduced to **mə**, thus *McCarthy* məˈkɑː(r)θi, *McCorquodale, McGill, McGonagall, McQueen*.

The problem with *McElderry*, and with several other names of three or more syllables, is knowing whether the second syllable is stressed or not. The BBC Pronouncing Dictionary of Proper Names regards the *El-* in *McElderry* as unstressed (which in turn triggers stress on the prefix), but Joe the singer treats it as stressed.

For what it's worth, the etymology of *McElderry*, according to Hanks and Hodges' Oxford Dictionary of Surnames (OUP 1988), is *Mac Giolla Dhorcha* 'son of the dark-haired lad'.

Why are *McIlwain, McIlwraith, McIndoe, McIntyre* stressed on the ˈmæk-, while *McInnes* is stressed on the -ˈɪn-? Why can *McElroy* and *McElwain*, not to mention *McGillycuddy*, go either way?

Although these surnames are now to be found throughout the English-speaking world (Joe the singer is a Geordie), the explanation of their stress patterns presumably lies in Gaelic phonetics, and perhaps in particular in dialect differences within Irish/Scottish Gaelic.

5.4 Eugenie

One of our minor royals is Princess Eugenie, the younger daughter of Prince Andrew, Duke of York; her mother is Sarah Ferguson and she is the Queen's granddaughter.

She pronounces her name as ˈjuːʒəni, as do other members of her family.

The only bearer of the name Eugenie that I know or knew personally was Eugénie Henderson (1914–1989), Professor of Phonetics in the University of London at SOAS. She was a former pupil of Daniel Jones and an expert on Thai, Karen, Chin, and other southeast Asian languages as well as an inspired theoretical phonetician/phonologist. I knew her as a cheerful, hard-working and helpful older colleague. The British Association of Academic Phoneticians awards a biennial Eugénie Henderson prize.

Professor Henderson pronounced her name as juˈʒeɪni, and so did we all. She also spelt it with a French acute accent on the vowel in the middle.

Ever since Jones's day EPD has prioritized juːˈʒeɪni, though also giving juːˈʒiːni and juːˈdʒiːni. The ODP gives BrE juːˈʒeɪni, AmE juˌʒeɪˈni. The Merriam-Webster Collegiate gives three possibilities, which in IPA would be ˈjuːdʒəˌniː, juːˈdʒeɪni, juːˈdʒiːni.

So our pronunciation authorities give no support to the form ˈjuːʒəni. Since that is indeed what her parents call Princess Eugenie and what she calls herself, it constitutes an innovation.

As Professor Henderson's spelling hints, the name is of French origin (and before that, of course, from Greek via Latin: Εὐγενία *Eugenia* 'well-born'). In French it is pronounced øʒeni. So although the ʒ must be French in origin, ju(ː)- is English rather than French, following words such as *eugenics, euphoric, euphemism*.

5.5 An Archiepiscopal Mnemonic

As of 2015, the current Archbishop of York is Dr John Sentamu.

You sometimes hear him referred to as Bishop senˈtɑːmuː. But, as those who consult LPD or the Oxford BBC Guide to Pronunciation will know, his own preferred pronunciation is ˈsentəmu.

The Archbishop has given us an easy way to remember how he would like us to say his name. He asks us to imagine three cows standing in a row. Each cow moos. On the left we have a left moo, on the right we have a right moo, and in the centre we have a centre moo. And he's like the centre moo, ˈsentəmuː.

(I'm sorry, this doesn't work for AmE or even for the Scots.)

A correspondent tells me that the original Luganda pronunciation would be **sːéːntámû** with a high tone on the first two syllables, a falling tone on the final syllable, and a long **s** at the start. (This is on the assumption that the Archbishop's name is actually *Ssentamu*, and that he's done what many Baganda do when they to move the UK and drop the double initial consonant in their clan name.)

5.6 Coetzee

Thirty or so years ago I was staying for a few days with a friend who lived in Antwerp, when I was struck down by illness. I was admitted into a local hospital and operated on for appendicitis.

The treatment I received was prompt, successful, and of course free of charge. Linguistically it was a very interesting experience. The surgeon who performed the operation talked to me in English. With the hospital chaplain I had to talk in French. But the nurses only spoke Flemish. Flemish is of course the same language as Dutch. My Dutch, though not non-existent, is not very good. I do remember being struck by the way the nurses pronounced the word for 'soap', *zeep*. I knew that this was basically **zeːp**, though in the Amsterdam-Rotterdam pronunciation to which I was accustomed the vowel tended to be realized as a closing diphthong, **zeɪp**. But in Antwerp the diphthongization was in the other direction, a Swedish-like **zeəp**.

Afrikaans is like Flemish in this regard (though in that language the word for 'soap' is spelt *seep*). According to Wikipedia, in Afrikaans

> /oə øə eə/ are also transcribed as long monophthongs /o: ø: e:/. /oə/ and /eə/ are also commonly realized as [uə] and [iə] respectively, and such pronunciation is already considered standard.

The Afrikaans vowel spelt *ee* (the one the Wikipedia article transcribes **eə**) is quite often mapped onto English NEAR. The writer J.M. *Coetzee*, accordingly, can appropriately be pronounced not only **kʊtˈsiːə** or **kʊtˈsiː**, but also **kʊtˈsɪə**.

My Polish colleague Piotr Gąsiorowski says he has met J.M. Coetzee in person, and heard him pronounce his own name many times when giving a talk on his family history. He definitely pronounced it **kʊtˈsɪə**. His native language is English, despite the Afrikaans surname, so the pronunciation can be regarded as anglicized.

5.7 Breughel

Not only are we uncertain about the pronunciation, we can't even agree on how to spell the name of the famous Dutch/Flemish painter(s): were Pieter B. the Elder and his relatives *Breughel, Brueghel, Breugel,* or *Bruegel*?

In Dutch this name is pronounced **ˈbrøːɣəl** (subject to the usual regional variation: possible diphthonging of the stressed vowel and devoicing of the velar, not to mention the variability in the second consonant), which is what you would expect for a spelling with *eu*. In turn, you would expect foreign-language **ø(ː)** to map onto nonrhotic English NURSE, as happens with French *deux* **dø** mapped onto BrE **dɜː** or German *Goethe* **ˈgøːtə** onto BrE **ˈgɜːtə**.

Yet on the whole we call the painter not **ˈbrɜːgl̩** but **ˈbrɔɪgl̩**. Why?

I can only suppose that our usual pronunciation is based on the *eu* spelling, interpreted according to the reading rules of German. If *Deutsch* is English **dɔɪtʃ** and *Freud* is **frɔɪd**, then *Breug(h)el* must be **ˈbrɔɪgl̩**.

For the same reason, even though several authorities prefer the spelling *Bruegel* (which would prompt us towards a pronunciation **ˈbruːgl̩**), most of us, I suspect, tend to spell the name with *eu*.

5.8 Kim Jong-Un

The deceased Dear Leader of North Korea, Kim Jong-il, was succeeded by his third son, Kim Jong-un. On radio and TV I have heard this name pronounced either as **kɪm dʒɒŋ ʊn** or as **kɪm dʒɒŋ ʌn**. Which is better?

In hangul it is spelt 김정은. In the Revised Romanization system, now official in South Korea, this transliterates as *Gim Jeong-eun*, or in the McCune-Reischauer system as *Kim Chŏng-ŭn*.

So the romanization *Kim Jong-Un* accords with neither system.

Given the Korean spelling above, we expect the pronunciation **g̊im d̥ʑʌŋ ɯn**. The vowels in the last two syllables are back and unrounded. The first, spelt ㅓ and conventionally shown in IPA as **ʌ**, tends to sound to British ears more like **ɒ**, despite being unrounded. So pronouncing *J(e)ong* in English (BrE) as **dʒɒŋ** (rather than **dʒʌŋ**) seems a good idea.

The vowel in the last syllable is more problematic. Spelt with the Korean letter ㅡ, and represented in IPA as **ɯ**, this is a vowel quality (close back unrounded) that appears exotic to us and for which we have no equivalent. Pronouncing it as English **ʌ** is wrong, since that is the sound we use for ㅓ. Using English **uː** would be inaccurate, since that is the sound we use for Korean ㅜ (as in the last syllable of 반기문 *Ban Ki-moon*). So I would vote for **ʊ** as the nearest English equivalent, giving **kɪm dʒɒŋ ʊn** as the best way of anglicizing this name, at least for BrE.

5.9 Voldemort

Lord Voldemort is Harry Potter's main enemy. He made his debut in the first novel of the J.K. Rowling series, *Harry Potter and the Philosopher's Stone* (1997) and appeared in most of the remaining novels and two of the films.

But how is his name to be pronounced?

We know that it's dangerous to pronounce it at all. Voldemort is so feared in the Wizarding world that it is considered dangerous to speak his name. Most characters in the novels refer to him as 'You-Know-Who' or 'He-Who-Must-Not-Be-Named' rather than saying his name aloud.

If we do choose to speak it aloud, though, the author – according to several press interviews with J.K. Rowling – intends his name to be pronounced with no final **t**.

> 'Is it Voldemort or Voldemor?' someone asked about Harry's evil nemesis.
> 'I say "Voldemor" but I'm the only one,' was her answer.

So I reckon the author intends it to be ˈvɒldəmɔː (or possibly ˈvəʊl-) for the English, ˈvoʊldəmɔːr for the Americans.

The name looks as if it is based on French *vol de mort* **vɔl də mɔʁ**. But this would mean 'theft of death' or 'flight of death', neither of which seems to make much sense.

One correspondent suggested that perhaps the etymology is Italian rather than French, *voglia di morte* 'death wish'. The problem with this is that Voldemort doesn't have a death wish: on the contrary, he fears death. In J.K. Rowling's reported words,

> Voldemort's fear is death, ignominious death. I mean, he regards death itself as ignominious. He thinks that it's a shameful human weakness, as you know. His worst fear is death ...

Does this justify the interpretation 'flight from death'? Voldemort's flight from death was his own quest for immortality, a theme explored throughout the whole series. The problem here, as I see it, is that French *vol* means flight as flying in the air. It does not mean flight in the sense of fleeing, running away (which in French would be *fuite*).

Though I suppose J.K. Rowling herself might have been misled by the polysemy of *flight*.

Or is the name something to do with grave robbery? Perhaps *vol de mort* (well, preferably *vol-de-morts*) could refer to 'theft of a dead body' as well as 'theft of death'. Indeed, in *Half-Blood Prince* Voldemort and the Death Eaters do engage in some grave robbery. He fills the underground lake with Inferii made from numerous men, women, and even children. So this may be the right solution.

A native speaker of French points out that in French *de mort* is found in phrases such as *instrument de mort* (= device that causes death), *engin de mort* (= vehicle or device that causes death), and *la machine de mort Nazi* (the Nazi scheme that causes death), etc. Hence the name *Voldemort* can be interpreted as something like 'deadly flight, murderous hovering, murderous soar'. There is indeed an episode in which Lord Voldemort performs an incredible act of broomless flight with the purpose of assassinating Harry, which supports this interpretation.

6 Places

6.1 Liverpool Suburbs

Non-Liverpudlians are sometimes flummoxed when confronted by the written name *Maghull* (a town or suburb located towards Ormskirk). They tend to think it might be ˈmæghʌl. But it isn't: it's məˈgʌl, even though you might think that that sounds like some unfamiliar Scottish surname *McGull*.

Another suburb, not too far from Maghull, is *Fazakerley*. This may look exotic, but its etymology is Old English and its pronunciation straightforward: fəˈzækəli.

Quite close to Fazakerley is *Kirkby*, a place you might be tempted to pronounce with two **k**s: but no, there's just one, because it's ˈkɜːbi.

Ah, *Aigburth* ˈeɡbəθ! Ah, *Widnes* ˈwɪdnɪs!

6.2 An Unwritten Possessive

In Montserrat in the West Indies there is a village shown on the map as *Frith*. Yet everyone pronounces it **frɪts**. Why should this be? It certainly surprises outsiders.

Many place names in Montserrat are taken from the names of former sugar estates identified by the surname of the erstwhile owner: *Blakes, Brades, Brodericks, Delvins, Drummonds, Dyers, Farrells, Gages, Geralds, Lees, Nixons, O'Garros, Sweeneys, Trants, Tuitts, Webbs, Whites*. The names of these villages obviously consist of the surname plus the possessive -*'s* ending. Occasionally they are written with an apostrophe, though more often not. The name of the village of *Molyneux* ˈmɒlɪnjuːz conforms to the same pattern. Some names pronounced like possessives are nevertheless written without the -*s* ending. The village shown on maps as *Farm* is actually pronounced **faːmz**. *Streatham* is ˈstrɑtəmz, which surprises people familiar with the London Streatham ˈstretəm. Omitting the possessive ending in writing is particularly usual in the case of stems ending in a sibilant. There are (or rather there were, before the volcano disaster of 1997) villages called *Harris* and *Weekes*. But they are generally pronounced ˈharɪsɪz, ˈwiːksɪz.

We would therefore expect the estate formerly belonging to Mr Frith to be called *Frith(')s*. However in popular Caribbean English there is no θ: the fricative of BrE and AmE is replaced by a plosive **t**. Just as θɪŋ becomes tɪŋ, so frɪθ becomes **frɪt**. Add the possessive ending, and we have the actual pronunciation **frɪts**.

Spoken Caribbean creoles are generally pretty cavalier about the possessive ending: you often hear things like *Mary mother* for standard *Mary's mother*. But anyone there who has learnt to read and write will have been taught that you mustn't omit the ending in writing. So it is all the more surprising that in these names people pronounce the ending but don't necessarily write it.

6.3 Pontcysyllte

One of the United Kingdom's UNESCO World Heritage Sites is the Pontcysyllte aqueduct in north Wales. This structure, built by Thomas Telford and William Jessop, is the longest and highest aqueduct in Britain.

Pontcysyllte is a lovely name, don't you think? I would transcribe its Welsh pronunciation as ˌ**pontkəˈsəɬte**. In Welsh, schwa is stressable, despite being mid central, and has the same quality in the penultimate syllable of this word as it has in the antepenultimate (see further in 6.11). In English, though, we map Welsh stressed ə onto our ʌ. So an appropriate anglicization, if you jib at attempting a proper ɬ, would be ˌ**pɒntkəˈsʌθlti**.

The first element of the name is the Welsh word for 'bridge', *pont*, an obvious Latin borrowing (*pons, pont-*, hence French *pont*) dating from the time before the arrival of the Anglo-Saxons in Britain, when the Latin-speaking Roman town-dwellers and legionaries interacted with an indigenous rural population that spoke British (= early Welsh). (That is why there are several hundred Latin loanwords in Welsh.)

What is the second element? It looks like a local dialect form of *cysylltau*, plural of *cyswllt* ˈ**kəsʊɬt** 'joint, junction'. This is related to the rather more frequently encountered verb *cysylltu* **kəˈsəɬti** 'join, connect'. So perhaps the name means something like 'junction(s) bridge'.

The nearby village is called *Froncysyllte*, 'junction brow'. Somehow it sounds less romantic when turned into English. *Bron* (when soft-mutated, *fron*) is the brow of a hill but the breast of a person or animal, hence the name *Bronwen* 'white breast'.

The stem of *cyswllt, cysylltau, cysylltu*, too, is of Latin origin. It is thought to be traceable to the Latin word *consolidus*, the stem of which has given us English *consolidate*.

The aqueduct is only two hundred years old, so did not exist in Roman times. It is nice to imagine, though, that there might have been a Roman bridge nearby, called *pons consolida*.

At the oral exam I took in Welsh after studying the language in evening class, I remember that the first question the examiner asked me was, *Beth yw eich **cysylltiad** chi gyda Chymru?* 'What is your connection with Wales?', to which I could only answer *Dim ond diddordeb ieithyddol* 'just linguistic interest'.

6.4 Bessacarr

My late aunt lived in a village on the edge of Doncaster called *Bessacarr*. You'd think it would be pronounced ˈbesəkɑː. But you'd be wrong: it's ˈbesəkə.

The weakening of unstressed vowels is one of the trickiest areas in the pronunciation of British proper names (and, of course, of English pronunciation in general). Those who first encounter them in writing tend to make them strong, while those who have local/personal familiarity with them know to weaken them.

Redcar is a much bigger place than Bessacarr. It is generally known as ˈredkɑː. But I am told that locals sometimes weaken the second syllable, making it ˈredkə.

The town of *Todmorden* in the Pennines is most usually ˈtɒdmədən or just tɒd, though you can also hear ˈtɒdmɔːdən.

In North Yorkshire there's a village called *Dishforth*. It has an RAF station generally known (I think) as ˈɑːr eɪ ef ˈdɪʃfɔːθ. But the locals call their village ˈdɪʃfəθ.

I was at school with a chap called *Spofforth* ˈspɒfɔːθ. But the village of Spofforth near Harrogate is ˈspɒfəθ, which according to the BBC Pronouncing Dictionary is also the usual pronunciation of the surname.

Most English villages called *Marden* are of course ˈmɑːdn̩. But the one in Kent, which has a different etymological origin, can be mɑːˈden.

Spelling pronunciation is a powerful influence. The place I know as ˈæskət, *Ascot* in Berkshire, is often heard as ˈæskɒt.

Even in America things are not necessarily as you might expect. Think of *Poughkeepsie* pəˈkɪpsi.

6.5 Slaugham

Just off the main A23 road from London to Brighton, near the intriguingly named Pease Pottage in West Sussex, there are signs to a village named *Slaugham*. Driving past, I've sometimes idly wondered how this written form is to be interpreted. How do the locals pronounce this name? Does it rhyme with *Maugham* mɔːm?

The answer is no, it doesn't.

I happened to be watching a traffic police video programme on television, when the action moved to this area. As the officers in the pursuit car reported their position over the radio I noted with interest that they called it ˈslɑːfəm. So it's like *laughter*, not like *slaughter*. The old BBC Pronouncing Dictionary of British Names says it can be either ˈslɑːfəm or ˈslæfəm, prioritizing the latter.

Not far away, *Laughton* in East Sussex, like the identically spelt surname, is straightforwardly ˈlɔːtn̩. But the name *Claughton* is more complicated: there are places in Lancashire so spelt that are ˈklæftən and ˈklaɪtn̩, while in Merseyside we have ˈklɔːtn̩, which is also the pronunciation of the surname.

6.6 Arnos Grove

Along the northern reaches of the Piccadilly Line in London there's a tube station called *Arnos Grove*. The etymology of the first part of this name is believed to be *Arnold's*, via an intermediate stage *Arnol's*.

How is the *Arnos* of *Arnos Grove* pronounced today? Given its etymology, we might expect ˈɑːnəʊz. The omission of the possessive apostrophe need not surprise us in the name of a London tube station, given other apostrophe-free Underground names such as *Canons Park, Barons Court, Carpenders Park, Golders Green* and *Colliers Wood*.

But I confess that I have always said the name to myself as ˈɑːnɒs, making it parallel to *chaos, ethos* and non-possessive names such as *Amos* and *Carlos*. (Note to Americans: I know that for you these names are ˈeɪməs and ˈkɑːrloʊs respectively. But in BrE they're ˈeɪmɒs and ˈkɑːlɒs.)

Checking with other Londoners, I find that most people, like me, say ˈɑːnɒs *Grove*. Even if once upon a time it was ˈɑːnəʊz, it isn't now.

6.7 Caol

There's a village in the Highland area of Scotland, called *Caol* (Scottish Gaelic for 'narrow'). It lies just to the north of Fort William. In Gaelic the name is reportedly pronounced kɯːɫ or kʉːɫ (accounts differ as to the roundedness of the vowel). In English we have no close back unrounded vowel, and the nearest we can get in RP and the like to ɯː is ɜː. Hence the English version of the village name kɜːl, making it a homophone of *curl*. However Scottish English has no ɜː, and typically pronounces *curl* as kʌrl. So it's just as well that the usual Anglicization is based on the variant with uː, making the village kuːl, a homophone of *cool*.

6.8 English Places

How should geographical names be treated in pronunciation dictionaries? I thought it might be useful if I tried to say what my policy was in LPD, at least as concerns place names in England.

I must confess that I did not set up a set of principles before starting work. Rather, what follows is a post-hoc attempt to express the principles I think I generally followed.

6.8 English Places

Let's start from the difficult fact that in England everything is complicated by social class factors. In 1900, most English people spoke with a local accent. Those who spoke with non-regional RP or something like it were a small minority. Still today it is the case that, broadly speaking, the lower your social class, the more your pronunciation diverges from RP; the higher your social class, the closer to RP (aka General British, etc). Whereas RP speakers can be found in all parts of the country (or could when I were a lad, when not only the local landed gentry but also the vicar and the doctor probably spoke RP or something very close to it), a 'local' or 'regional' accent implies non-RP. The local accent typically includes various features that are regarded as non-standard and have traditionally been considered unworthy of mention in normative reference works such as dictionaries.

So let's agree, for the purposes of argument, that most people who live in *Hull* call it ʊl. But in RP it's unquestionably hʌl. We can leave it to the sociolinguists to determine the precise details of who uses which of these pronunciations and under what circumstances, and to what extent there are also intermediate forms such as **hʊl, həl** and perhaps also ʌl.

I think there is very general agreement in England that we don't want dictionaries to tell us about h-dropped pronunciations. In any case, they can immediately be inferred once we know that in working-class England (except, it now appears, in multicultural inner cities) all aitches are subject to being dropped.

I think it's also generally agreed that we don't want to be told about the use of ʊ in all names in which RP has ʌ; again, this can be inferred by rule, once we know that in the north of England the FOOT-STRUT split does not apply, which means that there is no /ʌ/ and which makes *Hull* a perfect rhyme for *full* (as against RP, etc, in which **hʌl** has a different vowel from **fʊl**).

Those of us who, like me, grew up in relatively high-status families in the north have been aware of this variability since childhood. In the Lancashire village where I lived until I was a teenager, our neighbours drank from **kʊps** and ˈ**dlasız** (ˈ**glæsız**); but in our house we had **kʌps** and ˈ**glɑːsız**.

(As an aside, it wasn't until I went to boarding school in the south that I discovered that *fuck* has ʌ. We didn't swear in our family, and the only people I had heard using this word until then had pronounced it **fʊk**.)

The name of the village was *Upholland*. (Nowadays people often write it as two words, *Up Holland*. In those days we didn't.) Yes, our neighbours called it ʊpˈ**ɒlənd**. But we, of course, called it ʌpˈ**hɒlənd**. It is the latter that you would expect a dictionary of place names to show; the former can be inferred from it, but not vice versa.

Our nearest town was *Wigan*. We called it ˈ**wɪgən**, although quite a few of its inhabitants called it ˈ**wɪgɪn** (which caused some amusement: people would use it as part of a comical exaggerated local accent).

So it is with the BATH words. Our neighbours might have a **baθ** (actually, many had just a zinc tub in the kitchen, brought out as needed); we had a **bɑːθ**. Our neighbours had their TRAP vowel in the BATH words; we had our PALM-START vowel.

I have two younger brothers. All three of us grew up together and shared the same schooling (local primary school in Wigan, then fee-paying boarding schools in the south of England). I notice that one brother, who became a businessman in Birmingham, has switched to TRAP in the BATH words. The other, who has lived in Lancashire all his adult life and became a school teacher, has retained the PALM-START vowel in BATH words, as have I. (I moved to London as a postgraduate student and have continued to live in London all my adult life.)

One of my uncles lived in *Grasmere*, in Cumbria. His wife, my aunt by marriage, also happened to be aunt to the Attenborough brothers, the actor Richard (Lord A.) and the TV naturalist David. (You'll have heard how they speak: both are native RP speakers and grew up in Leicester, in the linguistic north.) They, and we, called the place ˈgrɑːsmɪə. For many local people, though, the first syllable had the TRAP vowel. *Grass* and the first syllable of *Grasmere* have the BATH vowel.

That's the background from which I felt confident in saying that the RP name of *Castleford*, Yorks., is ˈkɑːsl̩fəd, though the great majority of locals certainly give it the TRAP vowel in the first syllable. For *Doncaster*, on the other hand, all three possibilities -kəs-, -kɑːs-, -kæs- seem to me to be at home in RP, though probably in that order of preference.

As for London place names, I naturally gave the pronunciation of *Wapping* as ˈwɒpɪŋ, ignoring the ˈwɒpʔɪn you hear from many locals. Likewise *Harlesden*: ˈhɑːlzdən, not ˈɑːozdən.

And so to *Newcastle*. The RP form for all places with this name (in my view) is ˈnjuːˌkɑːsl̩. That is how I pronounce it myself. However, the size and importance of the city of Newcastle-upon-Tyne is such that I felt it appropriate to mention in LPD (following the BBC Pronouncing Dictionary of British Names) that locally it is -ˈkæsl̩, with a different stressing and different second vowel. (Here, of course phonemic /æ/ subsumes phonetic [a].) There is a similar note at *Carlisle*.

6.9 Where Was That Again?

Londoners are used to hearing overseas visitors struggling with what to us are very familiar names such as *Leicester* ˈlestə(r). We fail to realize how far from transparent the spelling is in such cases.

Sometimes, though, it's us Brits who are caught out by American names whose spoken form is just as surprising, in view of the spelling. We may know about *Houston* and even *Poughkeepsie* (Section 6.4) – but I was brought up short recently by *Ashtabula*, Ohio.

Given the antepenultimate stress of *nebula* and *fibula*, not to mention *tabulate*, I think I might be forgiven for expecting this name to be stressed on the **tæb** syllable. But it isn't: it's actually ˌæʃtəˈbjuːlə. (Thanks to Michael Ashby for this one. I'd better add it to LPD.)

On the other hand I'm told that *Temecula*, California, is pronounced **tə ˈmekjʊlə**. Well, of course, that's just what I'd have predicted.

A correspondent from Boston, Massachusetts, sent me a list of local shibboleth place names. They include *Quincy* **ˈkwɪnzi**, *Peabody* **ˈpiːbədi**, and *Billerica* **bɪlˈrɪkə**. (Compare *Billericay* in England, which is ˌbɪləˈrɪki.)

Bostonians pronounce their local *Gloucester*, *Leicester*, and *Worcester* just as we do their namesakes in England. English place names in southern New England, on the other hand, seem to have fared more poorly, with Rhode Island having *Warwick* **ˈwɔ(r)wɪk** and Connecticut having the *Thames* **θeɪmz** *River* (compare England's *River Thames* **temz**).

A British name that caught my attention recently is that of the village of *Wadeford* in Somerset. In a news report about flooding I'm sure I heard a local refer to it as **ˈwɒdɪfəd**. The BBC Pronunciation Unit tells me, however, that

> according to the parish council clerk, that is an older local pronunciation which isn't used quite as much now; most locals prefer **ˈwɒdfəd**.

Anyway, it's certainly not the ***ˈweɪdfəd** that the spelling would seem to suggest.

6.10 Penge

I have been browsing through the second edition of *A Dictionary of London Place-Names* by A.D. Mills (OUP 2012).

One of the things that Mills points out is that apart from various river names (*Lee* or *Lea*, *Brent*), the only London name of Celtic origin is *Penge*, the SE20 suburb, which is derived from a Celtic/British/Old Welsh compound corresponding to modern Welsh *pen* 'head' plus *coed* 'trees, wood', exactly as in *Pencoed* in south Wales, literally 'Woodhead'.

He comments further:

> Some make mock of **Penge** (an unusual name but not a pretentious place) by pronouncing it superciliously to rhyme with 'blancmange'.

That is, they jocularly call it not **pendʒ** but **pɒndʒ** (or perhaps **põʒ**).

I have a friend who lives in *Fulham* **ˈfʊləm**. Sometimes in jest he similarly refers to it as **flɑːm**. I've even heard *Clapham* called **klɑːm**. Another whimsical or jocular pronunciation distortion of this type is found in Liverpool, where the name of the district of *Blundellsands* ˌblʌndl̩ˈsændz (or in the local Scouse accent ˌblʊndl̩ˈsandz) is sometimes converted into the posher-sounding ˌblʌndl̩ˈsɑːndz, as if the final syllable belonged to the BATH lexical set (compare *Alexander* and *commands*, and see 6.1).

Mills tell us that the etymology of *Fulham* is the rather boring 'river-bend of a man called *Fulla'. In the Domesday Book (1086) it was spelt *Fuleham*, but in the Anglo-Saxon Chronicle (c. 900) *Fullanhamme*, with an OE genitive case ending *-n* on the personal name.

The street name *Piccadilly* has, Mills tells us, 'rather a bizarre' origin.

It seems that the name first appears as *Pickadilly Hall* in 1623, otherwise *Pickadel Hall* in 1636, as a (no doubt humorous) nickname for a house belonging to one Robert Baker, a successful tailor who had made his fortune from the sale of *piccadills* or *pickadillies*, a term used for various kinds of collars, highly fashionable at the time, for both men and women.

EFL teachers can use ˌpɪkəˈdɪli as a convenient demonstration of the 'stress shift' effect when we come to *Piccadilly Circus* ˌpɪkədɪli ˈsɜːkəs.

6.11 Machynlleth

Machynlleth in mid-Wales is quite a small town, not often featured in the national news. But when it did happen to be in the news recently I noticed the television presenters on the BBC1 Breakfast show handing over to their correspondent in what they called məˈkʌnlɪθ. The correspondent in question, who from his name appeared to be a Welsh-speaking Welshman, proceeded to refer to the town as maˈχənɬeθ.

Note the unreduced vowels in the first and last syllables and the schwa in the middle, stressed, syllable. In a manner strikingly unlike the Germanic languages, Welsh does not routinely reduce most vowels in unstressed syllables, while often having ə in stressed ones, but only if they are non-final (clitics such as the definite article *y(r)* count as non-final).

I was in my mid-forties when I sat my Welsh A-levels after studying in evening classes. I remember that in the English to Welsh translation paper, the passage set began 'The sign on the station platform read "Machynlleth"'. I dutifully recast my Welsh version so that *Machynlleth* was the first word of the sentence, as is required by Welsh syntax, rather than the last, as in English.

6.12 Acres

I've been reading David Abulafia's *The Great Sea: a Human History of the Mediterranean*. In the part dealing with the second millennium AD, one of the seaports frequently mentioned is the Levantine port known in English as Acre, in the north of what is now Israel.

I have always assumed that in English we pronounce this *Acre* identically with the common noun referring to the unit of measurement equivalent to about two-fifths of a hectare, i.e. ˈeɪkə(r). Wikipedia, however, asserts that it is ˈɑːkə(r). I see that Merriam-Webster gives both of these possibilities as well as a third one, ˈɑːkrə. In Hebrew it's עַכּוֹ, *'Akko*, in Arabic: عَكّا, *'Akkā*. The *r* in its English spelling evidently comes from its Greek name Ἄκρη *Akrē*.

There are various English place names that include the element *acre*, or rather its OE form *æcer* 'cultivated land': for example, *Sandiacre* ˈsændieɪkə in Derbyshire, and also *Castle Acre, South Acre* and *West Acre* in Norfolk, all with ˈeɪkə. On Merseyside, however, *Gateacre*, etymologically 'goat-acre', is ˈɡætəkə, with a weakened penultimate vowel.

The village of *Talacre*, not too far away but in north Wales, is properly tæl ˈækreɪ, being a Welsh compound of *tâl* 'end' plus the plural of *acer* from English *acre*. The standard Welsh plural form is, I believe, *aceri*; this *acre* must be a local variant *acrau*, with *-au* pronounced in the usual local way as **e**.

For the same reason *Acrefair* near Wrexham is properly ˌækrɪˈvaɪə (Welsh **akreˈvair**); but I am told people usually omit the **r** in the second syllable. Etymologically, the *fair* element in this name is the soft-mutated form of *Mair* 'Mary', so the name means 'Mary's acres'.

6.13 Beguildy

Beguildy in Wales looks as if it ought to be pronounced bɪˈɡɪldi, with the middle part being like the word *guild*. But actually it's pronounced bɪˈɡaɪldi, with a diphthong like in *guile*.

How come? As is often the case in Wales, it's because the name is an anglicization of what was originally Welsh. Its etymology, and its Welsh spelling, is *Bugeildy*, which in Welsh means 'shepherd-house'. *Bugail* ˈbɪɡaɪl is the Welsh for 'shepherd', and *tŷ*, here mutated to *dy*, means 'house'. We see the same ending in *Tonypandy* ˌtɒnəˈpændi 'lay-land of the fulling-mill'.

While the spelling of the erstwhile *Bugeildy* has been rearranged to look more English, the pronunciation has stayed essentially the same as it was before the English language arrived.

7 Abroad

7.1 Sichuan

There is a Chinese province known in English as Szechuan, Szechwan, or Sichuan. Although we are now encouraged to write this name as Sichuan, the older spellings Szechuan and Szechwan are still widely used, together with the pronunciation ˌsetʃˈwɑːn that they suggest. The OBGP calls this an 'established anglicization', but nevertheless recommends səˈtʃwæn. In LPD I give ˌsɪtʃˈwɑːn.

I have also, though, heard Americans speak of ˌʃeʃˈwɑːn. You can see how the spelling *Szechuan* might produce this – if we give *sz* its Polish value and *ch* its French value.

In tone-marked Hanyu Pinyin it is written *Sìchuān*. The Mandarin pronunciation is ⁴sɯ ¹tsʰwan, where the symbol **ɯ** represents an alveolar approximant with back unrounded resonance [zɯ] or an alveolarized back unrounded vowel [ɯᶻ] (the sinologists' phonetic symbol – not recognized by the IPA – for this unusual vowel is ɿ).

The Chinese written form of its name consists of the character for 'four', 四, followed by the character for 'river', 川. So the meaning is the straightforward 'four rivers'.

7.2 L'Aquila

In 2009 the Italian city of L'Aquila was devastated by an earthquake. To begin with, BBC presenters and newsreaders reporting this event called the city læˈkwiːlə, and even reporters on the spot got it wrong.

One, who had hastened to Italy to address us from among the ruins, gave it the more rarefied pronunciation læˈkiːlə, as if it were a Mexican liqueur. We ought, of course, to pronounce it with the stress on the first syllable. In Italian phonetics, it's ˈlakwila.

At the time there was some criticism of the BBC's Pronunciation Unit, whose proclaimed purpose is 'to ensure that pronunciations used on the BBC are accurate and consistent'. The fault lay, however, not with the Unit, but with newsreaders and reporters who had not bothered to consult the advice it provides. For *L'Aquila* the Unit recommends the anglicization ˈlækwɪlə.

Once upon a time any educated person had some knowledge of Latin. Not any more. But classicists will tell you that the Latin word for 'eagle', the origin of this name, is *ăquĭla* (with a short *i*). As many readers will know, a Latin word in which the penultimate vowel is short and in an open syllable is stressed on the antepenultimate. This Latin stress rule still works for Italian, as long as you know the Latin vowel quantity, even though vowel quantity has been lost as such in Italian. So *aquila* is one of the so-called *parole sdrucciole* (words with antepenultimate stress), like the word for 'liver', *fegato*, which catches out so many foreigners in Italian restaurants – being pronounced not **fe'gato** but **'fegato**.

And by the way, the Latin word for 'songs' is *carmĭna*, so this word too was/is stressed on the first syllable. As far as Orff's *Carmina Burana* goes, insisting on this stressing seems to be becoming a lost cause. Instead of the traditional **'kɑːmɪnə**, one nowadays hears British music lovers saying **kɑːˈmiːnə**.

7.3 Rock Law

A newspaper article about the Polish city of *Wrocław* reported that Brits who live there call it 'rock-law'. If true, this is a particularly egregious spelling pronunciation.

I've never heard **'rɒk lɔː** myself. English people in the circles in which I move call the place **'vrɒtslɑːv**, and that is what I put in LPD. Its pronunciation in Polish is actually **'vrɔtswaf**.

Two other interesting Polish cities are *Poznań* and *Kraków*. The latter has a traditional English name, *Cracow*, and a corresponding pronunciation – **'krækaʊ** – to set alongside its Polish name, which is pronounced **'krakuf**.

All three of these places are also known in English by their German names: *Breslau, Posen, Krakau*. The first is presumably the source of the surname of the comedy actor Bernard Bresslaw (1934–1993).

The capital of Poland is known in English only by its English name, *Warsaw* **'wɔːsɔː** (which unfortunately can easily be misheard as *Walsall*). The Germans call it *Warschau* **'vaʁʃaʊ**, the Poles themselves *Warszawa* **varˈʃava**.

7.4 Duisburg

Duisburg, near Düsseldorf in Germany, is in the news from time to time. Its name has an 'established anglicization' (OBGP), **'djuːzbɜːɡ**, which presumably implies variants **'duːzbɜːɡ** and **'dʒuːzbɜːɡ**. But I have also heard newsreaders say **'djuːɪzbɜːɡ**, an obvious spelling pronunciation.

In German its ordinary pronunciation is **'dyːsbʊʁk**, which does not exactly follow the spelling. Personally, given that I learnt German in Kiel in the far north of the country, I tend to pronounce it **'dyːsbʊʁç**, unless I remind myself not to.

There is no questioning established anglicizations such as *Berlin* (ˌbɜːˈlɪn) and *Hamburg* (ˈhæmbɜːg), different as they are from their echt German pronunciations (the German pronunciation of the first being bɛʁˈliːn and of the second ˈhambʊʁk). We call *Dresden* ˈdrezdən, even though in German its first vowel is long and the *s* voiceless, ˈdʁeːsdən. We call *Leipzig* ˈlaɪpzɪg, though in German it's ˈlaɪptsɪç. And we use French-derived names for *Cologne* kəˈləʊn (German *Köln* kœln) and *Munich* ˈmjuːnɪk (German *München* ˈmʏnçən). Some English speakers misguidedly imagine that the correct pronunciation of *Munich* must be ˈmjuːnɪx.

One or two other German cities have old-fashioned names now rarely heard in English, for example *Brunswick* ˈbrʌnzwɪk, in German *Braunschweig* ˈbʁaʊnʃvaɪk. In English the pied piper lured the children away from *Hamelin* ˈhæm(ə)lɪn, though the German name of that town is *Hameln* ˈhaːməln.

8 Home from Abroad

8.1 Agrément

We recently had the outside of our house treated with a protective spray-on coating. The salesman who persuaded us to allow his company to carry out the work pointed out to us that we could set our minds at rest about the quality of the product, because it was approved by the British Board of Agrément.

British Board of what? The salesman pronounced it ˈægrəmənt.

The Board's website explains:

> The BBA is the UK's major approval body for new construction products and installers. Our Agrément Certificates are recognized by specifiers and other industry decision-makers as proof that the products covered by them have been rigorously assessed, will allow compliance with Building Regulations to be achieved and will last for a defined period.

This word was not to be found in any of the dictionaries I had to hand at the time. Consulting the on-line OED, however, I find that the word is indeed recorded, but not in this meaning.

The OED gives three meanings. The first is as an alternative to *agreement* sense 9 ('pl. Agreeable qualities, circumstances, or accessories. Now treated as Fr., les agréments'). The second is musical ('pl. Grace-notes, embellishments'), the third diplomatic ('The approval given by the government of a country to a diplomatic representative of another country'). But there is no mention of the BBA's commercial sense.

You read it here first.

8.2 An Italian Wine

English people are so confused and ignorant about foreign languages and how to pronounce them that I sometimes despair about (a) trying to document the state of the language and (b) giving helpful guidance to EFL learners who want to know how to pronounce foreign words and phrases in English.

I heard someone on the radio saying what a good wine *pinot grigio* was. But she called it ˌpiːnəʊ ˈgriːgiəʊ.

55

Oh dear, oh dear. *Pinot* is French, and apparently means 'pinecone', being used of this variety of grape perhaps because of the appearance of the small clusters in which it grows. It is pronounced **pino**, which as you would expect becomes English ˈpiːnəʊ. So far so good. In French the full name of the grape in question is *pinot gris* ('grey pinecone').

The Italian for 'grey' is *grigio*, so the clone of pinot gris grown in Italy is known as pinot grigio. In Italian the second word is pronounced exactly as the spelling suggests (if you know the rules for spelling-to-sound in Italian), namely ˈgriːdʒo. This becomes English ˈgriːdʒəʊ or, if you must, ˈgriːdʒiəʊ.

But please not ˈgriːgiəʊ. What are we going to hear next? Lake ˌmægiˈɔːreɪ?

8.3 Ginkgo

In the front quad at UCL there are two ginkgo trees, which every autumn shed their distinctive leaves on the ground.

The origin of the name is not altogether clear. It is sometimes claimed that the Latin (and hence the English) specific name of the tree, *Ginkgo*, results from a combination of folk etymology and misreading.

All the OED tells us about the etymology of ginkgo is:

> [Jap., f. Chinese *yinhsing* silver apricot.]

In Chinese characters and Hanyu pinyin this Chinese etymon would be written 銀杏 *yínxìng*. The story is that when the tree was introduced into Japan from China, the Chinese name was borrowed into Japanese with the pronunciation *ginnan*. But the same Chinese characters can also be read in Japanese as *ichō* or *ginkyō*, which is where the folk etymology comes in.

Apparently Engelbert Kaempfer, the first Westerner to see the species in 1690, wrote down this latter version in his *Amoenitates Exoticae* (1712). According to one version (which some authorities dispute), his *y* was misread as a *g*, and the misspelling stuck: not *ginkyo* but *ginkgo*.

Our pronunciation follows the spelling, so that we call this tree ˈgɪŋkəʊ. If it had not been for Kaempfer's bad handwriting, we'd presumably be calling it ˈgɪŋkiəʊ. Because of the pronunciation, people also often misspell it as *gingko*. Confusingly, there is also a Japanese word *ginkō*, pronounced with -ŋ-. But it means 'bank'.

The second, specific, part of the scientific name *Ginkgo biloba* transparently means 'having two lobes', a reference to the shape of the leaves. You'd think that it would be pronounced in English as ˌbaɪˈləʊbə, since this is what we get for the Latin prefix *bi-* in *bisexual, bifurcation, bipolar* and other words. But in practice people who talk about the supposed medical benefits of *Ginkgo biloba* extract generally seem to say bɪˈləʊbə.

8.4 Liebestod

   Hearing a radio announcer tell us that we were about to hear Wagner's aria ˈliːbztɒd has provoked me into something of a rant about people's ignorance of how to pronounce words and names in foreign languages.

In German *Liebestod* ('love death') is pronounced ˈliːbəstoːt. German long vowels in spelling situations where they would be short in English cause particular difficulty to English learners: you hear *der Mond* moːnt (moon) mispronounced as mɔnd. Final obstruent devoicing, too, is a thing a lot of people don't know about. A reasonable anglicization might ignore it. For the Wagner aria I'd be happy in English with ˈliːbəztəʊd.

Our radio and TV announcers do try. The sports commentators are used to the idea that the letter *j* can stand for a palatal approximant rather than dʒ – they have no difficulty with the tennis player *Jelena Janković*. But then they overdo it by referring to Azerbaijan as ˌæzəbaɪˈjɑːn. (In Azeri that's *Azərbaycan*, with the usual Turkish spelling-to-sound correspondence *c* = dʒ.)

They know that Polish *sz* can be equated to English ʃ. They make a brave attempt at *Bydgoszcz*. But then they turn *Szeged*, Hungarian ˈsɛɡɛd, into ˈʃɛɡɛd (which sounds unfortunately like the Hungarian for 'your arse'). Just as Spanish spelling conventions don't apply in Italian or vice versa, so it is with Polish and Hungarian.

Chinese Pinyin continues to baffle them. Most of the sports commentators know that Chinese *x* is to be pronounced like English ʃ (actually it's more precisely ɕ or even **sj**). But then *Xie* comes out as **ʃaɪ** instead of the **ʃe** or perhaps **ʃeɪ** we ought to hear. You can't win.

We all know that German *s* is pronounced **ʃ** when followed by *p* or *t*, right? So *spät* is **ʃpeːt**, and *Stein* is **ʃtaɪn**, right?

Another radio announcer clearly knew this. What she didn't know was the constraint upon this German reading rule. She referred to the Wagner aria as the **ˈliːbəʃtoːd**.

In Standard German the rule *st* = **ʃt** applies only morpheme-initially. Elsewhere it doesn't. So *fast* is **fast**, *erst* is **eːɐ̯st**. In compound words, you have to know where the morpheme boundary lies. Thus *Backstein* is *Back* + *Stein* and pronounced **ˈbakʃtain**. But in the word *Liebestod*, the *s* and *t* are separated by a morpheme boundary (*Liebes* + *Tod*), hence **ˈliːbəstoːt**.

English words, of course, never begin with **ʃt**. Or at least, they used not to. Fifty-five year ago, when I were nobbut a lad fettling me English phonetics, my teacher John Trim gave us the usual lecture on phonotactics. In those distant days we could all agree that **ʃt** was ruled out, not possible, not well-formed, as an initial cluster.

But nowadays things have changed. You'll now find journalists using the words *schtick, schtum*, and *shtuck* (meaning respectively 'stage routine; gimmick', 'silent', and 'difficulty'). There's some uncertainty about their spellings, *schtick* or *shtick*, and *shtoom, schtoom, shtum* or *schtum*; but we agree in pronouncing them **ʃtɪk, ʃtʊm,** and **ʃtʊk**. (The spellings with *scht-* are a bit of a nonsense, anyhow, since the corresponding German words are spelt simply *st-: Stück* 'piece' and *stumm* 'mute' – see further Section 11.19.)

For the first two, the earliest citations in the OED, which prefers the spellings *shtick* and *shtoom*, are barely half a century old. These words probably entered English from Yiddish rather than from Standard German. The origin of *shtuck* is not clear: it is apparently not Yiddish. As far as its origin goes, we're in dead shtook.

There's may be some uncertainty, then, about spelling and etymology: But there's no hesitation about the pronunciation. All three words have the cluster that used to be impossible: **ʃtɪk, ʃtʊm, ʃtʊk**.

8.5 Women's Tennis

Two correspondents have written to me complaining about the way commentators for the Wimbledon tennis tournaments pronounce Maria Sharapova's name. As they pointed out, in Russian her surname bears antepenultimate stress: she is Шара́пова **ʃəˈrapəvə**, so in English we Brits ought to call her **ʃəˈræpəvə**, and the Americans perhaps **ʃəˈrɑpəvə**. But we don't, we call her **ˌʃærəˈpəʊvə** with penultimate stress.

Dismayed as purists and my correspondents may be, there's not much we can do about this. I am told that the tennis player herself is quite content to be given penultimate stress in English and to be known as BrE ˌʃærəˈpəʊvə, AmE ˌʃɑrəˈpoʊvə.

There were two other woman tennis players in the 2011 tournament the pronunciation of whose names perhaps deserves comment. One is Sabine Lisicki. She is German, born in Troisdorf, although her name must be of Czech (or some other Slavonic) origin. Neither of my German pronunciation dictionaries gives the pronunciation of her name. In Czech it would presumably be *Lisický* ˈlisitski:, and in Polish *Lisicki* liˈɕitski, though for her in each case with a feminine ending. The English commentators call her lɪˈzɪki, lə-.

The other is that year's women's single champion, Petra Kvitova. She is Czech, and in Czech her name is written *Kvitová* (with the obligatory unstressed feminine ending *-ová* borne by all Czech females) and pronounced ˈkvitova:. Our commentators have a problem with the cluster **kv-**, solved by inserting an anaptyctic schwa, giving kəˈvɪtəvə.

I am not sure why **kv-** presents such a problem to English speakers. We seem to manage to produce **sv-** without anaptyxis in *Svengali, svelte, Svalbard* and, um, *svarabhakti* (though you may feel the English versions of these words have **sf-** rather than **sv-**). We manage ʃv- in nazi-era mock-German *Schweinhund* as well as in *Schweitzer* and *Schwarzwald*. And **kw-** is an everyday cluster for us and not so very different from **kv-**. Furthermore Americans, though perhaps not most Brits, are familiar with the Yiddish word *kvetch*, happily borrowed into English as **kvetʃ** or perhaps **kfetʃ**.

8.6 Raw Fish

My Japanese colleague Masaki Taniguchi tells me he was on a train when he got talking, mostly in English, to a Swiss lady who was touring Japan with her family. She was from Lausanne and her first language was French. She mentioned that she loved sushi.

Sushi comes in many varieties. While westerners usually like most of them, not everyone is enthusiastic about those that include uncooked fish.

Masaki asked the Swiss lady 'Do you like raw fish?'.

Her unexpected reply was 'Oh, you speak German'.

It so happens that the (standard) German *roher Fisch* ʁoːɐ fɪʃ sounds very similar to the English *raw fish* ɹɔː fɪʃ.

This reminds me of a more complicated multilingual example, probably apocryphal. A visiting Frenchman in England went to buy an ice cream. The vendor asked him what size he wanted. The Frenchman understood the question but answered in French, *à deux boules* (with two scoops) **a dø bul**. Fortunately communication was not impaired, despite the interlocutors' ignorance of one another's language, because the English vendor heard it as *a double* ə dʌbɫ.

8.7 A Heavenly Haven

Peter Roach sent me an email:

> I wonder if you noticed the interview on Channel 4 News with Christine LaGarde, French Finance Minister. My wife and I were marvelling at her excellent English (including her pronunciation) but wondering why she kept referring to 'tax heavens' instead of 'tax havens'. We then remembered that the French for this is *paradis fiscal*. I hope somebody has put her right now.

Mme LaGarde's English is indeed much too good for her to confuse **eɪ** (as in *haven*) with **e** (as in *heaven*). But with *heaven* being a near-synonym of *paradise*, one can understand the confusion.

It suggests that she has learnt the English expression *tax haven* by hearing it used in context, rather than by encountering it in the course of reading.

English *haven* has moved away from its historical meaning 'harbour' to its current meaning, a refuge. Where English speaks of a *tax haven* for those reluctant to pay taxes in their home country, French, German, and Spanish speak of a *paradise* (*paradis fiscal, Steuerparadies, paraíso fiscal*).

8.8 Muchas Gratsias

Who pronounces the Spanish for 'thank you', *gracias*, as ˈgʁatsi̯as?
Having flown to and from Argentina with the German airline Lufthansa, I can tell you: it's Germans speaking Spanish as a foreign language.

In native-speaker Spanish, of course, the word is pronounced ˈgraθjas or, in Latin America, ˈgrasjas, ˈgrasjah.

This is a straightforward case of foreign learners being misled by the spelling. In German the letter *c* when followed by *i* or *e* stands for **ts**, as in *Circe* ˈtsɪrtsə. So the mispronunciation ˈgʁatsi̯as is a bit like French speakers of EFL saying *structure* with **y** (twice), using a vowel that plays no part in the English phonetic system but is what the French letter *u* typically stands for.

The most striking phonetic feature of Argentinian Spanish to my ears is the use of ʃ, ʒ for Spanish /j/, spelt *y* or *ll*. The voiceless variant is what one hears all around – for example, for *Callao* (street) you hear **kaˈʃao**. But all the Argentinians I spoke to claimed to themselves always use the voiced variant, **kaˈʒao**, which they judged more elegant. That's still not very like Castilian **kaˈʎao, kaˈjao**.

8.9 The Letter *z*

Just like *c* in certain positions (8.8), in German the letter *z* always stands for a voiceless alveolar affricate, **ts**. Thus *zu* 'to' is pronounced **tsuː**, *Zeit* 'time' is **tsait**, and *Herz* 'heart' is **hɛrts**.

Recently I enrolled for a refresher course in German. I was rather shocked to notice that when one of my fellow-students pronounced *zu* as **zuː** and *ausgezeichnet* as **ausgəˈzaixnət** the teacher did not correct her but on the contrary let the mispronunciations pass.

What this fellow-student was doing was to assume that German *z* stands for the same sound as English *z* or indeed IPA **z**.

Although I am in my seventies, this course was actually the first formal classroom instruction in German I had ever had. That's because as a teenager I was fortunate enough to be able to learn German under ideal conditions: not in the classroom, but by living with a German family for two months, with an exchange friend who regarded it as his duty to make sure that I emerged from the experience with a good command of German. Admittedly, in the month before I set off for Germany I did spend some time with a self-instruction textbook of German; but apart from that I learnt the language on the spot, ab initio and by total immersion. No doubt I benefited from being thoroughly familiar, from Greek and Latin, with languages in which nouns or noun phrases had to be put into an appropriate case depending on the syntax, while adjectives had to agree with the noun in gender, case, and number; and of course German is closely related to English.

My host family used to joke that when I arrived the only thing I could say was *Ich bin müde* 'I'm tired'. By the time I returned home to England, accompanied by my exchange friend who was now due to spend an equivalent length of time with us, I could speak pretty fluently as far as everyday topics were concerned.

Anecdotally, I remember how the fraught matter of adjectival endings (*ein neues Auto, das neue Auto*) suddenly became sort of automatic at three or four weeks in. That is, as long as I knew the gender of a noun, the accompanying article and adjectives would come out right without conscious mental computation.

Although English does not have words beginning **ts**, I do not recall ever having had difficulty with pronouncing words such as *zu* or *Zeit*. Partly that may be because I was hearing them spoken in a live situation rather than seeing them written in some textbook; partly it may be because I was fortunate enough to be blessed with a 'good ear' and hence to be alive to all sorts of phonetic subtleties even before I had begun to study phonetics formally.

Another reason may be that two years earlier I had taught myself Esperanto. In Esperanto the letter *c* stands for the affricate **ts**. Thus *paco* 'peace' is pronounced ˈ**patso**, and *celo* 'aim, purpose' is pronounced ˈ**tselo**. Although I didn't know it at the time, Zamenhof had based *celo* (the *-o* is just the ending borne by all nouns) on Russian цель **tselʲ**, Polish *cel* **tsel**, and German *Ziel* **tsiːl**, all with that same meaning. As a native speaker of Russian, Polish, and Yiddish, he may well not have been aware that for speakers of French, English, Spanish, and various other languages an initial affricate **ts** may present a bit of a problem.

But I did what my Esperanto textbook told me to, and carefully pronounced the letter *c* as **ts**. This even involved the difficult *mi scias* 'I know', **mi** ˈ**stsias**. Again, for Zamenhof models such as the international word *scena* 'scene' – Russian сцена ˈstsʲenə, Polish *scena* ˈstsena, German *Szene* ˈstseːnə – would have led him automatically to Esperanto *sceno* and therefore to other Latin-derived words with initial *sc*.

So I never thought twice about German words like *Ziel*. Ausgezeichnet!

8.10 Greek Politics

A note to newsreaders and others reporting on Greek politics.

The political party *Syriza* is not sɪˈrɪtsə. In Greek it's Σύριζα, pronounced ˈsiriza. The name is a punning acronym, short for 'Coalition of the Radical Left' but also meaning 'radically'. An appropriate anglicization would be ˈsɪrɪzə. The Greek letter zeta in its name, transliterated *z*, is read just like English *z*. It is not to be interpreted in a German way as **ts** or for that matter in a Spanish way as θ.

In Greek the name of its leader, Alexis Tsipras, is spelt Αλέξης Τσίπρας and pronounced aˈleksis ˈtsipras. If you can make the effort to pronounce a proper affricate **ts** at the beginning of *tsunami* you ought to be able to manage it in his name too.

Just saying.

PART II

Sounds and Letters

9 Allophones

9.1 Mysteries of Existence

Like other teachers of elementary phonetics to native English-speaking (NS) students, when teaching I would regularly set exercises in 'doing transcription'. I would give the students a passage of English in ordinary spelling. Their task would be to convert it into phonetic transcription.

This is a valuable exercise for NSs as much as for non-native speakers (NNS). It familiarizes them with the phonetic symbols. It makes them conscious of the difference between spelling and pronunciation. It alerts them to the characteristics of connected speech as opposed to individual words in isolation.

Good students sail through this task. The weaker ones often find it remarkably difficult. I would frequently have to point out that *write* does not actually begin with a **w**-sound, nor *looked* end with a **d**-sound (still less a syllabic **d̩**). The first vowel in *particular* is not normally pronounced ɑː, and the second vowel in *information* is not ɔː. Orthography has a distressingly dazzling effect on the phonetically unsophisticated.

Setting and marking (AmE 'grading') transcription can also be valuable for the teacher. Early in my career I noticed some students transcribing *exist* as ɪkˈzɪst (and similarly with *example, exhausted, exams*, etc). Since the usual pronunciation is ɪɡˈzɪst, I was inclined to mark ɪɡˈzɪst as wrong. (Initial e- or ə- rather than ɪ- in this word is OK, of course, though you might have to check that that's what the student genuinely says, and is not just spelling-driven.)

However some students protested: they really do pronounce the word as ɪkˈzɪst. I checked it out, and they appeared to be correct. I came to realize that some speakers in the southeast of England, at least, have an unexpected dissimilation of voicing in these words. Their **kz** in *exist* seems to be different both from the **ɡz** of *eggs* or *big zits* and from the **ks** of *exceed*.

Their **k** in this word, being a fortis plosive, is also a candidate for glottal reinforcement: ɪkʔˈzɪst.

Convinced now of their reality, I decided to include these variants in LPD. But no other dictionary seems to recognize their ɪkˈzɪstəns.

9.2 ʔ ≠ 0

My Japanese colleague Masaki Taniguchi tells me that he was seeking advice at the computer help desk at UCL when the IT person told him to click on the **stɑː** button, or so Masaki thought. But he couldn't see any *star* button. What had happened was that he had failed to notice the IT person's glottal stop after the vowel. It was not the **stɑː** button that he needed to click on but the **stɑːʔ** button (*start* button).

This is a nice example of the phonological function of the glottal stop in English, serving to distinguish words that might otherwise sound the same. The glottal stop, although consisting of no more than a silence, contrasts with its own absence. (OK, it may be more an effect on the phonation of the end of the vowel than just an instant of silence, but the point is the same.)

ˈstɑː bʌʔn̩ = *star button*
ˈstɑːʔ bʌʔn̩ = *start button*

Not all English people use a glottal stop at the end of *start* before another consonant. Nevertheless it is unusual to have an exploded **t**. If it's not glottal, the /t/ is likely to be assimilated to the following bilabial, producing an unexploded, indeed unreleased, **p̚**, thus ˈstɑːp̚ bʌʔn̩.

Pity the poor EFL learner. It is difficult to discriminate auditorily between unreleased stops at the bilabial, alveolar, velar, and glottal places. Fortunately, when speaking carefully for the benefit of foreigners, some of us tend to over-articulate and release all the stops. But not everyone, and not always.

It's not just people learning English. Those of us who are not native speakers of Cantonese find it very hard to hear the difference between final **p**, **t**, and **k**, all unreleased, in that language. (Hong Kong airport is called *Chek Lap Kok*, and each syllable ends in a no-audible-release/glottallized final consonant.)

9.3 Is Our Cake Archaic?

As I was chatting with some people at a party, one of them mentioned the possible minimal pair *archaic* vs *our cake*. We were trying to think of a context in which there might be a plausible confusion between the two. Finally someone came up with a scenario involving two daughters visiting their elderly mother. They had brought with them a cake as a gift, which their mother promptly stored in a tin. But she had numerous cake tins, all looking much the same, and tended to accumulate old cakes or pieces of cake and keep them in the tins for months. When it was time for tea, one of the daughters looked at all the cake tins, chose one, and asked her mother 'Is this one archaic/our cake?'

Perhaps not so plausible, after all.

Non-native speakers may be surprised that this is even considered a minimal pair. Surely **aʊə ˈkeɪk** is rather different from **ɑːˈkeɪɪk**. Well, yes, if that's what you say. But if you are one of the many native speakers who pronounce *our* as ɑː(r) rather than as aʊə(r), then the difference is only a matter of the vocalic material between the two velar plosives, **keɪk** vs **keɪɪk**, which comes down to a subtle question of timing.

There are two reasons why *our* might be monophthongal ɑː(r). One is through the operation of the optional process of smoothing, which deletes the second part of the diphthong aʊ when followed by another vowel, plus compression, which makes two syllables one. This is what gives us optional RP variants such as **pɑː** *power*, ˈ**gɑː strɪːt** *Gower St*, etc. (The quality of the resultant monophthong may or may not be identical to that of the ordinary ɑː of START words.)

But it might also be simply that ɑː is the speaker's default pronunciation of *our*. Not everyone has *our* as a homophone of *hour*. The two words are different for me, and for an unknown number of others. They make a possible minimal pair, ɑː *our* vs ˈaʊə *hour*. And for such speakers ɑː is not just a weak form for *our*: it's the strong form too.

When I was taught the Lord's prayer as a child, it began ˈɑː ˈfɑːðə, huˈɑːt ɪn ˈhevn̩.

I might ask you, *Did your bus come on time? We had to wait for* ˈa(ʊ)əz *for* ˈɑːz.

I don't think there are many non-native speakers who pronounce *our, ours* as ɑː(r), ɑː(r)z. On the other hand there may well even be a majority of native speakers who do. No one knows. Perhaps I ought to carry out a preference survey.

Kenyon & Knott included **ar** as a possibility for AmE *our* as long ago as 1953 (possibly even in 1944 – I haven't got the first edition to hand). For BrE priority goes, I think, to Jack Windsor Lewis, in whose Concise Pronouncing Dictionary (1972) ɑː is included just as a weak form. When still edited by Daniel Jones, EPD did not recognize the ɑː variant. It was only when Gimson and Ramsaran took over that it was acknowledged as a possibility. Now the OED, too, has caught up.

9.4 Bedroom Wardrobe

Over half a century ago, on 1 October 1962, I became Assistant Lecturer in Phonetics at UCL, where I remained on the staff until my retirement in 2006.

Back then when I first took up my post, one of the most discussed minimal pairs of English was *nitrate* vs *night rate*. Everyone agreed that they were distinct, despite consisting of the same phonemes in the same order. In the then dominant American 'structuralist' approach, the difference between the two was ascribed to 'juncture', or more exactly close vs open juncture, the latter symbolized /+/. So for Trager and Smith and their followers *nitrate* would be analysed /**náytrèyt**/, but *night rate* as /**náyt+rèyt**/. (There was also the more dubious *Nye trait*, /**náy+trêyt**/.)

In LPD I indicate these same differences by the use of spacing. So I transcribe *nitrate* as ˈ**naɪtr eɪt**, while for *night rate* (if that were a headword) I would write ˈ**naɪt reɪt**, and for *Nye trait* ˈ**naɪ treɪt**. You can interpret these spaces as indicating the boundaries of morphemes or (as I chose to) of syllables.

The reason we can 'hear' these junctures/boundaries is that the choice of allophones is sensitive to their presence/absence. Take another famous pair (one of Gimson's favourites), *great ape* vs *grey tape*. The **t** in *great ape* ˌ**greɪt** ˈ**eɪp** is a typical of **t** in final position: it has little or no aspiration, it causes pre-fortis clipping of the preceding **eɪ**; it is susceptible in BrE to becoming glottal, and in AmE to becoming voiced ('flapped'). None of this applies to the **t** in *grey tape* (or, to use American spelling, *gray tape*) ˌ**greɪ** ˈ**teɪp**, where the **t** is a typical initial one, being aspirated, not susceptible to glottalling or voicing, and not having any clipping effect on the preceding vowel.

(Brief excursus: other fun 'juncture pairs' suggested by correspondents as worthy of mention include *John said that all men could come* vs *John said the tall men could come*; *that ship's at anchor* vs *that ship's a tanker*. And *a great abbey* vs *a grey/gray tabby* makes for a better illustration than *ape/tape*.)

If **t** and **r** or **d** and **r** are contiguous, i.e. have no intervening juncture, then in English they are pronounced together as a postalveolar affricate, as in *train, drain, mattress, Audrey, entry, laundry*. Compare what happens when they are separated, as in *that rain, good reign, what result, saw drifts, ten trips, dawn drips*. For more on all this, see my article setting out the syllabification principles I applied in LPD. (You'll find it online at www.phon.ucl.ac.uk/home/wells/syllabif.htm.)

There are one or two exceptional cases where a putative or etymological morpheme boundary gets treated, by some speakers at least, as non-existent. I know that I do this in the word *wardrobe*. Although I know that etymologically it is a place for warding (keeping) robes (clothes), I pronounce its **dr** as an affricate, as in *Audrey*, not separated as in *board room*. Doubtless this is because I think of the word as a single item, not a compound. Personally, I do the same with *beetroot* and *bedroom*, though I am aware that some other speakers pronounce one or both of these with a boundary. I imagine that *wardrobe, bedroom* and *beetroot* are words that I knew well before I learned to read and write, and certainly well before I became aware of their etymologically compound status. (Note for Americans: in BrE a wardrobe is an everyday piece of bedroom furniture. You would probably use a 'closet' instead.)

This is what explains my different treatment in LPD of *bedroom* and *headroom*. I write their main pronunciations as ˈ**bedr uːm,** ˈ**hed ruːm**. (Let's ignore the irrelevant question of the vowel in *-room* – some people have **ʊ** rather than **uː**.) Although I ignore the boundary in the first, I think I usually preserve it in the second: *headroom* is a word I would not have learned before the age of nine or ten or so, and its compound nature as *head* plus *room* is fairly transparent. (Another note for Americans: *headroom* is the BrE for 'vertical clearance'.)

Furthermore, even when there *is* a boundary between **t** or **d** and **r**, people are not consistent in always reflecting it in their pronunciation. If I say *there is no good reason to think that*, I can still sometimes create an affricate out of the last consonant in *good* and the first in *reason*, even though there is an undoubted word/morpheme/syllable boundary between them. Similarly with the plosive and liquid in *what rubbish!*.

All this is rather good news for EFL learners. We can safely encourage them to treat all cases of **tr** and **dr** identically, namely as affricates.

But that's to ignore people like one of my correspondents, who had been listening carefully to the sound files that come with LPD and was dismayed by what he found in two words we have been discussing. 'The main pronunciation listed in LPD for *bedroom*', he wrote, 'is ˈ**bedr uːm**. On the other hand, the main pronunciation listed for *headroom* is ˈ**hed ruːm** and the pronunciation ˈ**hedr uːm** is visibly absent, but the recording shows clearly, for British English, ˈ**hedr uːm**. Please check the recordings from LPD. My query is, how should the discrepancy be resolved?'

What could I do but hold my hands up and congratulate him on his diligence and on the accuracy of his observations?

OK, I agree: on this occasion the actor who recorded *headroom* in the studio happened to pronounce it as an exact rhyme of (my version of) *bedroom*. That's life.

Of course, if I'd been in the studio monitoring the recordings (which I wasn't, though I was for most or all of those entries in LPD that are not also in LDOCE, and also for some that are), I'd have jumped on it and got it re-recorded. Possibly. Or possibly not.

9.5 Incomplete? Unreleased?

What does it mean to say that (ex)plosion is 'incomplete'?

Plosives are traditionally analysed phonetically as having three stages or phases:

(i) the 'approach' phase, during which the articulators move into contact;
(ii) the 'hold' (or 'compression') phase, during which the contact is maintained, blocking the escape of the air stream, so that air pressure builds up behind the closure; and
(iii) the 'release' phase, during which the articulators move apart, allowing the compressed air to escape explosively. In some cases the release may be followed ('accompanied') by aspiration, which means that after the release the vocal folds do not immediately start to vibrate.

By 'articulators' in these definitions we mean by default the primary articulators: for bilabials the two lips, for velars the back of the tongue and the soft palate (velum), or for alvelars and dentals the tongue tip or blade and the alveolar ridge or upper front teeth.

Sometimes these defaults do not apply. In the case of 'nasal release' (as in the **d** of *hardness*) it is not the primary articulators that move apart, but the soft palate that moves away from the rear wall of the pharynx, allowing the compressed air to escape nasally. In the case of 'lateral release' (as in the **d** of *sadly*) it is the side rims of the tongue (or more generally the side part of the primary articulators) that move, allowing the compressed air to escape laterally.

Logically, we can also speak of 'nasal approach' and 'lateral approach' for the variants of stage (i) in which it is not the primary articulators that move into contact, but the soft palate or side part of the articulator, respectively. Examples would be the **d** of *under* and the **d** of *elder*.

In the case of 'geminated' plosives, as in Italian *fatto*, the hold phase of the plosive lasts for an extra-long time. If you prefer to describe this event as consisting of two entities, corresponding to each of the phonemes involved (here, /**tt**/), you can say that the first has no release and the second has no approach. In that sense you can also say that in the English phrase *good dog* the first **d** has no release, the second **d** no approach. But at the physical level we really have just a single plosive with the same three phases as any other plosive, the hold phase simply lasting longer than usual.

In the usual relaxed English pronunciation in cases such as *actor* ˈæktə, *logged on* ˌlɒgd ˈɒn, the two adjacent plosive articulations (here, velar and alveolar respectively) overlap in time. (In a more carefully articulated version, such as you get when you put people in front of a microphone, this would not necessarily apply.) This means that the release of the first plosive is 'masked' by the second. The auditory signal shows us a velar approach, then a long hold, then an alveolar release. The first plosive is sometimes labelled 'unreleased', though a better term would be to say that it has 'no audible release'. (The second plosive could also be called 'unapproached', or better 'with no audible approach', but people don't often mention that.)

The IPA provides a special diacritic, [˺], meaning 'no audible release' (*Handbook of the IPA*, pp. 182, 204, and the IPA Chart). We could transcribe our examples narrowly as ˈæk˺tə, ˌlɒg˺d ˈɒn. See further Section 13.4.

Daniel Jones used to speak of 'incomplete plosive consonants' and to say that such consonants 'have no plosion'. What he meant was that they have no ***audible*** plosion. Nowadays we would say that they have no audible release.

Burmese, Cantonese, and Thai are examples of languages in which syllable-final plosives regularly have no audible release. This applies not only utterance-finally but also utterance-medially no matter how the following syllable begins. The explanation is usually a supervening (overlapping, masking) glottal closure, giving t˺ʔ, etc. But – utterance-finally, at least – it could theoretically also be because the lungs relax and so stop creating an airstream.

I would boycott the term 'incomplete plosion'. This expression is not to be found, as far as I can see, in any work by Gimson, O'Connor, Cruttenden, Roach, Ladefoged, Collins/Mees or in fact any British phonetician later than Daniel Jones (but see the following). I haven't checked American sources, but I don't think they use it either. So I was a little surprised when I found it in the draft of a textbook of English phonetics by a Chinese author that I was asked to read.

> When a plosive sound is immediately followed by another plosive sound, only the second plosive is fully exploded, but the closure of the first plosive sound (the second stage of the first plosive) is held for double the usual time. This is known as incomplete plosion.

Examples include such cases as the **k** *acting* ˈæktɪŋ or the **g** in *begged* **begd**. I commented,

> This is what I call 'no audible release' or 'masking' of a plosive. We also sometimes speak of 'overlapping plosives'. Because of the supervening second plosive, the release of the first plosive in such sequences cannot be heard, being masked by the hold of the second plosive. Acoustically, what you get in ˈæktɪŋ is the formant transitions of a velar approach, a long silence (the double hold) and the formant transitions of an alveolar release. (The assertion that the first plosive is held for double the usual time is simply wrong.)

I do remember Gordon Arnold, one of my teachers at UCL, when I was studying phonetics as a postgraduate in the early 1960s, telling me that the expression 'incomplete plosion' was strongly deprecated. The term 'incomplete plosive' was not quite so absurd, he said, but I should still prefer 'plosive with no audible release'. I was left with the general impression that these were unfortunate Jonesian terms which his successors were trying to eradicate.

Accordingly, in my *Practical Phonetics* (with Greta Colson, Pitman 1971, p. 73) I wrote

> Another term sometimes encountered, INCOMPLETE PLOSION, is misleading and best avoided.

In a quick search of Jones's major works, however, I can find no instance of 'incomplete plosion', only 'incomplete plosive (consonants)', e.g. at §§578–585 in the 1957 edition of *An Outline of English Phonetics*. Under that heading Jones deals not only with masked release but also with what we might now call gemination, zero release or unreleased plosives, in homorganic plosive sequences such as *red deer* and *eggcup*.

The only native-English-speaking phonetician in whose published works I can find the term 'incomplete plosion' is Patricia Ashby, who in *Understanding Phonetics* (Hodder Education 2011) writes on p. 137:

> ... The first plosive in the sequence effectively lacks a release phase and the second lacks an approach phase [. . .] The first in each sequence would be said to be unreleased or to have incomplete plosion.

It would appear that this terminology, now rare among phoneticians who are native speakers of English, lives on vigorously in the local tradition of English phonetics in the People's Republic of China.

Let's boycott the terms 'incomplete plosion' and 'incomplete plosive'.

10 Phonetic Processes

10.1 But …

A correspondent asked me about the pronunciation of *but* when it means 'except', for example in contexts like *I could come any day but Thursday, There's no one here but me, He was unable to swallow anything but liquids.* Would native speakers use the weak form **bət** here, as in most other contexts; or would they prefer the strong form **bʌt**?

My answer is that in these cases I would normally use the weak form, **bət**. A strong form would sound odd.

The only cases in which strong **bʌt** is usual would appear to be

- citation ('mention'), as in *no ifs and buts*;
- clumsy reading aloud;
- for special emphasis

It'll be difficult, | ∨<u>but</u> | it's still possible.

- and when stranded by a following syntactic boundary.

Perfect? It's anything but!
Before a pause you can have either a weak or a strong realization.
We are not yet ahead, but … er … one day we shall be.
For the weak form in fluent speech, where the following sound is a consonant, we commonly get the glottalled variant **bəʔ**. I have noticed, though, that in my own speech if the following sound is the **w** of a function word, as in *but what we ought to do, but when I arrived*, I tend to say just **bə**, i.e. to elide the **t** entirely. I do not know to what extent other speakers do this.

10.2 Spinach Sandwiches

The questions that no one can answer often involve *why*. A Japanese student asked me, 'Why do people pronounce *sandwich* with **dʒ**, given that the spelling is *-ch*?'

Not everyone does, of course. But in my BrE preference poll I found that 53% of respondents voted for **-wɪdʒ** in this word and only 47% for **-wɪtʃ**. Given the biasing effect of the spelling, the true figure for **-wɪdʒ** is probably quite a lot higher. (In AmE, on the other hand, I think we always get **-wɪtʃ**.)

The same alternation also seems to apply to all other words ending in *-wich*. Thus *Norwich* can be ˈ**nɒrɪdʒ**, *Woolwich* can be ˈ**wʊlɪdʒ**, *Dulwich* can be ˈ**dʌlɪdʒ**. More generally, we could say it applies to all words with possible final unstressed **-ɪtʃ**. (Well, not all. Probably not Harry Potter's *quidditch*.) As well as to those mentioned, it certainly applies to *Greenwich, Harwich, Horwich, Dunwich, (West) Bromwich*, and so on. (I think these all have both options, like *Norwich*. But it's difficult to be absolutely certain.)

Back to the common noun *sandwich*, the food item named after the Earl of Sandwich. The OED does not record anything except **-wɪtʃ**. EPD claims that some people have **tʃ** in the singular noun but **dʒ** in the plural and the verb. I don't know if there is any evidence for this.

Actually, *sandwich* is also unusual in that the historical **w** is not lost – unlike *Norwich, Greenwich*, etc, which in BrE, at least, have no spoken **w** in the suffix.

There are exceptions. *Ipswich* ˈ**ɪpswɪtʃ** retains **w** and has no variant with **dʒ**. Similarly *Nantwich, Middlewich, Droitwich*, and *Bloxwich*. You may notice something about the syllable weight of the first part of the name here.

Apparently *Colwich*, in Staffordshire, the location of a serious rail crash in 1986, is ˈ**kɒlwɪtʃ**, despite the light first syllable.

Strangely enough, the same hesitation between **-ɪtʃ** and **-ɪdʒ** is found in the common noun *spinach*. The OED tells us that in this case the variability extends as far back as its Old French origin, *espinage ~ (e)spinache*.

So can we speak of a neutralization of voicing in the case of affricates in final position? No, because *large* and *larch, edge* and *etch* are always distinct. Well, can we say there is neutralization just in the case of final affricates in weak syllables, then? No, because *Ipswich*, and so on never have **dʒ**, and because everyday words such as *marriage*, ˈ**mærɪdʒ**, *spillage, carnage, passage, cabbage, porridge*, etc, not to mention *Cambridge*, never have **tʃ** (or at least not in the kind of pronunciation recorded in LPD). Nor, for that matter, does *Prinknash* ˈprɪnɪdʒ (as my colleague Martin Barry points out).

The alternation seems to be restricted to just these odd *-wich* proper names with a light first syllable (short vowel, one single following consonant), plus the two oddities *sandwich* and *spinach*.

So why does this voicing happen? You can hypothesize about lenition of the affricate in this weak position, but not very convincingly. (Why does *which* not lenite in the same way when unstressed? Why do plosives, as in *gossip, rabbit, topic* not lenite, nor fricatives as in *sheriff, Lambeth, palace, radish*?)

10.3 Corn Beef and Fry Rice

There's a rivalry in English between *boxed set* and *box set* (or even *boxset*). Which is right? All three variants tend to be pronounced identically, anyway.

Tins of corned beef say just that on the label, even though we mostly pronounce the name of the stuff as if it were written *corn beef*.

The point here is that in English final **d** in a consonant cluster is susceptible to elision when the next word begins with a consonant sound. So kɔːnd biːf optionally becomes kɔːn biːf. In the case of a lexicalized phrase such as *corned beef*, people learn the pronunciation in its reduced form and may be unaware of the full form underlying it. They sometimes then spell it in accordance with the reduced pronunciation, which is for them the only pronunciation.

What Brits call 'skimmed milk' Americans call 'skim milk', in writing as well as in speech. But we all speak of 'roast beef', not 'roasted beef'.

However the elision is not equally possible before all consonants at the start of the next word.

This elision is less usual before **r**. I don't think I can omit the **d** from *boiled rice*. I certainly can't omit it in *fried rice*, where the final **d** is not in a cluster and therefore not a candidate for elision.

In Chinese English, however, *fry rice* seems to be quite frequent. So is *fry mushroom*, unknown in British or American English, which shows that these are not phonetic reductions, but morphological ones.

David Deterding found (2000, 'Deletion of final /t/ and /d/ in BBC English: implications for teachers in Singapore', *STETS Language & Communication Review*, 5(1), 21–23) that in a corpus of BBC recordings **d** was deleted from the end of a final cluster before a plosive in 60% of possible cases, before a fricative in 49%, before a nasal in 42%, and before an approximant in 16%.

It's not just at word boundaries, either: we can also delete **d** at a morpheme boundary, in cases such as *endless*, making it ˈenləs, or *soundly*, which can become ˈsaʊnli. Similarly *kindness* can be ˈkaɪnnəs and *amendment* əˈmenmənt.

10.4 The Irish Sea

A student wrote to tell me that his English teacher had said that ʃ could be assimilated to s before a following s, thus *bookish style* **bʊkɪʃ staɪl** assimilated to **bʊkɪs staɪl**. Did I agree? He couldn't find this possibility mentioned online.

My immediate reaction was that this type of assimilation simply doesn't happen. That's why correspondent could find no reference to it in his online search.

However, phonetic research is not just a matter of finding out what published descriptions say about this or that phenomenon (in this case, they indeed seem to say nothing). Genuine research involves making observations: observing and analysing what speakers actually say.

The phonetic context we are interested in is by no means unusual. Plenty of possible examples come to mind: *British citizen, cash some cheques, crash site, wash six pairs of socks, horseradish sauce, fish soup, rush suddenly, push something.*

Introspecting, I feel pretty confident in saying that full-blown progressive (= perseverative) assimilation, thus ˈ**brɪtɪʃ** ˈ**sɪtɪzn̩** → ˈ**brɪtɪʃ** ˈ**ʃɪtɪzn̩**, just doesn't happen. Nor does full-blown regressive assimilation, thus ˈ**brɪtɪs** ˈ**sɪtɪzn̩**. However some kind of intermediate allophonic regressive assimilation, perhaps ˈ**brɪtɪɕ** ˈ**sɪtɪzn̩** or something similar, seems possible.

My colleague Jack Windsor Lewis has for many years been making observations on the pronunciation used by BBC radio announcers, including those reading the early-morning shipping bulletin, and watching out especially for the expression *Irish Sea*. He has very occasionally heard it pronounced 'Iris Sea', but so rarely ('out of hundreds of tokens') that he would be inclined to classify it as no more than a slip of the tongue. He agrees with me that assimilation of ʃ to s before s is not a regular type of assimilation in English.

I stick by my view that in English progressive (anticipatory) assimilation is restricted to:

(i) morphological assimilation of voicing, producing **s** in *cats* and **t** in *kissed* (compare *dogs* with **z** and *raised* with **d**);

(ii) allophonic assimilation of voicing, always in the direction of voicelessness, as for example the possible partial devoicing of the **d** in *good things* **gʊd̥ θɪŋz**; and

(iii) assimilation of syllabic **n̩** to the place of a preceding obstruent, as in *ribbon* (ˈ**rɪbən** →) ˈ**rɪbn̩** → ˈ**rɪbm̩**.

In English phonology, features typically spread leftwards, not rightwards. Unlike the French, we do not tend to change *textbook* ˈ**teksbʊk** into ˈ**tegzbʊk**. (Compare *chaque jour* ʃak ʒuʁ → ʃag ʒuʁ.)

10.5 Aitches

Latin **h** tended to be dropped even in classical times, particularly in the middle of words. Thus *nihil* 'nothing' has an alternative form *nīl*, and *mihi* an alternative *mī*, while *dē-* plus *habeo* yields *dēbeo* 'I owe'.

In initial position it was more tenacious, though even here by classical times it was only the educated classes who pronounced **h**. At Pompeii, destroyed in the year 79 CE, there are inscriptional forms such as *ic* for *hic* 'this (m.)', and conversely *hire* for *ire* 'to go'. A century earlier, in his poem about Arrius, Catullus pokes fun at hypercorrections such as *hinsidias* for *insidias*. Even the educated sometimes got confused: the letter *h* in the regular spelling of *humor, humerus*, and *humidus* is apparently unetymological.

The Romance languages inherited no phonetic **h** from Latin. The **h** that we pronounce nowadays in English words of Romance or Latin origin reflects a spelling pronunciation: *habit, hesitate, horror* and for most speakers *humo(u)r, humid*. As we all know, in various other Latin-derived words we have not restored **h** despite the spelling: there is no **h** in *heir, hono(u)r, honest*. In *herb* Brits and Americans agree to differ.

I was thinking about this because I have been noticing people pronouncing *adhere, adherent, adhesion, adhesive* without **h**, thus ə'dɪə, etc. In LPD I give only forms that include **h** – əd'hɪə, etc. In this I follow Daniel Jones's EPD, though I notice that the Cambridge EPD now includes the **h**-less forms. Rightly so; on reflection, I think they are widespread enough to warrant inclusion, at least for BrE. Jack Windsor Lewis says he noticed ago, as evidenced by his 1972 pronouncing dictionary.

I have long been aware of the corresponding **h**-less pronunciation of *abhor*, which both LPD and the current EPD (but not the DJ EPD) include.

I don't think there is any tendency towards a spelling-inspired restoration of **h** in words with the prefix *ex-*, as *exhaust, exhibit, exhilarate, exhort*, which all have **-g'z-**. But *exhale* is a notable exception, always having **-ks'h-**, and so sometimes is *exhume*.

You sometimes encounter the hypercorrect spelling *exhorbitant* for *exorbitant*. I can't say I've ever heard the corresponding hypercorrect pronunciation, but presumably it exists.

10.6 Nonfinal Syllabic Consonants

We usually exemplify the syllabic consonants of English with words that end in one, for example, *muddle* ˈmʌdl̩, *hidden* ˈhɪdn̩.

A correspondent asked whether it is possible to find syllabic consonants in the middle or at the beginning of words. The answer is that they can occur in the middle of words, but not at the beginning of words spoken in isolation.

In LPD I intentionally chose to illustrate the Syllabic Consonants article (p. 799) with the word *suddenly* ˈsʌd n li, which has a syllabic n̩ in the middle of a word.

There are plenty of other words with medial l̩ or n̩: think *sandals, muddled, saddleback, Middleton, battlefield, rattlesnake, vitally; frightened, gardens, woodenly, hadn't, mightn't, ardent, woodentop, Attenborough, Hottentot, gluttony, Gordonstoun*, as well as the uncompressed versions of *rattling, dawdling, Madeleine, Middleham, fattening, gardening, Tottenham, Sydenham*, etc.

A more useful way of describing the restricted distribution of syllabic consonants is not by reference to their position in the word, but by reference to their relationship to strong (= stressable) syllables: syllabic consonants typically follow them. That explains why syllabic consonants never occur in initial position in words in isolation.

For syllabic consonants in initial position, all I can offer are cases such as *had a lot, had another* if pronounced with no schwa, i.e. as **hædl̩ɒt, hædn̩ʌðə**. You readily get this in connected speech: *I started early, because I had a lot to do before lunch. So I had another coffee and got cracking.*

Is that gʊd n̩ʌf?

Syllabic consonants are never categorically required in English. There is always an alternative pronunciation available, with ə and a nonsyllabic consonant. By this I mean that although the word *hidden*, for example, is mostly pronounced ˈhɪdn̩, it can also be said as ˈhɪdən. Most cases of n̩ can be replaced by ən, and vice versa, with no change of meaning. And the same applies to the other syllabic consonants of English. You can say əl instead of l̩ in *medal – meddle* (though that might sound odd or childish, depending on where you come from). For *hesitant* you can say ˈhezɪtənt or ˈhezɪtn̩t. For *blossom* you can say ˈblɒsəm or ˈblɒsm̩. For *gathering* you can say ˈgæðərɪŋ or ˈgæðr̩ɪŋ (= ˈgæðɚɪŋ), or indeed compressed as ˈgæðrɪŋ.

In terms of phonology, I would say that syllabic consonants are not phonemes, that is, not part of our underlying sound system. Rather, they are derived by rule from an underlying string of ə plus a nonsyllabic sonorant consonant. I call the rule Syllabic Consonant Formation, and it takes the general form

$$\text{ə [+son]} \rightarrow \text{[+syll] / } \ldots$$

Two segments are reduced to one, with the sonorant consonant retaining its various attributes (place, nasality/laterality, etc) as it acquires syllabicity.

The conditioning environment of the rule (shown here just as ' ... ') is pretty complex. It varies according to different accents and different speaking styles, and also depending on which consonant is concerned. For ən after a strong vowel plus d, as in *garden*, syllabic consonant formation is strongly favoured (though now becoming less so in some BrE). With a preceding fricative, as in *lesson*, it is still favoured, though perhaps less strongly. With an affricate, as in *kitchen*, it is disfavoured. In *common* and *lion*, that is, after a nasal or a vowel, it is so strongly disfavoured as to be virtually unknown in RP-style English. Although a syllabic nasal following a nasal is a no-no, a syllabic lateral, on the other hand, is fine: *channel* ˈtʃænl̩.

Although the AmE NURSE vowel could in principle be analysed as a strong (= stressable) syllabic r̩, this would not fit the above rule, which requires a weak ə as part of the input. So I treat the NURSE vowel in both BrE and AmE as a primitive, ɜː ~ ɝː. The second vowel of AmE *father*, however, does fit, and I analyse it accordingly: ˈfɑːðər → ˈfɑːðɚ.

This is the reasoning behind the notation I use in LPD, where potential syllabic consonants are shown either as ᵊl ᵊn ᵊr ᵊm or as *əl ən ər əm*, depending on whether a syllabic consonant is more or less likely as the output. The LPD notational convention is that a raised symbol denotes a possible insertion, an italic symbol a possible omission. So ᵊn implies a default n̩, as in *hidden* ˈhɪd ᵊn → ˈhɪdn̩, while *ən* implies a default ən, as in *hesitant* ˈhez ɪt ənt → ˈhezɪtənt.

A correspondent asked whether in a dictation exercise it would be wrong to include ə in words where the LPD writes it raised (= optional). I replied,

> Both pronunciations are possible. But on any given occasion the schwa is either there or not there.
>
> It is perhaps clearest in cases like *garden*. If there is no schwa between the **d** and the **n** (the usual pronunciation) then the tongue remains in contact with the alveolar ridge as we move from **d** to **n**, and the only change is the movement of the soft palate, which comes down to allow the air to explode through the nose. If, on the other hand, the tongue tip leaves the alveolar ridge at the end of **d** and then returns to the alveolar ridge for the **n**, then there is a schwa between the two consonants.
>
> In marking dictation, it is for you to decide your policy. I would not penalize presence/absence of schwa between a fricative or an affricate and **n** or **l** (as in *listen, heaven, kitchen; oval, puzzle, satchel*), but might penalize it after a plosive (as in *happen, garden, organ; apple, middle, eagle*), where the difference is perceptually more salient.
>
> On the other hand you could decide not to penalize this at all, since the two possibilities (i) schwa plus sonorant and (ii) syllabic sonorant are phonologically equivalent. Barring marginal cases, there are no pairs of words distinguished only by this difference.

The 'marginal cases' I was thinking of would be, for example, BrE ˈpætən, ˈbɪtən (*pattern, bittern*) vs ˈpætn̩, ˈbɪtn̩ (*Patton, bitten*), which a few non-rhotic speakers may have as minimal pairs, although they are normally homophonous for me as ˈpætn̩, ˈbɪtn̩. Compare also *modern* as a rhyme (or not) for *trodden*.

In the case of syllabic **l** there are the further complications of clear vs dark and the possible vocalization of the latter. *Trouble, people*, and so on are shown in the LPD as having ᵊl. As usual, this implies a default l̩, thus ˈtrʌbl̩, ˈpiːpl̩. As with ordinary nonsyllabic **l**, it will be dark unless immediately followed by a vowel sound. Usually, then, we have ˈtrʌbl̴̩, ˈpiːpl̴̩. Being dark, the **l** is susceptible in London English to vocalization (= becoming a vowel sound). If we represent the output of vocalization conventionally as **o**, that gives ˈtrʌbo, ˈpiːpo. In a transcription exercise (orthography to phonetics) I would be delighted to see these forms (particularly if phrase-final, or if the next word begins with a consonant sound). In a dictation exercise, however, I would not consider them correct if I had actually uttered l̩. In the general scheme of things, though, this would count as a very minor error. People who fail phonetic dictation do so because of multiple gross errors, not because of subtleties such as worried my correspondent.

More generally, my advice to the teacher giving a transcription or dictation exercise would be that optional symbols in the dictionary should not be shown as optional in these practical exercises. You may either include them or omit them; but choose which. They should either be there or not be there. Their inclusion in the dictionary is an abbreviatory convention. In real-life performance nothing is optional. You either do it or you don't.

10.7 Classical Elision

In Latin verse you have to avoid 'hiatus', that is two vowels with no consonant between them. If a word ends in a vowel and the following word begins with one, then the first vowel is disregarded ('elided') for purposes of scansion. This is where the use of the term 'elision' in English phonetics comes from.

Looking now at the Latin grammar book I learnt from at school (Kennedy's *Revised Latin Primer*), I am surprised to see that the whole matter is disposed of in a single paragraph.

> 474b A vowel at the end of a word was so lightly pronounced, if there was a vowel at the beginning of the next word, that it did not count as a syllable in Scansion: *Phyllid(a) am(ō) ant(e) aliās*; this is called Elision   (Synaloepha).
>
> A vowel and *m* were similarly treated at the end of a word: *Ō cūrās homin-(um) Ō quant(um) est in rēbus ināne*. This is called Ecthlipsis.
> A vowel unelided in such a position is said to be in Hiatus.
>
> *Ter sunt | cōnā|tī im|pōnere | Pēliō | Ossam*

(At my school we just called it 'elision', not 'synaloepha' or 'ecthlipsis'.)

So to form a regular hexameter (six feet, namely four spondees or dactyls, a dactyl, and a spondee; caesura in the third foot), a line such as *monstrum horrendum, informe, ingens, cui lūmen ademptum* has to be scanned as *monstr' 'or|rend', in|form', in|gens, cui | lūmen a|demptum*. Another example: the third line of the Aeneid is *lītora,| mult(um) il|l(e) et ter|rīs iac|tātus et | altō* with two elisions as shown.

I am one of that dying breed of people who spent many hours as a teenager having to compose Latin and Greek verse. By the time I was sixteen I knew the rules of elision and hiatus avoidance, and would apply them in my weekly task of putting English poetry into Latin hexameters (or sometimes elegiac couplets) and into Greek iambic pentameters. This is a skill I can safely say I have since lost.

The reason that a vowel plus *m* was subject to elision was that the spelling *m* here did not stand for any actual nasal consonant but just for nasalization of the vowel. So *monstrum* was pronounced **mõ:strũ:** (and ends up in Italian as *mostro*). The nasalized vowel, like any other vowel, would be in hiatus if immediately followed by another vowel and would normally be elided in this context.

In Latin, elision is not usually shown in writing (except sometimes in inscriptions, where you can get things like *scriptust* = *scriptum est*). This is different from the convention for classical Greek, in which elision is regularly shown by removal of the letters standing for deleted vowels, in modern texts with an added apostrophe to show the loss. Only short vowels could be elided in Greek.

Here's what it says in my Sidgwick and Morice, *An Introduction to Greek Verse Composition*.

> But whereas in Latin the elided vowel is elided only to the ear (e.g. we write *immane ingens* and not *imman' ingens*), in Greek it must always be elided to the eye also. Thus we must write ταῦτ' ἐξέπραξ' ἡ τῆςδ' ἔχουσ' ἀρχὴν πόλεως, and not ταῦτα ἐξέπραξε, etc.

In medieval Latin, by the thirteenth century, spelling pronunciation had restored the final **m**, and elision is blocked: there is a regular succession of eight trochaic feet (Hiawatha-style) in *Dies irae, dies illa, solvet saeclum in favilla*.

Since 2000, I have noticed the words *elide, elision* being used in a way that is quite different from how I would use them – particularly, I think, in the Guardian newspaper.

Here's an example. There had been some discussion whether the people who invaded England in 1066 are better described as 'French' or as 'Normans'. Correspondents had pointed out that the two terms cannot be regarded as synonymous. As the journalist summarizing the discussion put it,

> A correspondence on the letters page wrestles with the question of whether the French or the Normans invaded England in 1066, and whether there is any difference. As some contributors have pointed out, the elision of the French and the Normans is too crude.

This writer is clearly using *elision* here to mean something like 'confusion, conflation, confounding' of the two categories.

Another example of the same thing, this time involving the verb *elide*, is dated 12 April 2010 and bears the byline of Beatrix Campbell.

> ... towards the end of the 20th century within a single generation the numbers marrying halved, the numbers divorcing trebled, the proportion of children born outside marriage quadrupled. Intimacy, however, did not diminish and parenting – as commitment, care and companionship – has

flourished. Yet, Tories subliminally elide these changes with the collapse of civilisation as we know it.

As far as I can see, no dictionary includes this meaning. Every dictionary I can lay hands on defines *elision* as 'omission' or 'suppressing' of a sound/letter or syllable, or sometimes of a passage in a text. Correspondingly, *to elide* is to omit by elision.

That is how we use the term in phonetics, as when we refer to the possible elision of the **t** in *next* when we say *the next day* ðə ˈneks ˈdeɪ, or of the **h** in *him* when we say *I've seen him* aɪv ˈsiːn ɪm.

The 2010 edition of *guardianstyle*, the Guardian style guide [London: Guardian Books, 2010] says firmly:

elide, elision means omission, not the conflation of one or more things.

10.8 Initial Clusters

One of my favourite examples of metathesis is the Modern Greek verb βγάλω *vghálo* ˈvɣalo 'I take out' (aorist form).

To see how it came about we first have to dispose of one or two other sound changes en route from classical to modern. In Ancient Greek this stem took the form ἐκβαλ- *ekbal-* egˈbal-. The voicing assimilation of the consonant in the prefix ἐκ- *ek-*, making it voiced before a voiced consonant, appears to date from ancient times – see W. Sidney Allen's *Vox Graeca* (Cambridge University Press 1987), p. 18.

Ancient short unstressed vowels at the beginning of a word are lost ('aphesis') in Modern Greek. So for example the classical word ὄμμα *ómma* 'eye', or rather its diminutive ὀμμάτιον *ommátion*, stripped of its case ending -ον -*on*, loses its initial vowel to become Modern Greek μάτι *máti* ˈmati, still meaning 'eye'. Classical ἐξεύρω *ekseúrō* 'I will find out' yields Modern aphetic ξέρω *kséro* ˈksero 'I know' (probably: there is some difficulty with this etymology).

Classical voiced plosives became fricatives in Modern Greek ('spirantization'). Loss of the initial vowel in ἐκβαλ- *ekbal-* egˈbal-, the example we started with, left an initial cluster **gb-**. This duly became **ɣv-**. It was this cluster that then underwent metathesis to give the modern **vɣ-**. I do not know when the metathesis happened in popular speech. It was resisted in the katharevousa (puristic) form of modern Greek.

No parallel metathesis seems to have happened to γδ- from classical ἐκδ-. Homer's ἐκδύνω *ekdúnō* 'I undress' (as in modern English zoological *ecdysis* and fanciful *ecdysiast*) yields Modern Greek γδύνω *ghdhíno* ˈɣðino with the same meaning and unmetathesized.

I used to find Modern Greek useful for widening my students' appreciation of the phonotactic possibilities of language, and there was usually a native speaker conveniently to hand. Clusters such as word-initial **vɣ** are not difficult for speakers of other languages to pronounce, once they have mastered **ɣ**, but can seem very strange at first.

Greek has other interesting word-initial clusters involving a fricative plus an obstruent: φτάνω *ftáno* ˈftano or φθάνω *ftháno* ˈfθano 'I arrive', βδομάδα *vdhomádha* vðoˈmaða 'week', χτές *khtes* xtes or χθές *khthes* xθes 'yesterday', χτυπώ *khtypó* xtiˈpo 'I knock', σχολείο *skholeío* sxoˈlio 'school', σγουρός *sghourós* zɣuˈros 'curly'.

Polish, too, has some pretty complex initial clusters. Any Pole will demonstrate the tongue-twister that starts with the word *chrząszcz* xʂɔ̃ʂtʂ, as well as non-tongue-twister words such as *ptak* and *kto*, pronounced as spelt.

For really complex consonant clusters, however, you need to go to the Caucasian or Salishan languages. When I was teaching my phonological analysis class we never seemed to have any native speakers of those languages around.

10.9 I Must Haplologize

The other day I noticed a reporter on the BBC TV news pronouncing *deteriorate* as diˈtɪərieɪt. This pronunciation is a variant to which I attach a warning triangle in LPD ('pronunciation considered incorrect'), thereby grouping it with such other mispronunciations as ˈgriːviəs and prəˌnaʊnsiˈeɪʃn.

Googling around, I find people puzzled not only about the correctness or otherwise of 'deteriate' but also about why this (mis)pronunciation should have become popular.

> I have checked the dictionary and I can't seem to find this word 'deteriate', but I hear all sorts of people say it and I assume (from what they are talking about) this word really is 'deteriorate'. So why do you think these people think deteriate is a word?
> – I think it's probably just their accent or how they were raised to say it, because you're right 'deteriate' definitely isn't a word. A lot of people I know say it and it's really annoying. You should just show them the dictionary entry for *deteriorate*.

And

> I forgive anyone making mistakes . . ., but this pronunciation is not a mistake. It seems to be what a lot of people think is correct. What I wanted to know was, why?

So in this view a word 'exists' only if it's in standard dictionaries. And the word is its spelling.

And obviously the correct pronunciation is the one which follows the spelling.

There are difficulties with this popular view. No one would claim that we ought to say ˈkʌpbɔː(r)d for *cupboard*, although that is what the spelling suggests. No one argues that we ought to pronounce a **w** in *wrong* or a **k** in *know*. And what about words that have only just come into use, whether spoken or written, but are not (yet) recorded in dictionaries? How can we follow their established spelling, if they haven't yet got one? (I imagine all would agree that the onus is rather on the lexicographers to bring their dictionaries up to date.) What about words such as the BrE *scarper* 'run away, escape, make off in haste', where it is pretty clear that the usual spelling reflects the (non-rhotic) pronunciation ˈskɑːpə, rather than the other way round? The etymology is believed to be either Italian *scappa!* or by rhyming slang from *Scapa (Flow)*, neither of which would justify that spelling.

As for why people tend to simplify **diˈtɪərɪəreɪt** to **diˈtɪərieɪt**, the answer must lie in the tendency to eliminate one of two adjacent identical consonants – the same tendency we see in ˈ**prɒb(ə)li** for ˈ**prɒbəbli** *probably*, ˈ**laɪb(ə)ri** for ˈ**laɪbrəri** *library*, and so on (see *Sounds Interesting*, Section 2.15 for ˌ**sfɪgməˈnɒmɪtə** *sphygmomanometer* and ˈ**kwɒntətɪv** *quantitative*).

11 Spelling

11.1 Phrasebooks

There've been some interesting internet postings on the topic of how pronunciation is indicated in phrasebooks intended for travellers.

Phrasebooks aimed at an English-speaking readership typically use an ad hoc respelling system based on English spelling conventions. As Heidi Harley has pointed out in Language Log (http://languagelog.ldc.upenn.edu/nll/?p=283), many of them presuppose a British or at least non-rhotic accent on the part of the user. In her comparative test of three French phrasebooks, she reports that one of them offers:

>Where are the bus [coach] stops?
>Où sont les arrêts de car?
>oo sawng lay areh der kar

>How long does the trip [journey] take?
>Combien de temps dure le voyage?
>kawnbyang der tahng dewr ler vwahyazh?

Heidi doesn't supply an IPA version of these phrases, which in proper French would be

>u sõ lez aʁɛ d(ə) kaːʁ
>kõbjæ̃ d(ə) tã dyʁ lə vwajaːʒ

– or thereabouts. (As is customary, I use the IPA symbol ə to cover a range of varieties of mid central vowels. The French version is usually somewhat rounded, and not necessarily distinct from ɵ.)

By following the respelling, non-rhotic speakers would read *arrêts de car* as ɑːɹeɪ də kɑː (or with æ for the first vowel), which is perhaps not too bad. Rhotic speakers, though, would read it as ɑɹeɪ dɚ kɑɹ, in which the unwanted r-coloration of *de* is not good at all.

Another interesting article on the web, by Randy Alexander and now no longer recoverable, concerned English phrasebooks aimed at Chinese users. It included this sample phrase. The second line is the Chinese imitated pronunciation of the English phrase, repeated in the third line in Hanyu pinyin.

>Yes, of course.
>业丝 厄弗 靠斯
>yèsī èfú kàosī

86   11 SPELLING

In IPA that would be **jesɯ ɾfu kaosɯ** plus a lot of distracting prosody and alveolarization.

In the original article you can also hear sound clips of the results.

As Heidi says, and I agree with her,

> I find the whole phrasebook orthography situation pretty weird. It's another clear example of a situation in which providing English speakers with the rudiments of a linguistic education – in this case, a smidgen of basic phonetics and a bit of a clue about the IPA – would be useful in a seriously practical way. If that were generally part of the secondary education of most English speakers, phrasebook writers could stop inventing their own weird systems and standardize.

It applies equally to speakers of Chinese.

11.2 Spanish Phonetics for the Layman

It's depressing that so many writers of foreign language textbooks have little knowledge of phonetics. They don't know how to teach pronunciation (except by imitation). They don't have the understanding to describe speech sounds. They don't have the vocabulary to explain how sounds are made.

So when they come to write textbooks they can't give clear explanations of how to pronounce the sounds of the language.

Put yourself in the position of a naïve English would-be learner of Spanish, and see how much help you would get from this sort of thing (in a mini-phrasebook published by a reputable national newspaper).

> **g** if followed by an e or i, like the 'ch' in the Scottish 'loch'
> **r** pronounced by tapping the tongue against the roof of the mouth, like a less forceful 'd'
> **v** and **b** like b in bath, but softer and slightly aspirated
> ... all other consonants [apart from **g, j, h, ll ñ, rr**] sound the same as they do in English

What kind of sound would you take a less forceful 'd' to be? A fricative, perhaps, or an approximant? Or a very lenis plosive with no voicing? No, that's the description offered of the Spanish single *r* – which is actually a pretty forceful tap, [ɾ].

If you have even a very elementary knowledge of Spanish phonetics, you'll know that the voiced plosives /**b d g**/ have weakened allophones [β ð ɣ] intervocalically and finally. So you'd think the phrasebook would at least have mentioned that the *d* in *nada* sounds much more like the *th* (ð) in English *father* than it does like English **d**.

In the explanation of *b* and *v* we see a phonetic technical term, 'aspirated'. It's just that the author doesn't understand its meaning. For the record, no plosives in Spanish are aspirated in the phonetic sense of the term (= with an interval of voicelessness between the plosive release and the following segment). Let me try to explain the relevant facts as I understand them in terms that the ordinary reader might be able to understand. In Castilian Spanish, the letters *b* and *v* refer to the same sound. At the beginning of a phrase or after *m* or *n* this sound is just like an English *b*. (So *vaso* sounds like 'BAH-so', and *enviar* is 'em-bee-AHR'.) Elsewhere it is pronounced like an English *v*, except that you use the two lips rather than the lower lip and the upper teeth.

For a language learner with some phonetic training, it's easier. All we need say is that initially or after a nasal /**b d g**/ are plosives, [**b d g**]. Elsewhere they are realized as fricatives, [β ð ɣ] (or the corresponding approximants).

By the way, explaining the Spanish *j* as 'like *ch* in *loch*' may work satisfactorily for Brits, who even if not themselves Scottish are probably familiar with the Scottish pronunciation of this word; but it is likely to leave Americans simply puzzled. You have to tailor your advice to your audience, which may be hard in these days of globalization.

Contrary to the impression you may have formed from the above, I cannot actually speak Spanish, because I have never learnt it. But I certainly know how to pronounce it. And I know how to teach other people how to pronounce it. Oughtn't this to be part of the intellectual equipment of <u>all</u> teachers of Spanish?

11.3 Going Awry

A correspondent mentioned being misled by the spelling of the word *epitome*, which caused him to pronounce it 'eppy-tohm', i.e. ˈ**epɪtəʊm**, instead of the usual ɪˈ**pɪtəmi**. Greek ἐπιτομή *epitomē* has four syllables.

I hope he was indeed ˌ**mɪsˈled** rather than being ˈ**mɪzl̩d**.

I can remember once doing a double-take after misreading *seabed* (the ocean floor) as **siːbd**. Not to mention ɪnˈ**freəd** (*infrared*) rays.

Along with *epitome* we might mention *apocope* (Greek ἀποκοπή *apokopē*) and *syncope* (Greek συγκοπή *synkopē*). I have heard **-strəʊf** in *apostrophe* and *catastrophe*, but only as jocular intentional mispronunciations.

The OED comments that *apostrophe* in the sense of the punctuation mark, as opposed to the rhetorical figure, 'ought' to be pronounced with three syllables, as in French: it comes from the Greek ἀπόστροφος *apostrophos*, but has been 'ignorantly confused' with the rhetorical figure, which is from the Greek ἀποστροφή *apostrophē*.

Some of you may have been puzzled on seeing *sundried* tomatoes on the shelf at the supermarket. Nothing to do with *sundry*, not ˈ**sʌndrɪd**: they're *sun-dried*, ˈ**sʌn draɪd**. And the chemical *lanthanides* (the rare earth elements) are ˈ**lænθənaɪdz**, unlike the Greek *Eumenides* (the furies of myth and the Aeschylus tragedy), which are juˈ**menɪdiːz**.

I suppose the best-known case of a spelling pronunciation of this kind is seeing the word *awry* and saying it aloud as ˈɔːri. Strangely enough, the only word with orthographic *awry* actually pronounced ɔːri, as a model, seems to be *outlawry*, hardly an everyday word.

Pronouncing *awry* as ˈɔːri rather than as əˈraɪ is not a malapropism, since it does not involve the confusion of one word with another. I don't think we have a particular term for this kind of thing, such as would enable us to distinguish the *awry* type from run-of-the-mill spelling pronunciations such as *often* with a **t**, *falcon* with an **l**, or *Antigua* with a **w**.

Paul Carley comments that another case like *awry* is *askance*, sometimes misinterpreted as a derivative of *ask*.

Perhaps 'spelling misinterpretation'?

11.4   Yoo-Hoo

As we all know, English words spelt with *u* that come from Latin, or from Greek via Latin, regularly have a palatal semivowel in English. Thus Latin *futur-us* gives us BrE ˈfjuːtʃə, AmE ˈfjuːtʃɚ, while Latin *fūtĭl-is* gives us BrE ˈfjuːtaɪl, AmE ˈfjuːtl̩. Greek μουσικ-ή *mousik-ē* ends up as English *music*, pronounced ˈmjuːzɪk.

After alveolars the **j** was lost, or subject to coalescence, depending on the variety of English involved, giving the familiar variability in words such as *tube* tjuːb ~ tuːb ~ tʃuːb. In East Anglia the yod has been lost more widely, even in words such as *music, human* (and of course *beautiful* – as in the turkey adverts). There's some variability in weak syllables, too, as when *ambulance, executive*, or *regular* are pronounced without **j** in certain non-standard accents.

Disregarding these categories of exceptions, though, the rule applies pretty widely, and not only to Greco-Roman borrowings, but also to other long-established 'international' words (*butane, Cuba, pupa*). In more recent loans there may be more variability. So on the one hand Rudolf Nureyev (Russian/Tatar Нуреев, Нуриев **nu-**) often has **nj-** in BrE, while the late Sir Peter Ustinov (Russian Устинов uˈstʲinəf) was happy for his name to be anglicized as ˈjuːstɪnɒf; but on the other there is variability in *Lithuania, Nicaragua, jaguar*, and *muesli*. However *Zulu* is firmly yodless, and Japanese *futon* ɸɯton becomes English ˈfuːtɒn, never ˈfjuː-.

When it comes to acronyms (initialisms) we again see variability. When I was a student the University of London Union, ULU, was generally known as ˈjuːluː (and I think still is). We had BUNAC ˈbjuːnæk (the British Universities North America Club) to enable us to buy cheap flights to the United States, while CICCU ˈkɪkjuː (the Cambridge Inter-Collegiate Christian Union) tried to save our souls. I believe CUNY (the City University of New York) is known as ˈkjuːni. But the British medical insurance company BUPA (British United

Provident Association) is ˈbuːpə, and the GUI (graphical user interface) by which you operate your computer is a ˈguːi.

11.5 Habeas Corpus

I keep noticing the spelling mistake *habeus corpus* (instead of *habeas corpus*). The explanation is straightforward: the final syllable of *habeas* is usually pronounced in English just like the final syllable of *corpus*, namely as əs. If it's pronounced the same, there is an obvious temptation to spell it in the same way.

The word *habeas* is the second person singular present subjunctive active ('thou mayst have') of the Latin verb *habeō, habēre* 'have'. Its final vowel was long, *habeās*, so when I was taught Latin at school we pronounced it ˈhæbeɪɑːs (or ˈhæbiɑːs). English legal Latin gets both the initial and final quantities wrong, producing ˈheɪbiəs. But then legal Latin is something of a law unto itself, or *lēx in sē* as we might say.

The reason our Latin and Greek teachers were so insistent on our 'getting the quantity right', i.e. distinguishing between long and short vowels, is that the metre of classical versification is based on the idea of heavy ('long') vs light ('short') syllables. This is important in the appreciation of Latin poetry, but was even more important for us schoolchildren who were expected to compose Latin verse every week, usually by translating a set passage of English poetry.

We had a useful book called a gradus, short for *Gradus ad Parnassum*, 'steps towards Parnassus (the mountain sacred to the muses)' – Ainger A.C. and Wintle H.G., *An English-Latin Gradus*, London: John Murray, 1890. The gradus was a dictionary with a difference. It specialized in providing sets of homonyms or near-homonyms, all with the vowel quantities clearly marked, so that we could select a particular translation that would fit the scansion we wanted. Poetry translation became a kind of jigsaw puzzle, finding words that would fit the metre.

> MONEY – subst., *pĕcūnĭă* 1; *ārgĕntum* 2; *aurum* 2; *nŭmmŭs* 2 (H.); often = riches, *dīvĭtĭæ* 1 pl.; *ŏpēs* 3 f. pl.; *rēs* 5 pl.; *bŏnă* 2 pl.; = coinage, *mŏnētă* 1.

A hexameter line consisted of six feet, each of which was either a dactyl (ˉ ˘ ˘) or a spondee (ˉ ˉ). So if you wanted to put 'money' at the beginning of a line of verse, you could choose *argentum, aurum, nummus, res*, or *divitiae*; but not the commonest equivalent, *pecunia*, and not *opes, bona*, or *moneta*.

I don't suppose many schoolchildren have to do that sort of thing nowadays. But at least we who did have to ended up knowing how to spell *habeas corpus*.

11.6 Curly or Kicking?

I was listening to the commercial radio station Classic FM, when the announcer said that the next item would be Johann Sebastian Bach's *Air on a* gə *String*.

I thought at first that this was a twee joke, but it doesn't seem to have been: everything else was perfectly serious. Why he didn't say *on a* **dʒiː** *string*, as normal, I've no idea. (Anyhow, musicological pedants would insist on *Air on **the** G String*.)

Naming the letters of the alphabet in this way is something I've previously encountered only among primary school teachers and children learning to read, amongst whom it seems quite common to name the letters not **eɪ, biː, siː, diː, iː, ef** ... but **æ, bə, kə, də, e, fə** ....

I was wondering what they do when they get to *K*. How would it be distinguished from *C* **kə**? People who know tell me that C is called *curly* **kə**, while K is *kicking* **kə**.

11.7 A Spelling-Based Faux Pas

From the website of the Russian energy giant Gazprom:

> Gazprom Oil and Gas Nigeria and the Nigeria National Oil Corporation created NiGaz Energy Company Limited during the official visit of the President of Russia to Nigeria on 24th June 2009.
> www.freelanceuk.com/news/3164/shtml

It must have seemed like a good idea at the time. When Gazprom set up a joint venture to develop natural gas resources in Nigeria, they chose a name that from the point of view of Russian seems obvious and unexceptionable: Nigaz, i.e. Nigeria + Gaz. They would have expected to pronounce it in Russian as ˈnʲigas or ˈnʲigəs and in English as ˈnaɪgæz.

As people have pointed out, it seems unlikely that an English speaker was in the room when they chose this name – even though all educated Nigerians speak English. Because the natural way to read this spelling in English is as ˈnɪgəz, just like *niggers*. And that is not a respectful way for the Russians to refer to their African partners.

I blame the ambiguity of the English spelling system, where the letter *i* can in some positions arbitrarily stand for **aɪ** (as in *tiger*) or **ɪ** (as in *bigot*). Just like in the word(s) *wind*.

What a mercy that they didn't create the name from *Nig*(eria) plus *gas*. That would have left no ambiguity for the reader to untangle.

11.8 Sh!

As we know, English ʃ can be spelt not only *sh* but also in a number of other ways, as seen in the examples *ocean, machine, precious, sugar, conscience, compulsion, pressure, mission, creation*. However, *sh* is clearly felt as the basic way to spell this sound in English.

Why? Why did we choose this particular digraph for our voiceless palatoalveolar fricative?

Why do we need a digraph? Obviously, because there is no letter in our alphabet that regularly stands for this sound; so we have to represent it by using combinations of letters. Historically speaking, the basic problem is that classical Latin had no palatoalveolar sounds. In consequence, languages which use the Latin alphabet and which do have these sounds have not inherited any single way of representing them.

Greek, similarly, had and has no palatoalveolars. So the Greek alphabet, too, lacks a letter for the sound ʃ.

In Cyrillic, on the other hand, there is a letter used for just this purpose: Шш, presumably modelled on the Hebrew letter shin ש. This is also the origin of the Arabic ش. The Armenian and Georgian alphabets also have special [ʃ] letters, upper- and lower-case: Շշ and Შშ, respectively.

Getting back to the Roman alphabet, the predominant English way of writing ʃ is indeed the digraph *sh*. In Anglo-Saxon ʃ was written *sc*, but after the conquest this clashed with the habits of Norman scribes, for whom *sc* meant **sk**. For a time scribes wrote *sch* to resolve the clash, but by the end of the fourteenth century they had adopted the *sh* we use today.

French expresses the ʃ sound as *ch*. Words that in standard French now have ʃ were pronounced in Norman French with tʃ, and that is no doubt the reason we use *ch* in English for the affricate. Zulu and Xhosa logically write *sh* for the fricative, *tsh* for the affricate.

For the fricative ʃ German writes *sch* and Polish *sz*. Hungarian writes a simple *s*, reserving the spelling *sz* for the sound **s**. Czech, Slovak, Lithuanian, Latvian, Slovene, and Croatian all use the háček-bearing *š*. Romanian and Turkish use a subscript comma or cedilla, *ș*.

11.9 *rh* and *rrh*

I came across the words *mychorrizae* and *mychorrizal* in a science feature in a newspaper.

How did I know the words were misspelt, even though I'd never come across them before? Answer: because their etymology is obviously (to a classicist) Greek, and Greek double *rr* is always followed by *h*. Think of *catarrh*, *myrrh*, and *diarrh(o)ea*. Yes, they ought to have been *mycorrhizae* and *mycorrhizal*. The *h* was in the wrong place, and should have been after the *rr*.

Word-initial *r*, too, is regularly followed by *h* in words from Greek. We write *rhapsody, rheostat, rhesus, rhetoric, rheumatism, rhinoceros, rhizome, Rhodes, rhododendron, rhombus, rhubarb,* and *rhythm*, all being words derived from Greek; and there are no directly Greek-derived words in English from Classical Greek that begin with plain *r*. I say 'directly', because there are one or two scientific words from Greek via Latin or French for which this is not true, e.g. *raphe* (Greek ῥαφή *rhaphē*), *rachis, regolith*.

A mycorrhiza is a symbiotic association between a fungus and the roots of a vascular plant. Greek ρίζα *rhiza* means 'root'.

Why do Greek words have these apparently superfluous *h* letters? The reason can be traced back to an allophonic fact about Ancient Greek **r**, namely that it was voiceless in word-initial position and when geminated.

> Generally speaking [r] is a voiced sound, but in certain environments in classical Attic it seems to have been voiceless. What we are actually told by the grammarians is that ρ was 'aspirated' at the beginning of a word, and that when a double ρρ occurred in the middle of a word the first element was unaspirated and the second aspirated ... These descriptions are followed in the Byzantine practice of writing initial ῥ and medial ῤῥ, and are supported at an earlier period by Latin transcriptions such as *rhetor, Pyrrhus* ...
> [W.S. Allen, *Vox Graeca*, Cambridge University Press 1968]

Allen goes on to say that it can be shown to have been a single voiceless consonant **r̥** (rather than a cluster **rh**) by the fact that it was borrowed into Latin on the one hand as *rh* but into Armenian on the other hand as հɲ *hr̀*, thus հռետոռ *hr̀etor*, and similarly in Coptic.

When I did Greek at school, the transition from the fourth form to the fifth was marked by requiring us thenceforth to write the proper polytonic accents on our Greek, which we had until then been allowed to omit. So every initial rho had to be written with a 'rough breathing' ˈbriːðɪŋ (e.g. ῥήτωρ *rhētōr* 'orator'), though in line with modern practice we did not write breathings on doubled ρρ. All initial vowels or diphthongs require a breathing, either 'rough' (e.g. ὥρα *hōra*) to show **h** before the vowel concerned, or 'smooth' (e.g. ὤρα *ōra*) to show its absence.

The Greeks themselves did not bother with breathings and accent marks until the Hellenistic period. They first appear in papyruses in the second century AD, and then only sporadically. The Greeks finally stopped writing breathings only in the late twentieth century.

It seems a bit silly that now, well over a thousand years later, we have to go on including this unnecessary letter *h* after *r* in English spelling. But that's the power of tradition.

Oh, and since you were asking, the *cirrus* we know as a type of cloud is derived not from Greek but from Latin. Hence, unlike *Pyrrhus*, it has no *h* after its *rr*.

11.10 Prusiking Around

There are several English verbs that we can spell confidently in their base form, but which may throw us into uncertainty when we want to add an inflectional *-s*, *-ed*, or *-ing*.

Take the verb *to rendezvous* ˈrɒnd(e)ɪvuː. What's the 3rd person singular of the present tense? Clearly, it's pronounced ˈrɒnd(e)ɪvuːz. The Concise Oxford wants us to spell it *he rendezvouses with us*, but I cannot be the only one who feels very awkward with this. But then it would also be awkward to write *he rendezvous with us*. The other two inflected forms, *rendezvoused* ˈrɒnd(e)ɪvuːd and *rendezvousing* ˈrɒnd(e)ɪvuːɪŋ, are not quite so bad.

Then there's *to ricochet*, another French word. On the assumption that we pronounce it ˈrɪkəʃeɪ or ˌrɪkəˈʃeɪ, it would feel wrong to double the *t* when adding *-ed* or *-ing*. I certainly prefer *ricocheted, ricocheting*.

A former correspondent of mine got very excited about the verb *to prusik*, a technical term in mountaineering. When forming the present participle, he wanted to know, is it correct or not to double the *k*? He was disappointed when I declined to deliver an authoritative answer. I still don't know: in comparison I can only adduce *frolic, frolicking*, which doesn't really help. We do have *trek, trekked, trekking*; but that's a monosyllable. Americans, or at least those who write *worshiping* and *traveling*, may be confident with a single *k* in *prusiking*. But what about us Brits, who prefer to write *worshipping* and *travelling*? Does *prussikking* feel right to us? The third edition of the OED (2007) has a citation with the past tense *prussiked*, for what it's worth, which seems to imply an *ing*-form *prussiking*.

I once caught myself writing *stymieing*, only be struck by doubts whether it should not perhaps be *stymying*. (The COD gives both possibilities.) The word *stymie* ˈstaɪmi originated as a technical term in golfing, though I imagine most non-golfers know only its general meaning 'thwart, obstruct'.

11.11 The Digraph *zh*

In transliterating Russian names, the question arises what to do about Cyrillic ж, IPA ʒ, the voiced palatoalveolar fricative. The usual convention is to write it *zh*.

A former mayor of Moscow was called Yuri *Luzhkov* (Юрий Лужков). Since Russian assimilates voicing in consonant clusters, this *Luzhkov* is actually pronounced **luʃˈkɔf**. So it would be phonetically accurate to write it as *Lushkov* or indeed *Lushkof*. The usual *Luzhkov* is not a transcription but a transliteration.

How widely understood is the *zh* convention that *zh* stands for ʒ to a general readership? We all know about *Dr Zhivago*, or at least all of us who are over a certain age. (Pasternak's novel was published in 1957, and David Lean's film of it came out in 1965.) Some will remember *Brezhnev, Solzhenitsyn*, or other figures from Russian history or literature whose name includes this sound/digraph. The only familiar Russian place name that includes it is perhaps *Nizhny Novgorod*.

The logic behind the use of *zh* for this sound is transparent. As the letter *s* stands for the voiceless sound **s** and the digraph *sh* for the voiceless sound ʃ, so given that the letter *z* stands for the voiced sound **z**, the digraph *zh* must stand for the voiced sound **ʒ**.

Respelling systems deployed to show pronunciation in some monoglot English dictionaries (notably those published in the United States) represent **ʒ** as *zh* pretty much without exception. So one can say that writing *zh* is a well-established convention.

The only European language that uses *zh* for **ʒ** in standard orthography appears to be Albanian – not a language often learned by outsiders. I believe Navajo uses it, too.

In Breton (*Brezhoneg*) *zh* is used to represent a consonant which depending on the dialect involved may be **z** or **h** (but never **ʒ**).

This digraph is indeed used in the Chinese romanization known generally as Pinyin (properly Hanyu Pinyin). So we are all becoming familiar with names such as *Zhang, Zhou*, and *Zhu*. But here *zh* stands for a different sound! The corresponding sound in Mandarin is not fricative **ʒ** but an affricate **dẓ**, or more precisely its voiceless unaspirated counterpart **tṣ**. I notice that sports commentators who know very little about foreign languages often pronounce it **z** in the names of Chinese competitors. Those who are somewhat more sophisticated say **ʒ**. Only those who have bothered to find out the facts say **dʒ**, which is the closest English equivalent.

11.12 Speech and Writing

Speech is sounds, vibrations in the air arising from movements of the human organs of speech under the control of the brain/mind (or of an electrical device simulating this). Sounds can be heard, but not seen directly.

Writing is marks on paper or some other surface, or patterns of light and dark on a screen. Letters can be seen, but not heard directly.

It is incredible how difficult people find it to grasp the difference.

In public discussions of pronunciation, interviewers or commentators often raise the matter of text messaging and the innovative spellings associated with it. But that is not speech! Other than occasional initialisms such as *LOL* spoken aloud as **lɒl**, txtng has no effect at all on pronunciation. It is a matter of writing, not speech.

Other commentators, under the heading of pronunciation, complain about misplaced apostrophes. Apostrophes, whether misplaced or not, are not part of speech. They are part of our writing system. Why don't people get it? Even highly educated journalists?

Perhaps one reason for the confusion is the common sense of 'pronounce' in the sense of 'say letters aloud' (er ... you can't actually do that), i.e. 'say the sounds corresponding to written letters'.

> The letters *ng* are pronounced **ŋ**, or sometimes **ŋg** or **ndʒ**.
> Spanish has a letter *ñ*, which is pronounced as a palatal nasal.

But this rests on the fallacy that writing is primary, speech secondary. It implies that when we speak we are merely supplying sounds appropriate to the written form of the words we use.

If that were so, how could the illiterate ever speak at all? How is it that children learn to talk before they learn to read and write? How did humans manage to communicate using speech (which they did) before writing was invented?

Just as Magritte taught everyone that a picture of a pipe is not itself a pipe, so we need some genius to teach everyone that a letter depicting/representing/corresponding to a sound is not itself a sound.

I try to do my best for clarity by speaking of 'an **r**-sound', for example, as distinct from 'a letter *r*', and in writing, as in this book, by using bold type for sounds but italics for letters.

11.13 Pronunciation and Spelling

The inconsistencies of English spelling and the indeterminacies of its relationship to pronunciation mean that in English we frequently get the phenomenon of *spelling pronunciation*.

Spelling is, with rather few exceptions, fixed, while pronunciation varies. (That is why a high proportion of words in a pronunciation dictionary have more than one pronunciation shown.)

A speaker who is familiar with the written form of a word but not with its spoken form may, on the basis of the spelling, infer a pronunciation different from the traditional or generally used one. The word *posthumously* is usually pronounced ˈ**pɒstjʊməsli**. In November 2014 my colleague Paul Carley recorded someone on the BBC pronouncing it ˌ**pəʊstˈhjuːməsli**. This is an example of a new, previously unnoticed, spelling pronunciation.

Well-known examples of what were originally spelling pronunciations include *often* with a **t**-sound, *forehead* pronounced as *fore* plus *head* rather than rhyming with *horrid*, and *clothes* with **-ðz**. In the case of *backwards* the spelling pronunciation with **w** has entirely displaced the earlier ˈ**bækədz,** ˈ**bækɚdz**. In the case of *falcon*, formerly ˈ**fɔːkən**, my own pronunciation ˈ**fɔːlkən** and the newer ˈ**fælkən** represent successive stages of spelling pronunciation, as first the letter *l* and then the letter *a* receive their usual 'value'.

I particularly relish the Italian spelling pronunciation of *Colgate* toothpaste as **kolˈgaːte**.

There are two related phenomena. One is *pronunciation spelling*, in which a new spelling is applied, reflecting the pronunciation better than the traditional spelling does. Popularly this is sometimes called *phonetic spelling*. An example would be the proper name *Leicester* ˈ**lestə,** ˈ**lestɚ** respelt as *Lester*. Another is *though* respelt as *tho*. My colleague Jack Windsor Lewis uses nonce respellings such as *he'rd* for *heard* and *dou't* for *doubt*. Spelling reform projects typically involve systematic application of the principle of writing as we speak.

The other related phenomenon has no generally agreed name, but we could perhaps call it **'non-spelling pronunciation'**. This is the adoption of a new pronunciation that does not match the traditional spelling. An example is the mɪsˈtʃiːviəs variant of *mischievous*. Another is the widespread pronunciation of *Westminster* with -ˈmɪnɪstə instead of -ˈmɪnstə. Non-spelling pronunciation does particularly upset purists, and even from me tends to receive a warning triangle in LPD.

I suppose that if such pronunciations become established they are likely to lead to correspondingly changed spellings, thus *mischievious* and *Westminister*.

Non-spelling pronunciation followed by respelling is readily seen in the case of the word *pronunciation*, traditionally prəˌnʌnsiˈeɪʃn̩. Morphological regularization, given the base form *pronounce* prəˈnaʊns, produces prəˌnaʊnsiˈeɪʃn̩, which in turn gives rise to the unorthodox spelling *pronounciation*.

We Brits may laugh at Americans who use spelling pronunciations (with -hæm) of names such as *Nottingham* and *Cunningham*; but Americans have a corresponding right to laugh at us if we use a spelling pronunciation for *Poughkeepsie* (Section 6.5).

11.14 Latin Double Velars

Consider the everyday words *accelerate, accept, accident, success, vaccine*. They demonstrate the English spelling-to-sound principle that where double *-cc-* is followed by *e* or *i* the pronunciation is **ks**. Thus we have əkˈseləreɪt, əkˈsept, ˈæksɪdənt, səkˈses, ˈvæksiːn.

There are one or two rather rarer words where not all speakers follow this principle. One is *flaccid*, where ˈflæsɪd competes with the expected ˈflæksɪd. Another is *succinct*, where one occasionally hears səˈsɪŋkt rather than the səkˈsɪŋkt that I would say myself. Yet another is the anatomical term for the tailbone, the *coccyx*, which I call the ˈkɒksɪks, but for which I have also heard ˈkɒsɪks as well as ˈkɒkɪks. I can think of no reason why these words should be exceptions to the general rule. Like the others, they are of Latin origin. Their pronunciation goes back to a Latin double *-cc-*, which was classically **kk** but subsequently had the second velar 'softened' when it developed into **tʃ** or **s** in late Latin and the successor Romance languages.

As you would expect, this being English spelling, there are a handful of other words that violate the rule. *Soccer* ˈsɒkə, ˈsɑkɚ obviously 'ought' to be spelt *socker*. There's also *recce* ˈreki, short for *reconnoitre*, and *baccy* ˈbæki for *tobacco*. And lovers of classical music will be familiar with Italian names such as *Puccini* puˈtʃiːni and *Pagliacci*.

Strangely, the corresponding rule doesn't work in the case of the voiced etymological equivalent. In *exaggerate* ɪgˈzædʒəreɪt we have simple dʒ, not *gdʒ. In *suggest* Brits have simple dʒ, thus səˈdʒest, but most Americans have gdʒ, thus səgˈdʒest. Otherwise the velar remains unsoftened; there don't seem to be any other Latin-derived words with *-gge-* or *-ggi-*. Double *gg* stands for simple **g** in occasional non-Latin-derived words such as *druggist* and *digging*. And then there's *ciggy* ˈsɪgi, colloquial abbreviation of *cigarette*, which demonstrates the use of *-gg-* in informal spelling.

11.15 Bilding a Cubbard

I was pleased to see the Guardian newspaper arguing, with reference to English spelling, that 'the time has come to step back where we can from uniformity and let in variety and simplicity'.

> Some oddities in conventional spelling occur in only a few words, and could be changed without causing problems: *bild, cubbard, dubble, gost, gard, lam, bom, crum, autum, potatos, sope, foke, buty, canoo, frute*. These would be easier for native and non-native speakers, **but would have to become official – not alternatives to existing spellings** [emphasis added – JCW].

We might well add *bizzy* and *bizness*.

And we'd only be acknowledging texting reality if we were to allow the pronouns *I* and *you* to have alternat(iv)e spellings *i* and *u*.

On the assumption that we are content to allow reform of these 'oddities', I don't see the logic in insisting that the traditional spellings must no longer be permitted alongside the reformed spellings. Why not allow the two forms to co-exist, to compete if you will, until one or other becomes obsolescent and ultimately obsolete?

That is what has often happened in the history of our spelling.

Even within my own lifetime I can think of examples. As a boy I was taught that we could spell the word pronounced ʃəʊ either as *show* or as *shew*.

> Now the LORD had said unto Abram, Get thee out of thy country, and from thy kindred, and from thy father's house, unto a land that I will shew thee. Gen 12:1

No one would write *shew* today.

When I was at school in the 1940s it was still quite usual to write *no-one* and *to-day* with a hyphen. That hyphen is now obsolescent in the first, obsolete in the second. Nowadays (*now-a-days*), you will see mostly *no one* and nothing but *today*. In the nineteenth century our newspapers wrote *Oxford-street*; today it's *Oxford Street*. All those hyphens first co-existed with the unhyphenated forms, then finally lost out.

When I was a boy the spelling *gaol* (for *jail*) was still a frequent spelling in Britain. Not now: nowadays we all write *jail*.

In Britain we tolerate both *organise* and *organize*, and similarly with many other *-ise/-ize* words. (Some British people wrongly imagine that only *-ise* is correct for us. On the contrary, the Concise Oxford Dictionary, like many others, prefers *-ize*.) It does no harm to allow both forms. The same applies to *judg(e)ment* and various other cases.

And so we come to the Guardian's suggestions for *build* and *cupboard*. On the first, the OED comments (with its charming Victorian syntax)

> The normal modern spelling of the word would be *bild* (as it is actually pronounced); the origin of the spelling *bui-* (*buy-* in Caxton), and its retention to modern times, are difficult of explanation.

On the second, we all know that despite its etymology a modern cupboard is not a table or board for cups. It is a cabinet or closet in which we store all sorts of things. A 'broom cupboard' has nothing to do with cups or with boards.

So if people want to write about *bilding a cubbard*, let's allow them to do so. As for those who prefer *building a cupboard* – let's allow them too to continue to do so. Let a hundred or so improved spellings like these exist alongside the traditional forms. Let a hundred flowers bloom. And let's see what survives.

11.16 Stenotypy

The BBC news website carried an interesting article about stenography.

Or at least, that's what the headline said it was about. The topic it reports on was actually, as I understand it, not stenography as such but more precisely stenotypy.

'Stenography' is a general term that covers all forms of shorthand – handwritten shorthand systems such as Pitman and Gregg (the systems that are, or rather were, predominant in the United Kingdom and the United States, respectively), as well as machine shorthand. 'Stenotypy', on the other hand, refers specifically to the machine shorthand produced with the aid of a 'stenotype', which the COD defines as

> *n.* **1** a machine like a typewriter for recording speech in syllables or phonemes. **2** a symbol or the symbols used in this process.

As explained in greater detail in Wikipedia, the stenotype keyboard has a mere 22 keys, yet encodes the spoken material a full syllable at a time. This requires 'chording', i.e. the simultaneous depression of several keys. The left hand records the onset consonant(s), the right hand the coda consonant(s), and the thumbs the vowel. Many sounds are recorded by arbitrary key combinations, e.g. initial **d** as TK, initial **m** as P plus H but final **m** as P plus L, 'long E' (**iː**) as AO plus E, and so on.

In principle all English shorthand systems, as far as I am aware, including stenotypy, encode the pronunciation of the words direct, rather than via the traditional orthography. This means that shorthand writers have to be experts in instant on-the-fly phonetic transcription – though of course they do not have to pay attention to the way the given speaker says the word on the given occasion but rather to the citation form.

Both Pitman and Gregg, and also I assume stenotypy, require nonrhotic speakers to record the symbol representing **r** in words in which rhotic speakers use **r**. In Gregg, which I taught myself as a teenager, *stork* is written differently from *stalk* (though they are homophones for me), while *stalk* is written identically to *stock* and for that matter *stoke* (though they are not homophones for me).

However there are also numerous shortened forms (logograms, 'briefs') which make the relationship between sound and shorthand spelling less direct.

The Wikipedia article goes on to tell us:

> Some court reporters use scopists to translate and edit their work. A scopist is a person who is trained in the phonetic language, English punctuation, and usually in legal formatting.

Oh dear. How often do we have to say it? A writing system is not a language. English is still English, no matter whether you record it in traditional orthography, in Morse code, in IPA, in shorthand, or as a .wav or .mp3 file. Converting ordinary spelling into one of the other forms is not translating it into a different language.

Serbian is still Serbian whether written in the Latin or the Cyrillic alphabet. Kurdish is still Kurdish whether written in the Latin alphabet or the Arabic abjad.

So you cannot 'translate' a shorthand record of English words into English. If you convert it into ordinary spelling, you are transcribing it. That's also why we speak of phonetic 'transcription' when we use phonetic symbols to record utterances.

Compare converting an English utterance, word, sentence, poem, or book-length novel into French, Russian, or Japanese – or vice versa. That's translation.

11.17 Final *mb* and *mn*

Bombardier (1.37) is a derivative of *bomb*. The second *b* is silent not only in *bomb* **bɒm ‖ bɑːm** but also in *bombing* and *bomber*. However *bombard* is **bɒmˈbɑːd ‖ bɑːmˈbɑːrd** (or possibly **bəm-**), and *bombardier* is formed from that rather than directly from *bomb*.

Historically and etymologically the relationship between *bomb* and *bombard* is like that of *climb* **klaɪm** – *clamber* ˈ**klæmbə(r)**, *thumb* **θʌm** – *thimble* ˈ**θɪmbl̩**, *crumb* **krʌm** – *crumble* ˈ**krʌmbl̩**. In modern English most people do not feel the items in these pairs to have an obvious relationship to one another.

Other words spelt with a final silent *b* include *lamb, comb, dumb* **dʌm**, *plumb, limb, numb*, and (generally) *jamb* and *iamb*. Again, the *b* remains silent in inflected forms such as *combing, dumbest* ˈ**dʌmɪst**. This gives us the interesting pair of homographs written *number*: the one to do with counting, ˈ**nʌmbə(r)**, and the other the comparative of the adjective *numb*, ˈ**nʌmə(r)**.

Interestingly, most of the handful of words with final *mn*, in which the *n* is silent, have obviously related forms in which **n** is pronounced. Thus we have *condemn* **kənˈdem**, *condemning* **kənˈdemɪŋ**, but *condemnation* ˌ**kɒndemˈneɪʃn̩** and similarly *damn* **dæm** but *damnation* **dæmˈneɪʃn̩**, *autumn – autumnal, solemn – solemnity, hymn – hymnal. Column* follows the same pattern for those of us who pronounce *columnist* with -**nɪst**, but not for those who don't.

Phonologists in the Chomsky-Halle tradition see these stems as ending in a final underlying **b** or **n**, obligatorily deleted after **m** word-finally or before an inflectional ending, though not before a mere derivational boundary. But they would also see a similar relationship in pairs such as *sign – signal, (im)pugn – pugn(acious), (con)dign – dignity*. Let's not go there: in my view such alternations are orthographic, etymological, and pretty obvious to classicists, but not part of contemporary English phonetics.

11.18 Keeping Shtoom

Usually, when English borrows a word from some other modern language, we keep the spelling used in the source language and hesitate about the pronunciation. Thus we all agree on the spelling *restaurant* (from French), but disagree on how to pronounce the last syllable. We may take a cavalier line with diacritics, as when Swedish *smörgåsbord* becomes just *smorgasbord*. And with languages not written in the Roman alphabet we use a romanization, thus *perestroika* or *tsunami*. But generally speaking the spelling is not controversial, though the pronunciation may be.

There's a word **ʃtʊm** that has become quite well established in the United Kingdom (or perhaps particularly in London and environs; I don't think Americans ever use it). There is no question about its pronunciation. But we can't agree on how to spell it. This is the other way round from what is usual.

The word means 'silent', and is used almost exclusively in the phrase *keep* **ʃtʊm** or its variant *stay* **ʃtʊm** 'keep quiet (about something)'. (The OED also offers us a verb, *to* **ʃtʊm** *up*, but I don't think I've ever heard that.)

We agree on how to say it: but how do we spell it? There are quite a few candidates.

In 2012 I searched the *Guardian* newspaper website for various possible spellings of the word.

I found:

> 184 hits for *schtum*,
> 78 for *shtoom*,
> 41 for *shtum*,
> 21 for *stumm* (but some of these are for a proper name),
> 15 for *stum* (ditto),
> 5 for *shtumm*,
> 4 for *schtumm*,
> and 3 for *schtoom*.

The OED's first citation of this word is dated 1958. Its origin is Yiddish, the equivalent of German *stumm* ʃtʊm 'dumb, speechless, mute, silent'. (That's 'dumb' in the older sense, 'unable to speak', not the modern AmE sense 'stupid'.) But we see that the spelling used in German, *stumm*, comes only in fourth place in the Guardian statistics. The 2010 *guardianstyle* book prescribes *stumm*, eloquent testimony to how little attention Guardian writers pay to it.

In German the word-initial spelling *st-* corresponds to ʃt. The English spellings with *scht-*, which look German to us, aren't German at all.

11.19 Faustian

A correspondent asked me whether I knew of any English word, however obscure, in which *au* in the spelling has the sound of **aʊ** as in the proper name *Faust*?

After a little thought, and consulting Carney's *Survey of English Spelling*, I replied as follows.

> Lots of people say *traumatic* with the MOUTH vowel, though others use the THOUGHT vowel. The same applies to various other words of Greek origin (*claustrophobia, glaucoma, tau,* and *trauma* itself). You also sometimes get the MOUTH vowel in *aural*, to keep it distinct from *oral*. Then there are the actual German borrowings such as *meerschaum, sauerkraut*, as well as names such as *Audi, Schopenhauer, Strauss*, like the *Faust* you mention. There are also geographical names such as *Nauru, Palau*. And some people (though not Welsh speakers) use this diphthong in Welsh names such as *Blaenau* and *Dolgellau*.

I might also have mentioned other more or less exotic borrowings from various languages, such as *luau, pilau, Saudi (Arabia)*, and *Mau Mau*. And of course there are Latin words: *magna cum laude, gaudeamus igitur*.

Faust itself has a derived adjective *Faustian*, as when we say a Faustian bargain. This, of course, is not a German word: the German equivalent is *faustisch*. So it has to be counted as an English word. It usually has the MOUTH vowel.

But apart from these, as far as I can see, there are no pukka, echt, authentic native English words with *au* = indubitable **aʊ**.

Familiar words such as *author, cause, gauze,* and *taut*, all of which have the THOUGHT vowel ɔː, have established this as the normal spelling-to-sound correspondence for *au* in English. It means that foreign borrowings so spelt tend to be said in English with ɔː even if they have an **aʊ**-like diphthong in the language of origin. So *sauna*, which in Finnish is ˈ**saunɑ**, becomes ˈ**sɔːnə** in English.

On the other hand we use the GOAT vowel in French words and expressions such as *au fait, chauffeur, aubergine, de Gaulle, auteur*. In French they have **o**.

I notice that British television advertisements for the Toyota *Auris* car call it an ˈ**aʊrɪs**. I wonder if the company will succeed in stopping people call it an ˈ**ɔːrɪs**.

11.20 Digraphs in the Alphabet

A digraph is a sequence of two letters treated as a single grapheme. Familiar examples are English *sh* to represent ʃ, or *th* to represent θ or ð.

Other examples include DŽ, LJ, and NJ in Croatian, CH and LL in Spanish, and CH, DD, LL, NG, PH, RH, and TH in Welsh. They are somewhat different in how they behave.

I said 'treated as a single grapheme'. You could alternatively say that such sequences are considered individual letters or as single orthographic entities. They may have their own place in the alphabet; they may not be allowed to be separated into their constituent letters when sorting, abbreviating, or hyphenating; in crosswords they may occupy a single space.

This can cause difficulty for the unwary. In a Welsh dictionary, for example, NG is ordered between G and H, if pronounced [ŋ], but not if pronounced [ŋg], in which case it is treated as N plus G. So *angau* (death, [ˈaŋai]) comes before *ail* (second); but *dangos* (show, [ˈdaŋɡos]) comes after *damwain* (accident). In the first case we have the NG digraph, in the second case ordinary N followed by G.

There may be special rules for capital letters. If we need to capitalize a Bosnian word that begins with *lj*, we capitalize the initial *L* but not the *j* that follows it. This language can also be written in the Cyrillic alphabet, where the single letter Љ corresponds to it and can be capitalized like any other single letter. In Dutch, on the other hand, we have to capitalize both the *I* and the *j* at the beginning of *IJsselmeer*. (I had to fight my word processor to get this paragraph to come out right.)

Danish *aa* in proper names is alphabetized as if it were its modern equivalent *å*, i.e. at the end of the alphabet. Only the first letter of the digraph is capitalized. German *ae*, on the other hand, just like its modern equivalent *ä*, is alphabetized as if it were plain *a*.

11.21 English Spelling: What Should We Do?

In his book *Spell It Out* (Profile Books 2012), David Crystal has an upbeat message. Teachers of literacy must concentrate on the regularities, not on the anomalies.

- Above all, they should not set students the dispiriting task of learning the spellings of lists of difficult words presented out of context.
- The 'short word rule' for content words accounts for the doubled consonants of *inn, egg, add, odd, ill* and the final *e* of *eye, owe,* and *bye*. Compare function (non-content) words such as *in, up, to, if, as, by*. Arguably, though, awareness of this 'rule' lies behind the frequently encountered *add* for *ad*(*vertisement*).
- Pay attention to stress, which explains the doubling of the consonants in *preferring, preferred* but not in *proffering, proffered*.
- Be aware of the morphology (or that of the Latin origin), so as to understand, for example, the single *b* of *aberrant* (*ab* + *errant*) as against the doubling in *abbreviate* (*ab*+*brev*-). This even explains *accommodate* (*ad (ac)* + *con (com)* + *mod*-).

I would add the mnemonic value of related words, as when *definition* reminds us that *definite* is not *definate, while *substantial* and *residential* remind us how to spell the endings of *substance* and *residence*.

As far as reforming the system is concerned, Crystal declares baldly that 'there can never be a simple solution to the problem of English spelling'. On the other hand he twice refers to the fact that Google shows the non-standard spelling *rubarb* to be increasingly common online. 'If it carries on like this, *rubarb* will overtake *rhubarb* as the commonest online spelling in the next five years.' Then dictionary makers will 'eventually have to recognise that a change has taken place' (as they already have, for example, in the case of *miniscule* replacing *minuscule*).

If you are reading this in or after 2017 you will be able to judge how accurate Crystal's prediction was.

By this logic, dictionaries of the coming decade will also have to recognize *seperate, tounge, accomodation*, and so on ('misspellings' frequently encountered online), and abandon such distinctions as *lose – loose, rein – reign, sight – site, to – too, your – you're, its – it's* (all often confused on the web). Or perhaps ever more intelligent spell checkers and speech-to-text technology will prevent this from happening after all.

I think it's important to recognize that planned, systematic reform is not truly impossible. Consider the case of the chemical element *sulphur*. That's how it was standardly spelt, at least in the United Kingdom, until twenty years ago. But in 1990 the International Union of Pure and Applied Chemistry decided to adopt the spelling *sulfur*, and two years later the Nomenclature Committee of the Royal Society of Chemistry followed suit. In 1992 the Qualifications and Curriculum

Authority for England and Wales recommended the *f* spelling, which is accordingly now found in textbooks and GCSE exams. I think it's better for everyone to have an official change like this, so that we know where we are, rather than unofficial and chaotic *rubarb*-style changes.

Another similar example is the immunosuppressant drug of which the British Approved Name was formerly *cyclosporin* but is now *ciclosporin*. What used to be the correct spelling is now considered a mistake; what used to be a mistake is now correct. It might be better simply to allow both versions.

Unofficial changes do sometimes succeed, too, as with *today, tomorrow, tonight*, which have replaced the hyphenated *to-day, to-morrow, to-night* of my schooldays.

We could consider, for example, getting the QCA to make an official decision that all words with *rh* may alternatively be spelt without the *h*, just as we allow *likeable* alongside *likable* and (in Britain) *organise* alongside *organize*. That would take care not only of *rhubarb* but also of *rheumatism, rhythm*, and *rhino*.

Despite some commentators' alarmism, I think doctors, nurses, and health administrators would manage to avoid any resulting confusion between *resus* (*-negative/-positive* blood) and *resus*(*citation*).

11.22 Romeo Papa

In an on-line forum discussion about what language teachers need to know about pronunciation, one unusual suggestion made was this, from the phonetician David Deterding:

> We should teach them the Alpha Bravo Charlie Delta alphabet. Then, when they cannot be understood [when spelling a word out aloud], they could easily solve the problem. (And it would also be brilliant for telling someone your name.)

I agree that this is something that it is useful to know. I was taught it in my teens, as part of 'corps' at school (= officer cadet training corps, 'playing at soldiers'). I use it from time to time, particularly when giving information over the phone to travel agents, airline call centres and the like.

It is particularly useful for distinguishing letters whose traditional names are easily confused, such as F **ef** and S **es** or T **ti**: and D **di**:. How much clearer to say *foxtrot* and *sierra, tango* and *delta*.

That's why in LPD I decided to include the relevant 'communications code name' at the entry for each letter of the alphabet. Before we had the web it could be difficult to lay your hands on the list, though nowadays of course you can quickly access it on Wikipedia. For avoidance of doubt, as the lawyers say, it goes *Alfa, Bravo, Charlie, Delta, Echo, Foxtrot, Golf, Hotel, India, Juliett, Kilo, Lima, Mike, November, Oscar, Papa, Quebec, Romeo, Sierra, Tango, Uniform, Victor, Whiskey, X-ray, Yankee, Zulu.*

Although it's often known as the NATO Phonetic Alphabet, it is neither an alphabet (it's a list of letter names) nor particularly phonetic, and NATO is only one of a number of international organizations that have adopted it.

The list on the Wikipedia page includes a column headed 'phonic (pronunciation)', which explains the intended pronunciation of each letter name by respelling it in accordance with English spelling conventions, with all the ambiguity that can imply.

So, although *Delta* is keyed to 'DELL-TAH', it is normally pronounced by speakers of English as ˈ**deltə** (rather than the ˈ**deltɑː** that could be implied by this respelling). There is no indication of stress in the list given, so while anglophones will say *Uniform* ('YOU-NEE-FORM or OO-NEE-FORM') as ˈ**juːnɪfɔː(r)m**, francophones, for example, are apparently free to stress it anywhere or nowhere, in accordance with their native habits. On the other hand we English speakers are supposed to stress *Papa* with final-syllable stress and to say *Quebec* with no **w**. No one seems to take any notice of the instruction to pronounce *Golf* as if it were *Gulf*. The Wikipedia page has an analysis of the various versions to be found in officially recommended recordings.

The choice of letter names has changed slightly over the years. When I learnt them in the 1950s, N was called *Nectar*. Clearly, *November* is an improvement, being less likely to be confused with *Victor*.

The names of the digits are also covered. For *9*, we are supposed to say disyllabic 'niner', and for *5* monosyllabic 'fife'. This makes them less likely to be confused. Rather strangely, the pronunciation of *4* is prescribed as 'fower', though it is not clear exactly what that spelling means. Probably we are supposed to make it disyllabic, to rhyme with *slower*.

11.23 Going Up

Contrary to popular belief, neither the Korean script (hangŭl) nor the Japanese (kana) are phonetically opaque in the way that Chinese characters are. The Korean writing system is actually alphabetic, while the Japanese katakana is a straightforward syllabary. Both of them can be spelled out symbol by symbol.

The borrowed word *elevator* is written in Korean as 엘리베이터. It reads *el-li-be-i-tŏ*. When the Korean phoneme written ㄹ is between vowels it is pronounced as a tap, **ɾ**. But in syllable-final position, and when geminated (as here), it is pronounced as a lateral, **l**. As the *IPA Handbook* puts it, '/l/ is [ɾ] intervocalically; ... /ll/ is [ll] ... '.

Here is the same word in Japanese: エレベーター. It reads *e-re-be-ː-ta-ː*.

So the differences between the two languages in the treatment of this borrowing from American English are that in Korean,

- English **l** is correctly rendered as a lateral (but a geminated one);
- English **eɪ** is correctly rendered as a diphthong;
- the final AmE ɚ comes out as ŏ (ʌ);

while in Japanese,

- English **l** comes out as a tap **r**, not as a lateral (except by chance sometimes)
- the diphthong is rendered as a long monophthong (though Japanese no longer distinguishes between *ei* and *ee*, anyway);
- the final ɚ comes out as a long **aː**.

In both languages, English **v** is rendered as **b**. The two languages differ in how they treat the second, unstressed, vowel: but then so do native speakers.

(A correspondent tells me that previously, when under Japanese rule, Korean used a different form, *erebeta*, based on the Japanese version. There's also a Sino-Korean word for 'lift, elevator', *sŭng-gang-gi* 승강기; but it is not used in everyday speech.)

11.24 Family Words

I expect most families have private, family words, used only within the family and never with outsiders.

When I was growing up, we certainly did. And special family (mis)pronunciations, too. I'm not thinking just of nursery words for excretion and body parts, though of course we had those.

For example, my father and brothers and I (though perhaps not my mother) would often pronounce *jug* as **jʌg** ('yug') and *jump* as **jʌmp**. My father would tell me to get a ˈ**jʌg əv** ˈ**ɒlɪndʒ** (*jug of orange*, i.e. orange squash) to put on the table for a meal. Whether this betrayed some paternal or precocious filial awareness of IPA and historical phonology (confusion of liquid consonants) I do not know.

We also sometimes called *ice cream* ɪˈ**kekriæm**, obviously in a playful misinterpretation of the spelling.

The family dog was called Carlo, but we sometimes called him *Doggus* ˈ**dɒgəs** instead, so recruiting him to the Latin second declension masculine. (My brothers and I had all started Latin at a pretty tender age.) Interestingly, when my German exchange friend Klaus came to stay with us, at the end of my stay with his family when I was eighteen, I remember that he misinterpreted this name as *Doggers* ˈ**dɒgəz**, which would put it in line with *champers* 'champagne', *Johnners* (Brian Johnstone the cricket commentator), and the *Staggers* (the New Statesman periodical).

A correspondent tells me that his dog was a pug, and known as both Doggus and Puggus. Others have mentioned 'coinkidink' for *coincidence*, popularized by the Simpsons on TV.

They tell me that strawberries are variously known not just as 'strawbugs' (our school term) or 'strawbs', but also as 'struggleberries'.

11.25 Casing Clicks

The Namibian town generally known as Lüderitz has reportedly officially changed its name to !Nami╪Nûs. This is its name in the indigenous language Nama (aka Khoekhoe, formerly called Hottentot). The exclamation mark is the spelling for a voiceless retroflex click, IPA [!] and formerly [ꞓ], while the sign like a vertical doesn't-equal sign is the spelling for a voiceless alveolar click, IPA [╪] and formerly with no recognized IPA symbol.

The usual convention in languages that use the Latin alphabet is that the first letter of a proper name is capitalized (= written in upper-case). But what do we do if the first letter is not a part of the regular alphabet?

There's no problem with æ. It has an upper-case form Æ, and that is what we use if we so choose, for example, when writing the name of King *Æthelfrith* or Aldfrith of Northumbria. Likewise, the Icelandic letters thorn þ and edh ð have upper-case forms Þ and Ð, as in the Icelandic tourist destination *Þingvellir*.

But what are we to do with proper names beginning with punctuation marks or mathematical symbols? Answer: we ignore them, and capitalize the regular letter that follows. So the Calabrian version of the Mafia, the *'Ndrangheta*, is written with a capital N. Likewise, the scholarly transliteration of the Arabic name عمر is *'Umar*, in which we ignore the reverse apostrophe and capitalize the following *u*.

And that's presumably why Lüderitz's new name is correctly written as *!Nami╪Nûs*, not *!ami╪Nûs*. (I don't know why the second *N* is also upper-case, though.)

12 Transcription

12.1 Explicitness in Transcription

When I talk in public about pronunciation dictionaries one of the questions I am frequently asked concerns the level of phonetic detail that each dictionary entry ought to show.

Why don't we show the aspiration of the initial plosive in *time* **taɪm**, thus **tʰaɪm**? Why doesn't the dictionary show the glottal stop as a possibility in *right* **raɪt**, that is, **raɪʔ**? (After all, that's how it is frequently pronounced.) Why don't we show that the lateral in *sell* **sel** is dark, thus **seɫ**? (Or perhaps we ought even to write **sɛɫ**, showing what happens to the vowel in this environment. Not to mention such further possibilities as **sëo**.)

The usual answer is that each of these would constitute allophonic as opposed to phonemic notation. Despite the difficulties that modern linguistics has with the notion of phoneme, the point remains: the aspiration, the glottalling, and the velarization are predictable by rule, 'context-dependent'. Therefore they do not need to be symbolized explicitly each time they happen.

Furthermore, allophones at the edges of words typically apply only in certain environments. A glottal stop in *right now* **raɪʔ naʊ** will pass unnoticed in mainstream BrE or AmE. But in *right away*, thus **raɪʔ əweɪ**, it would convey a particular regional/social message. Different phonetic contexts demand different allophones.

The lateral at the end of *sell* is not dark in all contexts. In a phrase such as *sell it*, with a vowel following, it is clear. Marking it as dark in the dictionary entry would actually be misleading.

… But, you may say, in LPD you nevertheless show one predictable allophone, namely the voiced ('flapped') /t/ of American English in words like *city*, transcribed as ˈsɪt̬ i. My defence to this charge of inconsistency is that the conditions governing the use of this allophone are rather complicated, while arguably for some speakers it is anyway not an allophone of /t/ but an instance of the phoneme /d/ (many Americans reject this view, even though they may pronounce *atom* and *Adam* identically most of the time).

12.2 Syllabic Plosives

A correspondent wrote:

> I was put on the spot the other day when a student asked me if **p** in *potato* could be marked as a syllabic consonant – assuming there was no audible schwa after it. Thinking that **p** couldn't be the nucleus of a syllable because it's not sufficiently sonorous, I said no. Is this true, and if so, how would you transcribe it?

I agree that the answer is no, and I would transcribe it straightforwardly as **p**: for example, **hæv əpˈteɪtəʊ**. Phonetically, the **p** might either be released, [pʰ], or not [p̚], just as applies to the **p** in *kept* **kept**.

In principle, I would say that plosives can never be syllabic. People have sometimes tried to claim that a very reduced form of *thank you*, **kkju**, has two syllables, the first consisting of an inaudible and unreleased syllabic **k**. And in Romanian there are high vowels which become devoiced or disappear after voiceless plosives, giving contrasts such as Romanian **lupi̥** vs **lupu̥** (or better **lupʲ** vs **lupʷ**, respectively the plural and singular of the word for 'wolf') – but I would say that historical or underlying disyllables were reduced to monosyllables by this process. It's the same with the Japanese pair **kiˈɕi** (**kʲɕi**) *kishi* 'coast' and **ku̥ˈɕi** (**kʷɕi**) *kushi* 'comb'. (Compare the final vowels in these words, which are accented and therefore are not devoiced or elided.)

Nevertheless I agree that there is a fine line between devoicing a vowel and deleting it entirely, perhaps leaving behind a secondary articulation on the preceding consonant.

I have often had to correct beginners who thought it correct to transcribe *wanted*, for example, as ˈwɒntd̩, imagining that the final sequence **ɪd** or **əd** was a syllabic **d**. But it isn't.

There are various languages for which linguists have posited the existence of syllabic obstruents. Among them are the Salishan languages (especially Nuxalk or Bella Coola, in which you can get long strings of consonants without any intervening sonorants; some words are entirely voiceless). But this raises the thorny question of how we define the syllable.

12.3 happY Again

It seemed like a good idea at the time, but it clearly confuses a lot of people.

Like many other phoneticians of English, for the past twenty-odd years I have been using the symbol **i** to represent the weak 'happY' vowel used in positions where the FLEECE-KIT distinction, **iː** vs **ɪ**, is neutralized, and where an older generation of RP speakers used a lax [ɪ] but a younger generation tend to prefer a tense [i]. (See *Sounds Interesting*, p. 52ff.)

A puzzled correspondent asked:

> Is there any rule for the use of **i** and **u** (neither long nor short?) ... In the case of *bizarre* LPD uses ɪ and for *behind* **i**. What is the difference?

The symbol **i** does not mean 'neither long nor short'. It means that RP traditionally has lax ɪ in these positions, but that many speakers nowadays use a tense vowel more like iː. Therefore the EFL learner may use one or the other indifferently in these cases, because it does not make any difference whether the vowel is tense or lax. See further the discussion in LPD under 'Neutralization' (3rd edition, p. 539). You might also like to try a YouTube search on 'the happY vowel song'.

In LPD I use the symbol **i** in those cases where some people have a tense vowel in place of the traditional RP lax vowel: namely, in weak positions that are:

(a)   word-final, as *happy, coffee, valley,*
(b)   prevocalic, as *various, euphoria,*
(c)   in the unstressed prefixes *be-, de-, pre-, re-* and certain word-like combining forms such as *poly-*.

As far as I know, no one uses a tense vowel in *bizarre*, whereas in *behind* and other *be-* words some people do. That is why I treat the first syllables differently in the two words.

If all this is too complicated to teach, learners of EFL should be advised to interpret **i** (without length marks) as just an unstressed FLEECE vowel. They won't sound quite like me, but then I am now elderly, and RP has moved on.

Actors aiming at an early-twentieth-century RP, on the other hand, can treat it as meaning the same as ɪ (the KIT vowel). So can those aiming at an American southern accent. Those aiming at the local accent of some parts of the English midlands or north may even need to identify it with the local DRESS vowel; or of Scotland with the local FACE vowel. (Leave that to the specialists.)

I might have gone on, but won't, to discuss the theoretical idea that English has a weak vowel system as well as a strong vowel system; the weak vowels are found exclusively in unstressed positions, and are those vowels which can result from vowel weakening in the lexicon. Pairs such as *vary, variety* demonstrate that **i** acts as the weak counterpart of **aɪ** (PRICE). The strong and weak forms of *me, she*, etc demonstrate that **i** also acts as the weak counterpart of **iː** (FLEECE).

All the above applies, mutatis mutandis, to **u** as in *sit<u>u</u>ation* and *thank<u>you</u>*.

Perhaps for the lexicographer this is another case of the conflict between on the one hand trying to accurately document the phonetics and phonology of English and on the other hand presenting a convenient simplified distillation for pedagogical EFL purposes.

There are various words in which it is not clear whether the dictionary entry should show ɪ or i. What, for example, about the second syllable of *helicopter*? Americans usually weaken it, but not all Brits do. Etymologically, *heli-* is not a separate morpheme (combining form); but modern coinages such as *heliport*, *helipad* show that it can be treated as if it were.

12.4 False Alarm

I quite often get emails like the following:

I am a student of applied linguistics doing a PhD on L2 phonology in Iran. I'm investigating the phonological problems of Persian speaking L2 learners of English (focusing on American English). I have one question with regards to the American English liquid /ɹ/ (or [ɹ]).

As you know, in Persian we have the alveolar trill /r/ while in American English we have the alveolar approximant /ɹ/. Now for the purpose of my research, I want to know that whether we should take both of them as allophones of /r/, therefore put them in square brackets (i.e. [r] in Persian and [ɹ] in American English) or we should consider them as two distinct phonemes in the two languages, hence putting them in slashes (i.e. /r/ in Persian and /ɹ/ in American English).

My idea is that they are two distinct phonemes, as 'r' in American English is approximant in all word-positions so the concept of complementary distribution for allophones doesn't work for it.

I replied:

I think you need to consider how the term 'phoneme' is defined and used. Technically, a phoneme is a phonological unit **in a particular language, dialect, or idiolect**.

It is therefore meaningless to ask whether a sound of one language belongs to the same phoneme as a sound of a different language.

The choice of phonetic symbols to notate particular phonemes is a separate issue. You can write the English r-sound as /r/, even though its commonest realization is the postalveolar approximant [ɹ]. You can write the German r-sound as /r/, even though its commonest realization is the uvular approximant [ʁ]. You can write the Farsi r-sound as /r/ even though its commonest realization is, according to you, the trill [r] – though I suspect it is more usually the tap [ɾ].

Similarly, we write /t/ for the voiceless coronal plosive of English (where it is usually alveolar and aspirated, though sometimes glottal), of French (where it is usually dental and unaspirated), of Dutch (where it is usually alveolar and unaspirated), and of Swedish (where it is usually dental and aspirated) – and also of Russian (where it is laminal rather than apical). Please consult the *IPA Handbook* (Cambridge University Press 1999) on this point.

Learning to pronounce a foreign language well means understanding that it does ***not*** use just the same sounds as your mother tongue.

> How you choose to symbolize English /r/ for EFL learners is really a pedagogical issue rather than a phonetic or phonological one. Personally, I would write /r/ while also training the learners to hear and produce the English sound, i.e. [ɹ] – and to be aware of the difference between it and their Farsi /r/. Equally, if teaching Farsi to native speakers of English I would write Farsi ر as /r/, while training the learners to hear and make the difference between it and their English sound.
>
> By the way, /r/ is not always an approximant in English. In the clusters /**tr**/ and /**dr**/ (as in *train* and *drain*) it is fricative and thus different from the /r/ in *rain*.

As often happens, the student who had asked this question did not acknowledge or react to my careful answer, on composing which I had spent well over an hour.

Some issues never go away. Another worried correspondent asked:

> Is there a recent change in the depiction of English r sound from **r** to **ɹ**? If I understand it, now the regular English character **r** (the lowercase of the eighteenth letter of the Latin alphabet) is used for depiction of the Spanish **r** sound (a trill), and the upside down **ɹ** is assigned to represent the English r sound.
>
> In case I failed to express myself here is what I mean: For the word *solarium* IPA pronunciation was **səˈlɛərɪəm**, now should we write it as **səˈlɛəɹɪəm**?
>
> If my assumption is correct does your book's latest edition reflect that change?

No need to panic. It's a false alarm.

Needless to say, there has been no such change in the IPA, recent or otherwise. I have not changed the transcription of this consonant in LPD, nor do I plan to. The writer's assumption is not correct. Oh, and by the way, *solarium* is not transcribed as **səˈlɛərɪəm** in any edition of LPD. (For BrE I write **səˈlɛərɪəm**. In other books you may also find **səˈlɛːrɪəm**. All represent the same pronunciation.)

I haven't bothered to track down exactly when the symbols **r** and **ɹ** received their current IPA definitions, but it was certainly more than a century ago.

IPA symbols have always had to be interpreted in accordance with conventions implicitly or explicitly defined by the transcriber who uses the symbols. In the words of the *IPA Handbook* (Cambridge University Press 1999, p. 29),

> Any transcription is connected to a speech event by a set of conventions. In the case of an impressionistic ('general phonetic') transcription, the conventions are precisely those lying behind the IPA Chart, indicating for instance that the phonetic value of [ʔ͡k] is a simultaneous velar and glottal closure. In the case of a phonemic transcription, the conventions also include the 'phonological rules' of the particular language which determine the realization of its phonemes, such as the fact that for some varieties of English the lateral phoneme /l/ is realized with an accompanying secondary articulation ([ɫ]) when not followed directly by a vowel or /j/ in the same

word. Likewise, the realizational information which is not explicit in a particular allophonic transcription is, in principle, provided by conventions.

It is convenient (= practical and sensible) for us to use the same phonemic symbol **t** for the unaspirated dental plosive of French, the aspirated dental plosive of Swedish, the unaspirated alveolar plosive of Czech, and the aspirated alveolar plosive of English.

In general, phonemic symbols should be as simple as possible. That means letters of the ordinary lower-case Roman alphabet in preference to special letters such as ɛ ɹ ɫ, and the avoidance of diacritics as far as possible. For detailed discussion of the issues involved, see, for example, Appendix A (Types of Phonetic Transcription) of Daniel Jones's classic *An Outline of English Phonetics*, or Part I (Introduction) of David Abercrombie's *English Phonetic Texts* (London: Faber and Faber, 1964), or of course the *IPA Handbook* or its predecessor, the 1949 *Principles of the IPA* booklet.

So the English consonant at the beginning of *red* can be written phonemically as **r** or allophonically, impressionistically, or general-phonetically as ɹ. Both ways of writing it are 'IPA'; both are equally 'scientific'; both convey the same information.

The problem is how to convey this point clearly to non-specialists such as my correspondent.

I checked the transcribed texts of the 1902 *Maître Phonétique*. The symbol **r** is used there for all the various r-sounds of both English and French, even though at that date the notion of 'phoneme' in the modern sense had not yet been developed.

Yet another correspondent then commented:

> I think the problem is that most people don't know that dictionaries use phonemic transcriptions (and they don't even know what a phoneme is), and the symbols used do not represent actual speech sounds. If they look up what sound **r** stands for in the IPA chart, they'll find it's a trill. No wonder they're confused. On the other hand, decades ago it was more difficult to use such special symbols in typing, but today it no longer is an issue. It may be time for dictionary makers to reconsider using phonemic symbols that resemble actual speech sounds more accurately to avoid misleading less trained readers.

But what are 'phonemic symbols that resemble actual speech sounds'? I know what you mean, despite being obliged to remind you that written symbols are (visible but inaudible) marks on paper or on a screen, while actual speech sounds are (invisible, but audible) vibrations in the air.

What might this suggestion imply? Admittedly, we could write ɹ passim for **r**. But what other symbol(s) might replace **t**? Or **l**? Or **h**? Or any other consonants of English?

We could also change some of the vowel symbols, as various authors suggest from time to time. But I can't see that any such change would genuinely 'avoid misleading less trained readers'.

To interpret symbols in a dictionary or textbook for language learners, consult the book's list of symbols and keywords for the language in question, not the IPA Chart.

> Writing **ɹɛd** instead of **red** may be less convenient for the author, but more informative and less misleading for the reader, and I think a dictionary should aim to be as informative as possible without being too informative. You know, the golden mean.

It's not a question of the author's convenience. I reiterate: the information conveyed by **ɹɛd** is exactly the same, no more and no less, as that conveyed by **red**. Any transcription is connected to a speech event by a set of conventions. It is true that phonemic transcription is a kind of respelling: we could also write, for example, **rĕd** or use the kind of non-IPA phonemic transcription to be found in American dictionaries. We can represent the pronunciation of *face* as **fes** or **feɪs** or **fejs** or **feys** or **fayss** or **fās**. Any set of symbols conveys the information if we follow the set of conventions, stated or unstated, that applies to it.

For the bulk of the EFL market (the principal market that publishers of pronunciation textbooks and dictionaries target), **red** and **feɪs** seem to be preferred.

> '... more informative and less misleading ...'

For a tiny minority of readers, maybe. But EFL students, the majority of the market, would certainly reject **ɹɛd**, and so on as not worth the trouble. And the majority of EFL teachers would follow suit. Using such special symbols would make the textbooks and dictionaries less easy to consult for those who have not made a special study of phonetics.

12.5 Ram's Horn and Gamma

I have often had to remind people not to confuse the phonetic symbols ɤ and ɣ.

The first, ɤ, is the symbol for a back close-mid unrounded vowel, cardinal 15. This is the vowel heard in Mandarin Chinese 刻 *kè* **kɤ** 'carve'.

The second, ɣ, is the symbol for a voiced velar fricative. This, or the corresponding approximant, is the consonant heard in the middle of Spanish *fuego* ˈ**fweɣo** 'fire', Greek εγώ e'ɣo 'I', etc.

Confusion of these two symbols was something I repeatedly had to correct in authors' manuscripts when I was the editor of the *Journal of the International Phonetic Association*. Since other copy editors may not have been so symbol-obsessed as me, the confusion is found uncorrected in quite a few printed books, including some from publishers who really ought to know better.

At its 1989 Kiel Convention the IPA discussed this issue. At the time the vowel symbol was usually printed with straight sides (although on the line, x-height), making it very similar to the consonant symbol (which descended through the line).

12.6 Constraints on Diacritics

A graphic designer wrote to me enquiring about phonetic letters and diacritics. What constraints are there on the combination of particular base characters with particular diacritics?

Is there anything wrong with the combination θ̥? or with ʋ̥ or ʔ̥?

In my view, for a phonetician's use of the International Phonetic Alphabet to symbolize actual sounds, the only constraints on combinations of diacritics and base characters are logical ones. (People using the symbols for typographical decoration can do whatever they like, of course.)

For example, the 'voiceless' diacritic U+0325 COMBINING RING BELOW can logically only be applied to a base character that stands for a voiced sound, e.g. **m, b, ɓ, u**, but not **t, θ, ç, Θ**. So **m̥** and **b̥**, for example, are fine, but **t̥** is not. There is a variant, U+030A COMBINING RING ABOVE, used if the base character has a descender, e.g. **ŋ̊, ɟ̊, g̊**.

Similarly, the dental diacritic U+032A COMBINING BRIDGE BELOW would usually only be applied to a base character standing for an alveolar sound, e.g. **t, n, s**. However if someone wanted to use it with, say, **b** to show a labiodental stop **b̪**, that would also be acceptable. But combined with, say, **k** it would presumably be meaningless.

There is no formal constraint against having multiple diacritics on the same base character.

The aspiration diacritic, ʰ, is most commonly deployed after symbols for voiceless plosives. The *IPA Handbook* also shows it with **d**, although the article about Hindi in the body of the book instead uses ɦ for the voiced aspirated series, thus **bɦ dɦ dʒɦ ɖɦ gɦ**. Korean has two kinds of alveolar fricative, one of them often transcribed **sʰ**, and I suppose in principle any affricate or fricative can be aspirated. Can approximants? Can vowels? You could call the preaspiration of Icelandic, Scottish Gaelic, etc aspiration of the preceding vowel, and certainly transcriptions of the type **kʰaʰt** are in use for such cases.

'Breathy voiced' and 'creaky voiced' can only combine with symbols for voiced sounds, which means that **t̤**, for example, is presumably a logical contradiction. Nasals can't be nasalized. And so on.

Are 'advanced' and 'retracted' only for vowels? No, because they are sometimes used to show dental as against alveolar consonants, or prevelar as against velar. What about 'centralized'? Vowels only, I think. Is 'syllabic' only for consonants? Normally yes, and then only for nasals and liquids (as with **n̩** and **l̩** in English and German, and **r̩** in Czech and Serbian). Some students imagine that the English word *looked* should be transcribed **lʊkd̩** (with 'syllabic d'), but they are confusing phonetics with morphology. Syllabic plosives are generally speaking a no-no (see Section 2.2), though we may have to make exceptions for Berber and one or two other special cases. Syllabic fricatives do exist, but are rare.

What about combining the syllabicity mark with a vowel symbol? Normally we don't do that, because vowels are inherently syllabic, so it would be tautologous. But Abercrombie, in his *English Phonetic Texts* (1964), used a transcription for English in which the syllabicity mark sometimes appeared under schwa to show that it was not part of a diphthong, thus **kənˈtɪnjwə̩s** (aka **kənˈtɪnjuəs**).

My colleague John Maidment comments:

> More years ago than I care to remember, I and some others in an idle moment tried to pile as many diacritics on a single symbol as we could. We started with ð, added a lowering diacritic to turn it into a voiced dental approximant, added a nasalisation tilde and a wiggle through the middle to velarize it, then a labialization diacritic, a breathy voice diacritic and a length mark. I am sure we had more than those six, but I can't figure it out now. It is quite possible to produce the sound, but I take no responsibility for physical injury or mental anguish if anyone wants to try.

12.7 Ban Legacy Fonts!

Do you remember the bad old days before Unicode? The time when there was no standardized way of encoding phonetic symbols? When word processing was single-byte and fonts were 8-bit, so that any given font was limited to under two hundred characters? When the various phonetic fonts available all used different encodings, so that where one person had input ɥ another might see ɦ or ʰ or something else entirely arbitrary? When if you transferred a document to a different computer you would as likely as not get garbage for your phonetic symbols? When your PowerPoint presentation using the computer supplied by local organizers would probably fail to display your phonetic symbols properly?

Thank goodness those days are past. Nowadays we all use Unicode, the internationally-agreed-upon industry-wide font-encoding standard for all alphabets and scripts, covering all the languages of the world as well as all the phonetic (and other) symbols we might need. A single font can now contain thousands, indeed tens of thousands, of different characters. So we no longer have to keep switching fonts merely in order to include phonetic symbols. In preparing the manuscript of this book I was confident that when I input a particular phonetic symbol you would see that same phonetic symbol in the printed book, no matter which typographic font the designer might choose. (Even in web documents, the worst failure you are likely to come across nowadays is an unusual symbol being presented as a blank square or something similar – you won't see the wrong phonetic symbol or some ludicrous webding, as used to happen.)

But people haven't all caught up.

In the mid-1990s I created the IPA-SAM computer fonts. Building on SIL software, they were 8-bit fonts that enjoyed some considerable popularity because the encoding and therefore the keyboarding fitted in nicely with the way phoneticians actually use phonetic symbols. Nevertheless, once Unicode became available it rendered these and other specialist 8-bit fonts obsolete. Now that Unicode phonetic fonts are widely available and most word processing software is Unicode-compatible, I have been actively discouraging people from using these and other non-Unicode, 8-bit fonts. Most of the 'core' fonts supplied with new computers these days include all the IPA symbols (though some fonts do a better job than others in their typographical design).

So everyone should now use Unicode rather than the old 'legacy' fonts. Conference organizers, journal editors, and publishers should require their use, no ifs and buts.

The 'manuscripts' of this book and of its predecessor *Sounds Interesting* started life as MS Word files in Unicode. As you can see, the typesetting and printing of the phonetic symbols proved seamless and unexceptional.

The only problems that can occasionally remain concern the rendering of certain letters with diacritics, if the combination required is not available as a single precomposed Unicode character, as for example the ash symbol æ with a tilde, thus æ̃, represented in Unicode by two successive characters, U+00E6 and U+0303. But such cases are pretty rare.

Phonetic-symbol anoraks/nerds/geeks can have hours of fun browsing the Unicode Standard, the repository of all the characters that can be displayed on a modern computer screen. You'll find it online at www.unicode.org.

Every few years a new version of the Standard is published. Unlike previous versions, versions 6 and 7 were not published as printed books, but are available only online.

To give a flavour of recent changes, what was new in version 6.0? In brief: 2,088 new characters, including (I quote):

- over 1,000 additional symbols – chief among them the additional emoji symbols, which are especially important for mobile phones
- the new official Indian currency symbol: the Indian Rupee Sign
- 222 additional CJK Unified Ideographs in common use in China, Taiwan, and Japan
- 603 additional characters for African language support, including extensions to the Tifinagh, Ethiopic, and Bamum scripts
- three additional scripts: Mandaic, Batak, and Brahmi

There are also extensive technical changes to do with character properties and format specifications.

118   12 TRANSCRIPTION

Two new Cyrillic characters cater for Azerbaijani. Two new Arabic characters and ten new Devanagari characters cater for Kashmiri. Thirty-two new Ethiopic characters cater for Gamo-Gofa-Dawro, Basketo, and Gumuz. Complete new blocks of letters cater for Mandaic, for Batak, and for Brāhmī.

Is there anything of particular interest to phoneticians and IPA users?

How about a symbol for a voiceless retroflex lateral fricative? A sort of combination of ɭ and ɬ? It's not (yet) an official IPA symbol, but it's a logical combination of two. Its Unicode number is, U+A78E. (Unicode numbers are given in hexadecimal and prefixed with the identifier U+.) You can see it on-line by looking up the code charts at www.unicode.org.

Phonetic symbol

| A78E | ɬ̢ | LATIN SMALL LETTER L WITH RETROFLEX HOOK AND BELT
• voiceless lateral retroflex fricative
• used to transcribe Toda |

If you've always wanted a COMBINING DOUBLE INVERTED BREVE BELOW, it's now available (U+1DFC). But unless you're a Uralic Phonetic Alphabet aficionado, you'll have managed without. Do you have a use for subscript ₕ ₖ ₗ ₘ ₙ ₚ ₛ ₜ? I doubt it. Even if you do, you'd probably simply subscript the ordinary small letters, as I have just done. In Unicode 6.0 they're ready-made at U+2095 to U+209 C.

Students of the minority languages of China may welcome three new Bopomofo characters to cater for Hmu and Ge. (Bopomofo is a phonetic notation system based on Chinese characters.)

It's one thing to have a symbol recognized in Unicode and assigned a U+ number. It's something else for the new symbol to become included in an available font. We'll just have to wait and see if and when these new characters make an appearance in documents on our display screens and elsewhere.

Version 7 adds fourteen new diacritics especially for German dialectology, including parentheses to enclose diacritics above or below a letter. It also contains two additional diacritics for ExtIPA, one for 'faucalized' and one for 'open-rounded'. Not to mention the 160-odd characters of the as yet undeciphered Minoan Linear A script.

12.8   What [a] Means

A correspondent was under the impression that

> the symbol **a** in IPA is reserved for a phoneme which occurs rarely in European languages (if it occurs at all), whereas the common continental *a* has got to be transcribed **ä**.

I say no it isn't, and no it doesn't.

The vowel **a** occurs extremely commonly in European languages (and of course in non-European languages). The Northern English TRAP vowel, too, is very satisfactorily represented by the symbol **a**, with no diacritics. The contrary claims reveal a basic misunderstanding of how phonetic symbols are used when we represent the phonemes of a language or language variety. Let's see why.

The symbol **a** is one of the set of symbols representing the 'Cardinal Vowels' **i e ɛ a ɑ ɔ o u** defined by Daniel Jones.

No language is actually spoken with cardinal vowels: they are idealized reference points not defined by what happens in any particular language. (They are, however, suspiciously similar to a subset of the vowels of standard French as spoken in Jones's day – though the quality of French ɔ, at least, was and is considerably different from that of cardinal ɔ. In passing we may note that the articulatory-auditory theory behind Jones's cardinal vowel scheme is no longer accepted.)

Rather, these symbols are used for vowels in the general area concerned. Like all IPA symbols, they allow some considerable leeway. A typical French **e** is not identical with a typical Italian **e** or a typical German **e**, although all share a general similarity and all can be characterized as unrounded, front, and close-mid ('half-close'). Compare colour terms, where we happily refer to shades of crimson, scarlet, vermilion, and so on all as 'red'. We are dealing not with discrete entities but with points in a multidimensional continuum.

In those languages it so happens that the close-mid **e** is distinct from an open-mid ('half-open') ɛ. (This claim is subject to qualification: for many French speakers the choice of one or the other can be more or less predicted from the phonetic environment, although others distinguish e.g. *les* **le** from *lait* **lɛ**; not all Italians make the distinction between *venti* 'twenty' with **e** and *venti* 'winds' with ɛ; in German the vowel quality distinction is accompanied, in stressed syllables at least, by a length distinction.)

There are many other languages in which there is only one unrounded mid front vowel: they include Greek, Spanish, Serbian, and Japanese. Qualititatively this may lie anywhere between cardinal **e** and cardinal ɛ. In each case the appropriate symbol, though, is **e**. In the words of the 1949 IPA *Principles* booklet (§20),

> When a vowel is situated in an area designated by a non-roman letter, it is recommended that the nearest appropriate roman letter be substituted for it in ordinary broad transcriptions if that letter is not needed for any other purpose. For instance, if a language contains an ɛ but no **e**, it is recommended that the letter **e** be used to represent it. This is the case, for instance, in Japanese.

Similarly, the symbol **a**, which as a cardinal vowel symbol denotes an unrounded front open (low) vowel, is also appropriate to denote an unrounded open vowel of any degree of advancement (anywhere from fully 'front' to fully 'back') if that is the only open vowel in the language. This is the case in Spanish, Italian, Greek, Serbian, German, and Polish, to mention only a handful of

European languages. It is also the case in thousands of other languages around the world.

In RP I say **ðə kæt sæt ɒn ðə mæt**. If I switch into northern (I was bidialectal as a child), I say **ðə kat sat ɒnt mat**. That's how I would transcribe it. I'll leave someone else to measure the formant values of my northern **a** to determine just how central it might be.

A few years ago the Council of the IPA, rightly in my view, rejected a proposal to recognize an additional vowel symbol, small-cap ᴀ, to represent a quality between cardinals **a** and **ɑ**.

This question of whether the son-of-RP ('General British') vowel of TRAP is best transcribed **æ** or **a** is a separate issue.

12.9 Old Nonsense

In the early sixties I was a postgraduate student at UCL doing a master's in phonetics and linguistics.

I have been digging around in one of my old notebooks dating from those days. One of the things I found was a collection of nonsense words used for ear training in general phonetics. I received this kind of training from J.D. O'Connor, Marguerite Chapallaz, Hélène Coustenoble, and A.C. Gimson.

Here are fifteen of O'Connor's nonsense words. He would have dictated them for us students to write down phonetically. I assume that the page of my notes from which I reproduce them was a fair copy rather than my own attempts at recognition.

1. k'oβɓaŋ͡jyʔ
2. ɽɛyxəːmʔmʒ
3. ɕæ̪t̪əʟɑɣajl
4. ǵ͡ʗɔhtɥɵʂcɑʕ
5. ijœʔʂpl̩'uːʄ
6. ʔɤːm̥ʙɢɵːẓdʐ
7. ts'ʁ̥qəldjəux
8. tn̪æɹhuɾœʂ
9. gɥɒχɡ͡ʝaç
10. ɬɯɣəc'ɑqœʉ
11. ɳʀɛʔʂoːʄʁʔ
12. ṣʋɛɪzẽɓɔht̪'
13. gjɑːgŋɒʟæɯ
14. pmɯhʉːnɖnsᶠ
15. ɴʒit̪oœdʐ̪

In the first word, you will see that four different airstream mechanisms are involved. As well as the default pulmonic egressive, they are glottalic egressive for the ejective **k'**, glottalic ingressive for the implosive **ɓ**, and velaric ingressive combined with pulmonic egressive for the nasalized dental click ŋ͡ʇ (which nowadays we write ŋ|).

Among other points of interest are

- further pre-1989 click symbols, retroflex ʗ (now !) and lateral ʖ (now ǁ).
- in 5, an ejective cluster, with a bilabial plosive and an alveolar lateral combined in a single 'ejection': I don't know of any language that has this kind of combination.
- in 7, the symbol **ɐ** with a 'more open' diacritic, to represent a fully open vowel halfway between cardinal 4 **a** and cardinal 5 **ɑ** (this diacritic has now been superseded by the 'down tack', thus **ɐ̞**). Compare this with the 'advanced' **ɑ** in line 3, which shows that we were operating in terms of five degrees of backness among open vowels: cardinal 4, retracted 4, this central one, advanced 5, cardinal 5.
- in 8, the symbol ɹ with a subscript dot (= closer), standing for the fricative rather than the default approximant (or 'frictionless continuant', as we used to call it in those days). The post-1989 equivalent of this diacritic is the 'up tack', thus ɹ̝.
- in 10, a velarized voiceless alveolar lateral fricative. I have not been able to reproduce the symbol very clearly here: it is meant to be a 'belted l' with a superimposed tilde. Nowadays we would write it ɬˠ.
- in 14 the symbol **s**ᶠ stood for a labiodentalized **s**. ExtIPA (see the *IPA Handbook*) now writes this as **s**ᶹ.

How many phoneticians in today's universities are lucky enough to receive this kind of meticulous ear training? Speech and language therapy and speech pathology curricula are too full of other things. Some linguistics students? And who else? Perhaps it's nowadays more or less confined to trainee missionaries and Bible translators taught by Pike's successors at SIL.

PART III
Applying Phonetics

13 Classification

13.1 Fricative or Approximant?

A correspondent mentioned that she had come across a textbook in which English **h** was described as a voiceless glottal approximant. Given that in LPD I classify it as a voiceless glottal fricative, she wondered which is right, approximant or fricative.

I am not alone in classifying **h** as a fricative. That is how it is categorized on the IPA Chart; that is how Cruttenden, Roach, Collins, Ashby and Maidment, and other respected writers on English phonetics categorize it.

It is clear, however, that **h** is different from the other English voiceless fricatives **f, θ, s, ʃ**, in that it does not involve a constriction within the mouth cavity. Conventionally we classify it as a glottal fricative; but the constriction giving rise to the turbulence that we hear as friction may be not so much located at the glottis itself as distributed throughout the whole of the upper vocal tract. That is why Ladefoged and Maddison in *The Sounds of the World's Languages* (Blackwell 1996), at the beginning of their chapter on fricatives, comment:

> Forms of **h, ɦ** in which a turbulent airstream is produced at the glottis are also sometimes classed as fricatives [...], but it is more appropriate to consider them in the chapter on vowels.

At the end of the vowels chapter they mention the possible description of **h** as the voiceless counterpart of the vowel that follows.

> In such cases it is more appropriate to regard **h** and **ɦ** as segments that have only a laryngeal specification, and are unmarked for all other features.

But in some languages, including Hebrew and Arabic, a glottal constriction is observable during the production of these sounds.

One problem with classifying **h** as an approximant is that voiceless approximants are by definition inaudible. (At least if approximants are defined as having no audible friction, i.e. no turbulent airflow and thus no audible aperiodic noise. Approximants used to be known as 'frictionless continuants'.) If there's no friction and no voicing, there's nothing to hear. Anything you can hear during a voiceless **h** must be some sort of weak friction, resulting from some sort of weak turbulence, which must mean that **h** is some sort of weak fricative – but still a fricative.

Not only phonetics is relevant here, but also phonology. The English **h** phoneme does not behave like a vowel. We say *a house*, not **an house*. We say ðə *house*, not ði *house*. You get a linking r in *you're out*, but not in *your house* – except among non-standard speakers who drop h.

The tradition in generative phonology is to class **h** as a 'glide', along with **j** and **w**. That's fine phonologically, but not very helpful phonetically. Its traditional name in English is 'the aspirate', which similarly avoids the question of possible friction.

For practical teaching, it's convenient to call **h** a fricative. But you do have to emphasize that there is no friction at the uvular or velar place (of the sort you get in χ and x). Many EFL learners can be helped by thinking of **h** as just a voiceless onset to the following vowel.

Advanced students can be asked to write an essay on the problem of defining the terms fricative and approximant.

13.2 VOT Is That?

A correspondent asked about VOT (voice onset time), wanting in particular to know how English and Spanish differ in this respect. He added,

> While smoking a cigarette, I think I found a difference when pronouncing some words. I mean, the smoke came out from my mouth differently, I think.

As a non-smoker, I cannot comment on this last remark.

The **p** in English *pair* is 'aspirated', i.e. has a long VOT. That means there is a substantial delay after the lips separate (= the primary closure is released) before the vocal folds kick in with voicing. During this time, air from the lungs escapes unobstructed through the oral cavity, sounding 'like a little **h**'. More narrowly, we could transcribe it [pʰeə].

The Spanish **p** in *perro*, on the other hand, is 'unaspirated', i.e. zero VOT (or a very short VOT). That is, there is very little or no delay between the labial release and the onset of voicing, so no 'little **h**'. More narrowly, we can transcribe it [p̄erro].

Differently from *pair*, the **p** in English *spare* is unaspirated. The effect of the preceding **s** is to suppress aspiration of the plosive. We say [sp̄eə].

In words like *pray, play, twin, cure* the aspiration is manifested in the voicelessness of the liquid or semivowel, thus [pr̥eɪ, pl̥eɪ, tw̥ɪn, kj̊ʊə]; but in *spray, splay, obscure* in principle this does not apply (because the **s** inhibits aspiration): [spreɪ, spleɪ, əbˈskjʊə].

Aspiration affects all three English voiceless plosives, **p, t,** and **k**.

Spanish **b, d,** and **g** are voiced throughout. English **b, d,** and **g** are only partially voiced, unless surrounded by voiced sounds.

So far, this is the information given in all textbooks of phonetics. You will find schematic VOT diagrams in Cruttenden, *Gimson's Pronunciation of English*

(8th ed., Hodder 2014, p. 165) and elsewhere. If you want measurements of VOT in milliseconds, consult a textbook or measure a waveform. The usual value given for English VOT in words like *pair* is of the order of 40–75 ms.

But there's more that can be said. So far we have considered only initial consonants and initial consonant clusters: more precisely, plosives located at the beginning of a stressed syllable. That means the English aspiration of **p** in words such as *page, pick, appear, spin, price, pure, display*, of **t** in words such as *time, top, attack, stand, tree*, and of **k** in words such as *coffee, key, account, scanner, cross, clean, accuse*.

But what about **p t k** in other positions? In those positions that I (but not everyone) would consider syllable-final?

It is unfortunately the case that English aspiration is not a matter of all or nothing. In some positions voiceless plosives may have a certain amount of aspiration, but not enough to call them fully aspirated. The VOT in such cases is intermediate between that of 'aspirated' voiceless plosives and that of 'unaspirated' ones.

As I put it in LPD,

> English [p t k] are **aspirated**:
> - when they occur at the beginning of a syllable in which the vowel is strong.
>
> They are **unaspirated**:
> - when preceded by s at the beginning of a syllable
> - when followed by any FRICATIVE, as in lapse læps, depth depθ
> - if immediately followed by another plosive as with the k in doctor ˈdɒktə ‖ ˈdɑːktᵊr. The release stage of the first plosive is then usually inaudible ('masked').
>
> Otherwise, they are unaspirated or just **slightly aspirated**. For example, ripe raɪp, shut ʃʌt, lake leɪk; happy ˈhæpi, writer ˈraɪtə (BrE), lucky ˈlʌki; wasp wɒsp ‖ wɑːsp, resting ˈrestɪŋ, Oscar ˈɒskə ‖ ˈɑːskᵊr, lifted ˈlɪftɪd, today təˈdeɪ.

Peter Roach suggests the useful word *potato* pəˈteɪtəʊ (BrE). The initial **p** is unaspirated (because a weak vowel follows). The first **t** is aspirated (at the beginning of a stressed syllable). The second one is weakly aspirated (at the end of a syllable, I would say; or you could alternatively say because followed by an unstressed vowel).

Spanish **p t k** are always unaspirated. They have zero VOT.

Another phonological feature sometimes claimed to be involved is [spread glottis]. Aspirated stops and voiceless sonorants are then said to share a common feature of aspiration (or [spread glottis]). This helps account for the fact that in some languages unaspirated and aspirated voiceless plosives contrast in word-final position (see the waveforms for Armenian final [k] and [kʰ] in Ladefoged and Maddieson's *The Sounds of the World's Languages*). It's no use talking about

VOT there: in sentence-final position both possibilities have trivially infinite VOT (there's no VOT because there's no voice onset).

13.3 Labiodentals

As we grow older, our teeth and gums deteriorate, and so does our fine motor control. When I was young I used to be able to make labiodental plosives, **p̪ b̪** – but I can't now. I can no longer get a hermetic seal between my lower lip and upper teeth: there's always some escape of air through the gaps between my teeth. (Some people have gaps between the teeth even when young.)

This is no doubt one of the reasons that no language has distinctive labiodental stops.

It means that when I try to make the labiodental nasal **ɱ**, the usual allophone of **n** before **f** or **v**, as in *information* or *emphasis*, I end up with some sort of **ṽ**. Inevitably some air escapes through the mouth.

What this is leading up to is that I used to think that I would normally pronounce *seventy* as ˈ**seɱn̪ti** (with the alveolar nasal somewhat dubious). I am sure plenty of other people still do. But what I now say is ˈ**seṽnti**. And that must have been an intermediate stage in my previous nasal-assimilated pronunciation.

Underlyingly it's still ˈ**sevənti**, and always has been. And I can still manage the option of realizing it as ˈ**sebm̪ti**.

Since my stroke I also find I can no longer make a bilabial trill **ʙ**. Fortunately, since I am no longer teaching, I don't need to, either.

13.4 Unreleased

A correspondent asked about the meaning of the term 'unreleased' when applied to a plosive.

For a plosive to have literally no release at all, the speaker would have to stop breathing, or at least discontinue the airstream mechanism underlying the production of the plosive.

In the middle (compression) stage of a plosive, air pressure builds up in the cavity behind the primary articulators. Something has to undo that pressure build-up: if not the release of the primary articulators, then either some other release (notably nasal, by lowering the soft palate) or a zeroing of the pressure (if the intercostal muscles and diaphragm creating the egressive airstream stop compressing the lungs).

That is why the diacritic in [t̚] is defined on the IPA chart not as 'unreleased' but as 'no audible release'. An unreleased stop or unreleased plosive is a plosive consonant without an audible release burst.

Unfortunately, the Unicode Standard glosses this diacritic as 'IPA: unreleased stop'. And it is true that English **k** in *actor* is sometimes termed 'unreleased', as are final stops in some languages. I think this terminology is inappropriate.

Why would a plosive have a release that was not audible? Usually because a new primary place of articulation takes over the task of retaining the compressed air: most typically the glottal place. When we say a word such as *out* aʊt at the end of an utterance we often bring in a glottal closure to reinforce the alveolar closure for the final consonant. When the tongue tip then ultimately separates from the alveolar ridge there is no audible 'burst' (noise of release), because the air pressure is held behind the glottal closure. Then later we either produce a glottal release or, more usually, just stop pushing with the lungs. The result can correctly be transcribed t̚. (It is also possible, of course, to release the **t** normally, or to entirely replace it by a glottal articulation, ʔ.)

In phrases such as *stop me* and *at noon* it is possible to use nasal release, i.e. to release the **p** or **t** by lowering the soft palate. In that case there will be an audible release as we move from **p** to **m** or from **t** to **n** without moving the lips or the tongue tip respectively. Daniel Jones called this 'nasal plosion', and judging by his description it appears to have been the norm in the RP of a hundred years ago. The IPA symbol is **pⁿ, tⁿ**.

Nowadays nasal release in this phonetic environment would tend to sound a bit prissy or over-careful: in Britain we mostly either just use a glottal stop, **stɒʔmi, əʔnuːn**, or else we render the nasal release inaudible by covering ('masking') it with a glottal closure.

What do I mean by this 'masking'? It can be notated **stɒpʔmi, ətʔnuːn**, or if you prefer **stɒp̚ mi, ət̚ nuːn**. Instructions for making **pʔm** (which could also be written **p̚ m**) would be:

1. As you finish making the vowel, switch off voicing and bring the lips firmly together, thereby cutting off the air escape and thus creating the first stage of the plosive (the 'approach'). The air builds up in the pharynx and mouth behind the lips.
2. While the lips remain together, close the glottis. This cuts off the air pressure from the lungs, isolating the supraglottal cavities so that there is no longer much pressure differential between the oropharynx plus mouth on the one hand and the nasopharynx and outside air on the other. Air pressure remains in the subglottal tract. This is the middle stage of the plosive (the 'hold' or compression stage).
3. Lower the soft palate. We don't hear any nasal release because there is no great pressure differential involved. The oropharynx and the nasopharynx now communicate.
4. Release the glottal closure. This is the third stage of the plosive, the 'release' – but it is inaudible as such. The lips are still together. As the vocal folds (= glottis) cease to be firmly closed they start to vibrate, giving voicing. Air escapes through the nose. We have **m**.

You could abbreviate all this description by just referring to it as 'p with no audible release'.

A further possibility that might be called 'no audible release' is the kind of thing we get in *grab bag, bad dog, big girl*, where articulatorily there is just a single plosive with a long hold: narrowly [**græb:æg, bæd:ɒg, bɪg:ɜ:l**]. Phonologically, of course, there are two plosives involved each time, /**bb, dd, gg**/. The /**d**/ at the end of *bad* is literally unreleased, just as the initial /**d**/ in *dog* is 'unapproached'. There is just one plosive approach, as **æ** ends, and one plosive release, as **ɒ** begins. The extra duration of the hold phase, as the primary articulators remain in position and air builds up, signals to us that this counts as two successive consonants, not one.

A student asked me:

> Do you think an unreleased stop can sometimes appear in intervocalic contexts? E.g. in phrases like: *that itchy goose, that area was, she measured out a lot.*

Clearly, **t** in these phrases can sometimes be pronounced as a glottal stop **ʔ**. But it can also be pronounced in a way that involves an alveolar articulation with complete closure, yet without the noise burst associated with alveolar release.

Physiologically, you can't have a fully 'unreleased' plosive between vowels. In any plosive there is a compression stage, during which the air stream gets compressed behind the closure. Either this compressed air is ultimately released (by the removal of the oral closure, or alternatively by the removal of the velic closure as the soft palate moves) – or the initiator of the airstream (the lungs, usually) ceases to provide the pressure.

In utterance-final position you might have a truly unreleased plosive, with the lungs ceasing to maintain the air pressure. But not in mid utterance.

If it sounds like an unreleased plosive, perhaps it is really an oral plosive with a supervening glottal closure. After the oral closure is complete, the glottis closes, thereby holding the air pressure from the lungs. When the oral closure is released, the closure is inaudible because there is no air pressure behind it.

So I would call it 'no audible release', not absence of release. That's what we mean by the term 'unreleased'.

13.5 Implosives and Ejectives

In modern phonetic terminology, an 'implosive' is a sound made with a glottalic ingressive airstream mechanism. That is, the airstream is initiated by sharply lowering the glottis, thereby creating negative pressure in the supraglottal cavity.

Along with ejectives (glottalic egressive airstream) and clicks (velaric ingressive airstream), implosives are a sound-type taught to all serious students of phonetics. At UCL I used regularly to train budding phoneticians not only to recognize implosives, ejectives and clicks, but also to produce them to order.

13.5 Implosives and Ejectives

Most of the implosives found in the world's languages are voiced. That means that the rarefaction in the pharynx and mouth (the glottalic ingressive mechanism) is combined with a simultaneous vibration of the vocal folds dependent on a pulmonic egressive airstream. So you could say that they have a mixed glottalic ingressive and pulmonic egressive airstream mechanism.

Interestingly, in my experience learners generally find this combined airstream easier to produce than the purely glottalic one that is needed for voiceless implosives.

The IPA chart lists five symbols for implosives, all voiced: ɓ ɗ ʄ ɠ ʛ. It is also possible to make voiceless implosives, produced purely with the ingressive glottalic airstream mechanism.

But does what we teach in the classroom agree with what we find in real languages?

Examples of implosives from relatively familiar languages are the ɓ ʄ of Zulu and the ɓ ɗ ʄ ɠ of Sindhi (the second of these is retroflex). According to Ladefoged and Maddieson (*The Sounds of the World's Languages*, Blackwell 1996), the Igbo labialvelar spelt *gb*, often considered a voiced pulmonic plosive with double (labial-velar) articulation, i.e. simultaneous **b** and **g**, is more accurately described as a voiceless bilabial implosive, ɓ̥.

On the web you can find various sound clips of people speaking or singing in Zulu or Xhosa, languages in which implosives, ejectives, and clicks are all to be found. Here you can confirm that the implosives are only very mildly implosive and the main auditory difference between them and the plain voiced plosives is that plain [b] and [g] are depressors (see Section 13.15), while weak-implosive [ɓ] and [ɠ] are not. (In singing, though, such tonal subtleties are naturally lost.)

Take the Zulu song *Thula sizwe*, which you can find on YouTube (www.youtube.com/watch?v=LSBvvlg-cVM). Listen to the third word in the song, *ungabokhala* uŋgaɓɔˈkʰala. The *b* in this word is pronounced as a bilabial implosive ɓ. Notice, though, that its 'implosiveness' is much weaker than in the exaggerated versions we tend to get in phonetic demonstrations of airstream mechanisms. Mea culpa, perhaps. We see the same thing in the last word, *uzokunqobela* uzɔʄuˈŋ!ɔɓɛla, with both velar ʄ and bilabial ɓ.

The implosives of Sindhi seem to be similarly weak.

I wonder if there are any languages with really strong, noisy implosives.

In the *World Atlas of Language Structures* data (wals.info), implosives are found in 75 of the 567 languages studied (= 13%), most of them in Africa or southeast Asia. (Ladefoged and Maddieson, however, say that implosives are found in 'about 10% of the world's languages'.) By far the commonest implosive is the voiced bilabial ɓ.

The OED reveals that as a phonetic term 'implosive' goes back at least as far as Sweet, who wrote in 1890 that:

Some sounds are produced without either out- or in-breathing, but solely with the air in the throat or mouth. The 'implosives' are formed in the former, the suction-stops or 'clicks' in the latter way.

There is one other usage of this term that you may occasionally come across in older works, in which an 'implosive' stop is an ordinary pulmonic stop with no audible release stage, or in which the release is not taken into account, as against an 'explosive' one which has no audible approach stage, or in which the approach stage is not taken into account. The OED has a quotation from Bazell in 1953:

> If all initial occlusives are explosive and all final occlusives are implosive, it is obvious that two distinct conventions (explosiveness of initials and implosiveness of finals) need not be postulated.

We can regard this meaning as obsolete.

We pair implosives with 'ejectives', sounds made with a glottalic egressive airstream mechanism. They have an airstream initiated by the raising of the closed glottis, which compresses the air in the supraglottal cavity. The OED's first citation for this term is Daniel Jones in 1932.

In IPA ejectives are written with an apostrophe diacritic, thus **p' t' k'**, etc. They are 'not at all unusual sounds, occurring in about 18 percent of the languages of the world' (Ladefoged & Maddieson). Although they are not contrastive in English or any other European language, many speakers in Britain use ejectives as optional phrase-final variants of **p t k**.

Apropos of implosives, one correspondent asked

> How does one pronounce a vowel that immediately follows an implosive? Is the airstream for the vowel also ingressive, or does it suddenly change direction to be egressive?

The answer is that in every case – as far as I know – the vowel following an implosive consonant has an unremarkable pulmonic egressive airstream. Note though, that this means that not only does the direction of airflow change, but so in principle does the identity of the initiating cavity. Since voiced implosives (the usual kind) actually involve a combination of airstreams, we can say that in the sequence **ɓa** there is a constant pulmonic egressive airstream, but that in the first segment it is accompanied by a glottalic ingressive component.

In a vowel-ejective-vowel sequence such as **ap'a** the air flow is egressive throughout, but the initiating cavity for the consonant is glottalic – and takes place during a glottal closure, **ʔ**, that interrupts the egressive pulmonic airstream used for the surrounding vowels.

Clicks have a velaric ingressive airstream, but this is always combined with a velar articulation that interrupts what is normally an egressive pulmonic airstream. So in **a|a** (= old **aʇa**) we have an ordinary pulmonic-air sequence **aka** with the velaric ingressive operation taking place entirely during the hold phase of the velar plosive.

Ejectives never cluster with implosives. The ingressive pulmonic airstream mechanism appears always to characterize entire utterances rather than individual segments. Reverse clicks are only paralinguistic: they certainly never cluster with ordinary clicks. So we can formulate the universal that we never get an abrupt reversal of the direction of airflow within the same initiating cavity as we pass from one segment to the next in speech.

One striking historical development is revealed in the regular correspondence between the pulmonic-airstream **z** of Zulu and the ejective (glottalic-airstream) **t'** of the closely related language (si)Swati. We see this in the name of the latter language, which is also known by its Zulu name of Swazi.

The Wikipedia page on Nguni languages gives these example sentences meaning 'I love your new sticks':

Zulu   Ngi-ya-zi-thanda izi-ntonga z-akho ezin-sha
Swati   Ngi-ya-ti-tsandza ti-ntfonga t-akho letin-sha

in which all four instances of Zulu *z* correspond to Swati *t* (= **t'**).

So how did this correspondence come about? What kind of consonant could historically have given rise on the one hand to a pulmonic-air voiced fricative and on the other hand to a glottalic-air voiceless plosive? (I can confirm from my own observation that this Swati consonant is indeed ejective.)

It may be relevant that Zulu **z** is a 'depressor' consonant, one of the set that cause the pitch of the following vowel to start lower than it would otherwise do (see Section 13.15). Like other depressors, it has breathy voice rather than modal voice. That perhaps provides a link to the change at the glottis, but the possible pathways of change still seem pretty obscure.

13.6 Guttural

In the boys' adventure stories I would read in my childhood, the baddies often spoke in 'guttural' tones. Not only German and Arabic, but also Welsh, Hebrew, and Dutch are still occasionally popularly referred to as 'guttural' languages.

A hundred and fifty years ago *guttural* was in use as a technical term in phonetics, as a descriptor for a place of articulation. In 1869 A.J. Ellis wrote, "The guttural nasal seems to have been the regular pronunciation of *ng* in English."

A helpful note in the OED tells us:

> By non-phoneticians any mode of pronunciation which is harsh or grating in effect is often supposed to be 'guttural'; with this notion the designation is popularly applied by English-speakers to the German *ch*, but not to *k* or *g*, though technically it belongs equally to them. As a technical term of phonetics, the word was first used to denote the Hebrew spirant consonants

ע ,ח ,ה ,א; it is now commonly applied (inaccurately, if its etymological sense be regarded) to the sounds formed by the back of the tongue and the palate, as /k/ /g/ /x/ /ɣ/ /ŋ/.

As a phonetic term 'guttural' has now been entirely supplanted by more precise terms: mainly 'velar', but also 'uvular', 'pharyngeal' and 'glottal', as appropriate. The non-technical use of 'guttural' has declined in parallel, and has not been replaced by 'velar' or any other phonetic term.

The OED's first citation for *velar* in the phonetic sense is dated 1876. Its definition for the noun sense of this word reads 'a velar guttural'.

13.7 Trilling

It is notoriously difficult to learn to make an alveolar trill, [r]. It took me nearly a year to acquire this skill myself, even though I was a highly motivated postgraduate ambitious to become a proper phonetician, professionally required to be able to make all the sounds on the IPA chart.

By 'trill' I mean a sound in which an active articulator strikes a passive articulator several times in quick succession. A trill can be bilabial, alveolar, uvular, or perhaps epiglottal. You need it for Italian, Spanish, Serbian, Czech, and various other languages.

The teacher who finally helped me conquer this hurdle was Marguerite Chapallaz, and she did it by getting me to **relax**. I was lying on my back in the bath at the moment I first succeeded in producing an alveolar trill, so it might be worth experimenting with different body orientations.

What it comes down to is that you have to hold the organs of speech in the right place, relax, and then produce an airstream. You don't actively move anything to make the separate vibrations: it's all done by aerodynamics. (Physicists will tell you it involves the Bernouilli effect.)

As Ladefoged and Maddieson put it (*The Sounds of the World's Languages*, p. 217),

> This is very similar to the vibration of the vocal folds during voicing; in both cases there is no muscular action that controls each single vibration, but a sufficiently narrow aperture must be created and an adequate airflow through the aperture must occur.

One useful hint is to start with trills you *can* make. Most people can manage a voiced bilabial trill, *brrr* [ʙ], or its voiceless counterpart. Some can make a uvular trill (think Edith Piaf, **nɔ̃, ʀjɛ̃ də ʀjɛ̃, ʒə nə ʀəgʀɛtə ʀjɛ̃**). Use these to get a feel of how trills work.

(If you can switch off voicing to make a voiceless uvular trill [ʀ̥], too, it's fun to do it while whistling. It makes you sound like a referee's whistle.)

If you still can't manage an alveolar trill, it may be a consolation to know that there are tens of thousands of native speakers of Spanish and Italian who can't make one either, but who replace it by something or other that is easier. Yet they manage to function in those languages.

If you can make [r], and want a further challenge, try the retroflex trill of Toda. Only the onset is retroflex; the actual trill is alveolar.

Sorry, class: I haven't got a magic bullet.

13.8 Ooh!

Students of phonetics in Britain have to learn to recognize the Cardinal Vowels established by Daniel Jones: at least the primaries (**i e ɛ a ɑ ɔ o u**) and four of the secondaries, namely **y ø œ ɯ**. Masters' students have to learn not only to recognize them but to produce them, too.

Some readers may be surprised to learn that the cardinal vowel that generally proves most difficult for English and Scottish students to produce is primary number 8, **u**. These students have to learn to make a vowel sound that is considerably backer and rounder than their English GOOSE vowel (which in England, as we know, is becoming steadily fronter and less rounded).

If simple imitation fails, I generally find that the most helpful technique is to start from the English word *wall*. The BrE vowel in this word is reliably back. More importantly, so is the close and rounded **w** at the beginning. If you prolong this **w** instead of immediately gliding away from it, the result may be an acceptable cardinal-style **u** – properly close, back, and rounded. It may need to be made a little 'tighter' (i.e. with a greater degree of tongue raising). Once the learner has produced that satisfactorily, you just need a few fluency and catenation exercises. Then you can compare and contrast English *boot* with cardinal **but** and *moon* with cardinal **mun**. (NB cardinal vowels have no inherent length. They can be prolonged or not at will.)

The same difficulty faces the English-speaking learner of German. German long **u:** is just about cardinal. If I were teaching German **u:** I would apply the same technique. I'd emphasize the difference in sound between German *du* **du:** and English *do*, German *Hut* **hu:t** and English *hoot*. Learners of German also have to master the front-back distinction in *Brüder – Bruder* ˈ**bryːdɐ** – ˈ**bruːdɐ**. (These are the plural and singular forms, respectively, of the word meaning 'brother[s]'. Both tend to get mapped onto English *brooder*.)

The word *Stuhl* **ʃtuːl** 'chair' is particularly interesting. For many English people their vowel in English *stool*, because of the following dark lateral, is not very different from the German vowel. However the German final clear **lʲ** is strikingly different from the usual English dark **ɫ** used in this position.

The German bird *der Uhu* ˈ**uːhu**, 'eagle owl', has an onomatopoeic name. It hoots in a cardinal way. (And it's also a brand name for a glue.)

13.9 A Multiplicity of Schwas

If you study the official IPA chart closely, you may be intrigued by one of the vowel symbols to be found there, namely ɘ – not the usual schwa symbol, ə, but a differently reversed lower-case letter e. It appears in the middle of the vowel chart and is described as a close-mid central unrounded vowel.

You may well never have seen it actually used except in lists of symbols. So what's it for?

I would say that it can be seen a consequence of some theorists' wish for excessive phonetic precision and their reluctance to use flexible ('vague') cover symbols.

The English ə phoneme, as is well known, varies considerably in vowel quality depending on its phonetic surroundings. In particular, it is somewhat more open (ʌ-like) at the end of a word than elsewhere. When it's *not* at the end of a word (more precisely, of a word said in isolation or at the end of a phrase), English ə is approximately half-close, central, and unrounded – i.e. exactly where the current official IPA chart places [ɘ]. Examples would be the ə in words such as *along, about, breakfast, method*. In his *Outline of English Phonetics* (Heffer 1956), Daniel Jones says it can be indicated, 'where necessary', by attaching a subscript figure 1 to the schwa symbol, thus ə₁. He calls this the principal member of the English ə phoneme. The current standard textbook, Cruttenden's eighth edition of Gimson's Pronunciation of English, writes it narrowly with an uptack, thus [ə̝]. Very sensibly, Cruttenden prefers to use a diacritic rather than the unfamiliar, though now IPA-recognized, ɘ symbol. Jones also mentions, by the way, that this variety of schwa is 'almost identical with the North German sound of *e* in *bitte*'.

What about the narrow notation of the rather opener English schwa used in final position? That's the one at the end of words such as *comma, villa*, and non-rhotic *collar, better*. Jones writes it with a subscript figure 3, ə₃, while Cruttenden implicitly treats it as the 'principal member' (default allophone) and writes simply ə (it's also possible that he intended to attach a downtack, thus ə̞, which would have been consistent, but that his printers messed up).

These two English schwas, then, are positional allophones: the choice between them is determined by the phonetic environment.

This is strikingly different from the phonology of German, a language in which there is a phonemic contrast between a closer schwa, as at the end of *bitte* ˈbɪtə 'please', and an opener schwa, as at the end of *besser* ˈbɛsɐ 'better', or indeed *bitter* ˈbɪtɐ, meaning the same as in English.

On the IPA chart both of these symbols, ə and ɐ, are conveniently vaguely positioned, the first between close-mid and open-mid, the second between open-mid and open. Neither symbol is used to denote any cardinal vowel.

In my view the middle of the current IPA chart represents an excessive enthusiasm for a non-Jonesian extension of the Cardinal Vowel scheme. In this scheme Daniel Jones first gave us the primary cardinal vowels **i e ɛ a ɑ ɔ o u**, supplemented by the secondary cardinals **y ø œ ɒ ʌ ɤ ɯ**. Later the missing one, the open front rounded secondary 4 (c.v. no. 12) was assigned the symbol **ɶ**, though it is not clear whether there is any use for this symbol in transcribing a real language. (The best candidate for it known to me is the open allophone of Danish /œ/ used next to the Danish uvular **r**. But no language, as far as I know, distinguishes four front rounded vowel phonemes.)

Considerably later than he first proposed his Cardinal Vowel scheme, Jones added the two close central vowels to fill the gap between **i** and **u, y** and **ɯ**, namely **ɨ** and **ʉ**. Their inclusion is justified by languages such as Russian, which needs the symbol **ɨ**, and Swedish, which needs **ʉ**. But Jones never defined any non-peripheral cardinal vowels. For most languages there is at most one mid central vowel, which can be adequately represented by the schwa symbol, **ə**, which has always been rather vaguely defined. A few languages have two mid central vowels. German, as we saw, distinguishes a higher/closer **ə** from a lower/opener **ɐ**. Non-rhotic English distinguishes a strong long **ɜ**ː (as in the noun *insert* ˈɪnsɜːt) from the weak short **ə** (as in the noun *concert* ˈkɒnsət). English and German justify the presence on the chart of two other non-peripheral lax vowel symbols, **ɪ** and **ʊ**. Certain other languages (e.g. Dutch) may need the symbol **ɵ**, for a distinctively rounded schwa. But as far as I can see we don't need **ɘ** and we don't need **ɞ**. The only reason to include them on the chart is a desire to label every intersection of lines on the chart, rounded and unrounded.

At UCL we have never taught the symbols **ɘ** and **ɞ** or drilled the corresponding sounds. I wonder if students have been taught them and drilled on them anywhere else. I suspect not. Let's continue to boycott these upstarts. We don't need them. In fact, let's go further and remove them from the Chart.

13.10 A Controlled Rolling Grunt

Anyone who studies phonetics at a British university, and no doubt in many other countries too, has to learn to recognize and produce a number of 'difficult' or 'exotic' consonants, among them the one that we transcribe **ʕ**, which is classified on the IPA Chart as a voiced pharyngeal fricative.

For a language that includes this sound, people usually think first of all of Arabic, where the sound associated with the letter ع (*ʻayn*) has traditionally been classified by phoneticians as a voiced pharyngeal fricative and written **ʕ**. (The IPA symbol was chosen to be reminiscent of the top half of the Arabic letter.)

However, Robin Thelwall argued in 1990 (*JIPA* 20.2:37–41) that the Arabic sound is actually not a pharyngeal fricative but a pharyngealized glottal stop. I think he is probably right. When pronounced by native speakers of Arabic, this sound often seems to involve, as well as a constriction in the pharynx, a momentary cessation of the vibration of the vocal folds.

The Hebrew alphabet, too, includes a letter *ayin* (ע), which in some kinds of Hebrew is pronounced in the same way. Apparently this was its historical pronunciation, but nowadays many Israelis just pronounce it as a glottal stop, ʔ (which also has its own letter in the Hebrew alphabet, *aleph* א).

The foregoing discussion assumes that you, the reader, have enough familiarity with phonetic terminology and classification to be able to follow it. I hope you do. Those who don't are forced into inventive but incoherent descriptive attempts such as this one that a correspondent came across in a wiki about Hebrew. He sent it to me as a 'gem for your collection of examples of the complete inability of the phonetically naive to describe speech sounds'.

> Ayin is not pronounced the same as Aleph. Ayin has a gutteral sound applied to it, a gutteral sound void of tonality – almost a controlled rolling grunt.

My correspondent commented, 'I don't mean to mock people for knowing nothing about phonetics, but the sheer desperate inventiveness (and uselessness) of the description was striking.'

Lance Eccles mentions a rather ad-hoc description of how to pronounce *'ayn*: 'Sing the lowest note you can, then sing one note lower. It sort of works.' Others have drawn attention to its lengthening and/or pharyngealizing a preceding vowel.

13.11 Initial ŋ

What makes velar nasals so special? Why are they so more restricted in distribution than **n** and **m**? For example, why doesn't English have words like **ngail, *ngight, *ngine*, and **ngoon*? Why do many languages not have velar nasals at all, except perhaps as positional allophones of **n** before a following velar stop?

Velar plosives are unproblematic, and nasals are unproblematic, so why is the intersection of velarity and nasality somehow exceptional?

I don't know whether anyone has a really satisfactory answer. I haven't got one myself. The usual explanation in terms of markedness theory seems to me to be post hoc and circular (because X is rare, we say it's marked; then it is the markedness of X that's responsible for its rarity).

There are plenty of languages in the world that do have initial velar nasals, particularly those of central Africa, southeast Asia, and the Pacific. The Nguni ŋˈguːni group of languages in South Africa illustrates this possibility in its very name; this group includes Zulu and Xhosa, both with millions of speakers, though velar nasals in these languages are always followed by a velar stop. But in the Dinka language of Southern Sudan the word for 'who' is ŋa, while in Luganda ŋaːŋa means 'ibis'. In the Nivkh of Sakhalin the number 'seven' is ŋamg. In Māori the definite article is ŋaː. Australian languages typically have many words beginning with ŋ followed by a vowel. The very frequent Vietnamese name *Nguyen* (*Nguyễn*) is phonetically ŋʷĩʔən or ŋʷĩəŋ. And *Ng*, pronounced as a syllabic ŋ, is a well-known Cantonese surname (possibly the shortest surname in the world?), corresponding to Mandarin *Wu*.

Of the 234 languages in the World Atlas of Language Structures database that have a velar nasal as an independent phoneme, there are more that allow it in initial position (146) than that disallow it (88), which you may find surprising.

Remember that the languages familiar to Europeans are by no means representative of the world's languages in general. Even in Europe, an initial velar nasal is regularly found in Welsh and Irish, though only through mutation of an initial velar plosive: e.g. in Welsh *fy nghi* 'my dog' və ŋhiː, from *ci* 'dog' kiː; and *fy ngardd* 'my garden' və ŋarð, from *gardd* 'garden' garð. In colloquial spoken Welsh the *fy* və bit can be dropped, leaving the velar nasal initial in the whole noun phrase. So 'I'm digging my garden' becomes just *rw i 'n palu 'ngardd* ru in pali ŋarð.

13.12 The Palatal Nasal

While we're on the topic of nasals, it's interesting to note that there's one nasal that is pretty common in the world's languages in general, but which we don't have in English: the palatal nasal, ɲ.

When we borrow words containing a palatal nasal from languages that have one, we have two possible anglicization strategies: map it onto **nj**, or map it onto simple **n**.

In final position, there's no choice: it has to be **n**. So French *Charlemagne* ʃaʁləmaɲ becomes ˈʃɑː(r)ləmeɪn (mostly), and *champagne* ʃɑ̃paɲ becomes ˌʃæmˈpeɪn. When speaking about the German city of *Köln* kœln we use its French name, namely *Cologne* kɔlɔɲ, which we pronounce as kəˈləʊn. In *Boulogne* bulɔɲ, on the other hand, we transfer the palatality to the vowel and say buˈlɔɪn.

Medially, we have **nj** in *poignant, cognac, vignette*. French doesn't have words beginning with ɲ, so the question of what to do with it doesn't arise; but Italian does have it, and when confronted with *gnocchi* ˈɲɔkki I think most people just say ˈnɒki, unless they are among the few linguistic sophisticates who know it 'ought' to be ˈnjɒki. There's a phonotactic problem there, though, in that in a stressed syllable English Cj- is on the whole restricted to positions before the vowel **uː** or something derived from it.

When it comes to Spanish, I think most British people ignore the diacritic in *piña colada* piɲa koˈlaða and just say ˈpiːnə kəˈlɑːdə. But Americans know more Spanish, and say ˈpiːnjə. In the case of *cañon*, we decided to anglicize its spelling to *canyon*, so everyone says **nj**. Few British people know any Portuguese, so *piranha*, BrPort piˈraɲa, is usually just pəˈrɑːnə.

As we see, the palatal nasal ɲ is spelt as *gn* in French and Italian, as *ñ* in Spanish, and as *nh* in Portuguese. In Catalan and various African languages it is spelt *ny*. You might think that this last spelling would be straightforward for English speakers to process, but experience shows this isn't necessarily the case. *Canyon* may be unproblematic; but Malawi (or Malaŵi, to be pedantic) used to be called *Nyasaland*, where *Nyasa* ɲasa, also spelt *Nyassa* or *Niassa*, means 'lake' in various Bantu languages in that part of Africa: what is now known as Lake Malawi was then called Lake Nyasa. But would the British say ˈ**njæsə(lænd)**, as intended? No, they tended to go for **naɪˈæsə**. That is, they misinterpreted the letter *y* as standing for a vowel rather than a consonant. They did the same with the Tanzanian political leader Julius Nyerere. Compare today the name Myanmar, which we're meant to pronounce ˈ**mjænmɑː**, but for which you will sometimes hear **maɪˈænmɑː** or the like.

Quite apart from its use to spell a palatal nasal, the digraph *gn* is well known to be ambiguous in English. The *g* is silent (or 'zeroed') in *sign, reign, impugn*, but not in *signal, pregnant, pugnacious*.

Most English-speaking classicists, I think, say **gn** in Latin words such as *agnus, dignus, regnum*. But choral singers and Catholics attempt Italian ɲ and usually end up with **nj**. In classical Latin, however, *gn* appears to have stood for neither **gn** nor ɲ, but rather for **ŋn**, thus **aŋnus, diŋnus, reŋnũ**.

A discussion of *gn* would not be complete without mention of the *gnu*, immortalized by Flanders and Swann with the jocular pronunciation **gəˈnuː**. We don't use this word in ordinary conversation, since we usually call the animal in question a wildebeeste. According to the COD, *gnu* originated as a Bushman word *nqu*. As far as I know, modern Khoisan orthographies do not use the letter *q*; but if we interpret it following the spelling conventions of Zulu and Xhosa, that would mean a retroflex nasal click ɳǃ at the beginning.

13.13 Lateral Fricatives

People asked me for advice on how to learn and teach the sound [ɬ], the Welsh *ll* as in *Pontcysyllte* (1.16), *llaw* 'hand', *Llanelli* and many other words and names.

This consonant is a voiceless alveolar lateral fricative. To make it you have to control the voicing (voiceless), the place of articulation (alveolar), and the manner of articulation (lateral fricative). I would teach each of these features separately, and then combine them.

To get awareness of voicing, pronounce **fvfvfv θðθðθð szszsz ʃʒʃʒʃʒ** and then **m̥mm̥mm̥m n̥nn̥nn̥n ɬlɬlɬl**. As you do so, check the voicing by covering your ears with your hands or by feeling the front of the larynx with your fingers. As you alternate between voiced and voiceless, make sure that everything in the mouth remains unchanged: the only difference should be at the larynx.

Concentrate now on l̥l̥l̥l̥l̥l̥. Alveolar place should not be a problem, for native speakers of English at any rate. Resist any well-intentioned but misguided suggestions involving placing the tongue between or against the teeth, unless this is just part of making the learner conscious of the placement of the tongue tip: yes, the tip should be in contact while the side rims are down (as for any English l), but the contact should be with the alveolar ridge, i.e. just behind the teeth.

Try the English words *please, plum, clear, claw*. Observe that the l-sound in these words is actually devoiced, [l̥], because of the effects of aspiration. Isolate this sound. It is a voiceless lateral approximant. Note how the air escapes over the side rim(s) of the tongue. (Over both sides? Or just one, and if so which?)

Some may find it helpful to compare the English word *subtlety* ˈsʌtl̩ti. But beware: this word has lateral release of the preceding alveolar plosive, which introduces an entirely unnecessary complication. Its lateral is only slightly devoiced and is not fricative. Furthermore, it is dark, which will be inappropriate for most kinds of Welsh. Welsh *ll*, [ɬ], on the other hand, is a fricative. It does not have lateral release, just lateral escape.

After *please* and *claw*, your remaining task is to change the sound from a lateral approximant to a lateral fricative. This means that you have to narrow the gap between the side rims of the tongue and the side teeth. Try to do this while saying a long l̥. It should change into ɬ.

Feel the air escaping turbulently over the side of the tongue. Keeping everything else constant, change from breathing out to breathing in. Check that you can feel a cold airstream at the side (not in the centre line). Go back to breathing out.

Lastly, we need to check the place of articulation. If you have carried out the above steps successfully, the place of articulation is still alveolar. The *ll* sound is a single phonetic segment, and should not have any accompanying elements. There should be no element of velar friction before, during, or after the lateral fricative. There should be no central friction (s or θ) before, during or after it. The pronunciations xɬ, θɬ, often used by non-Welsh speakers, are not acceptable.

Try the words *llaw* (hand), *lle* (place), *llo* (calf), *llwybr* (path). Then try *pell* (far), *twll* (hole). Then *allan* (out), and *felly* (thus). Like the other Welsh voiceless consonants, ɬ is considerably longer intervocalically than would be the case in English: but there is no change in quality.

Make sure that you can hear and make the difference between *dallu* (to blind) ˈdaɬi and *dathlu* ˈdaθli (to celebrate).

Practise some place names: *Llangollen, Llanelli, Machynlleth*. (The last one is maˈxənɬeθ.)

For fun, try using ɬ in place of English s. This produces a common type of lisp (lateral sigmatism). Try ɬɪkɬ piːɬɪʒ (six pieces). Don't be afraid of ɬaʊndrɪŋ ɬɪli.

Lastly, it is perhaps only fair to mention that there seem to be some native speakers of Welsh who replace ɬ by ç. Other native speakers don't notice anything odd about this, as long as everything else is native-like.

You are now equipped to pronounce not only Welsh but also Icelandic and Zulu words with this sound. Icelandic has a voiceless lateral affricate, though the second element is usually thought of just as l̥. It sound to me like ɬ, but I suppose the friction may be optional as long as the sound is voiceless and lateral. Try *fjall* **fjatl̥** (mountain) and *Þingvellir* ˈθɪŋgvetl̥ɪr (the site of Iceland's first parliament).

Zulu has voiceless ɬ and also a voiced alveolar lateral fricative, ɮ. Use your control of voicing to switch between them: ɮɬɮɬɮ. Then alongside -*hlala* ˈɬaːla (sit) and *Hluhluwe* ɬuˈɬuːwe you should also be able to manage -*dla* ɮa (eat), not to mention *Isandlwana* **isandɮwaːnə** and *amandla* aˈmaːndɮa (power). The spelling *dl* denotes ɮ except after *n*, where it denotes the affricate dɮ.

Lastly, do not fall foul of the 'exotic sounds syndrome'. For speakers of languages that have it, ɬ and ɮ are perfectly ordinary sounds that do not require any special effort. You, too, must use them effortlessly.

13.14 Russian ж

What is the correct way to represent in IPA transcription the Russian consonant written ж in orthography? Like most phoneticians, I write it ʒ. But, asks a correspondent, isn't it actually a retroflex, so shouldn't we use IPA ʐ?

This suggestion risks opening a whole can of worms.

If you compare a typical French ʃ or ʒ with a typical English ʃ or ʒ, you may notice that the French ones sound slightly 'darker' than the English. As Armstrong and Ward put it,

> The palatal (i.e. j-like) quality which is often heard in English ʃ and ʒ is absent from the French sounds. [*The Phonetics of French*, 1932]

If you compare the Russian sounds written ш and ж, transliterated *sh* and *zh*, respectively, you will notice that they are darker still. Here is Daniel Jones.

> English ʃ . . . is a somewhat palatalized sound . . . in comparison with Russian ʃ, and does not have the characteristic 'dark' or 'hollow' quality of the latter. [. . .] English ʒ differs from Russian ʒ in exactly the same way that English ʃ differs from Russian ʃ. [Jones and Ward, *The Phonetics of Russian*, 1969]

All three ʒ sounds (English, French, and Russian) are 'darker' than the 'alveolopalatal' ʑ of Polish. On the other hand none of them are as 'dark' as the 'retroflex' ʐ of Standard Chinese (Pinyin *r*, as in 人 *rén*).

So what we are dealing with is a continuum of possibilities. I used to make my students first produce with their usual ʃ (or ʒ) and then prolong it while modifying the articulation so as to make it sound first clearer then darker, and then to slur backwards and forwards between the extreme points of ɕ ʑ and ʂ ʐ, passing through a range of subtly different varieties of ʃ and ʒ.

Providing a language has no phonemic contrasts of place within this range, it is entirely acceptable, indeed recommended, to use the symbols ʃ and ʒ. The precise coloration does not matter: we write ʒ in transcriptions of French and of English without causing any confusion (even though the sounds are not exactly identical).

In cases where a language does have a contrast within the range, we can discuss which symbols to use. So for Polish it is usual in the IPA tradition to write ɕ ʑ for the clearer pair (orthographic *ś, ź*) and ʃ ʒ for the darker pair (*sz, ż*), though some prefer ʂ ʐ for the darker.

Russian is an interesting case. There is no simple direct contrast of place, but the fricatives spelt ш and ж are dark (non-palatalized) and very different from the palatalized fricative spelt щ, which tends to be longer and can also be interrupted by a plosive element, so ɕɕ or ɕtɕ. (Jones and Ward use the obsolete IPA symbols ʆ, ʆʆ, ʆtʆ.) For the non-palatalized ones Jones and Ward write ʃ and ʒ, e.g. nʌˈʒa ножа 'knife (gen. sg.)'.

Ladefoged and Maddieson, in *The Sounds of the World's Languages* (1996), have a long discussion of the articulatory postures involved in sounds of this general type. They categorize the Polish sound spelt *rz*, which I equate with Russian ж, as 'flat post-alveolar (retroflex)'. Yes, somewhat retroflex. But they are nowhere near as retroflex as the 'genuinely retroflex gesture' that they (Ladefoged and Maddieson) report in the Toda language, or in other Dravidian languages.

Perhaps we would do best to confine the use of the retroflex symbols to those languages where there are not only fricatives but also plosives and nasals that are distinctively retroflex. For Russian ж I'm sticking with ʒ.

13.15 Depressors

In Zulu and other Nguni languages some consonants are 'depressor' consonants. It might be worth summarizing what I learnt of this topic in the Introduction to Zulu course I followed at SOAS in the 1970s. It was taught by the late David Rycroft and A.B. Ngcobo.

Zulu has two (or three) phonological tones: High tone (H), shown in the examples by an acute accent (ˊ), Falling (F) (ˆ), and unmarked or Low. However the actual pitch contour of a syllable is affected by several additional factors, notably tone assimilation, depression, and of course intonation, downdrift, etc.

1. Assimilation: unmarked syllables standing between two marked ones adopt the same pitch as the previous H (subject to certain exceptions).
2. Depression: a vowel following a depressor consonant, if H or F, begins with a rising-pitch onset and reaches a lower high point than would otherwise apply. If it is unmarked (low), it receives low pitch, overriding the Assimilation that would otherwise apply.

Among the depressor consonants are the voiced obstruents, including the voiced clicks, but excluding the consonants written *b* and *k*, which in certain contexts are voiced implosives **ɓ, ɠ**. There are paired depressor and non-depressor semivowels, glottal fricatives, nasals, and nasalized clicks. There is also a free-floating depressor effect characterizing certain vowel-only syllables. Rycroft claims the depressors all have breathy voice, and writes them **d̤, z̤**, etc. Auditorily, the greatest difference between the implosives **ɓ, ɠ** and the plain *bh, g* **b̤, g̤** is the depressor nature of the latter but not the former.

Here is a nice example of the depressor effect. Zulu has borrowed the English word *spoon*, but has modified it so as to conform to the usual Bantu noun pattern of 'classifier' prefix plus stem: *isi-punu*. (The **s** is taken to be the classifier *isi-*. The English **p**, unaspirated in this position, is duly mapped onto Zulu **p'** rather than onto aspirated **pʰ**.) The English stress on a monosyllable is mapped onto Zulu H tone; internal Zulu rules then impose an H on the first syllable of the classifier prefix. The result is that the word for spoon (singular), *isipúnu*, is pronounced with a high level pitch for the first two syllables, then with automatic downstep to a not-quite-so-high pitch for *pú*, and a fairly low pitch for the final *nu*. Nouns that have *isi-* in the singular regularly form their plural by changing the prefix to *izi-*, making spoons (plural) *izipúnu*. The plural prefix contains a depressor consonant, **z**, although the singular prefix has no depressor. The consequence for the pitch pattern in the plural is that although the initial **i** still has a high level pitch, the **zi** syllable is markedly lower; the remainder of the word has the same pattern as the singular. The *-si-* syllable of the singular is assimilated to high pitch, while the depressor consonant in *-zi-* overrides that effect and causes low pitch.

Another example involves the words *abántwana* (children) and *amádada* (ducks). These words have the same tone pattern (H on the second syllable, otherwise unmarked). There are no depressors in the first word (the spelling *b* denotes a non-depressor implosive **ɓ**); but the second word has two depressor consonants **d**. The pitch pattern of *abántwana* has a medium-high initial **a**, a high second syllable **ɓá**, then a tonally partially assimilated gradual downward movement on the tonally unmarked remaining syllables **ntwana**. In *amádada*, on the other hand, the depressor consonants (**amád̤a:d̤a**) trigger a sharp fall to a low level pitch for the last two syllables.

In *Thula Sizwe* (Section 13.5), the pitch of unmarked *-la* in *thúla* is tonally assimilated to highish, but then in *sízwe* there is abrupt drop to low pitch on *-zwe* caused by the depressor **z̤**. In *úngabókhâla* the **g** of the second syllable is a depressor, but not the implosive **ɓ** of the third. In *úJehóva* you hear the depressor effect of the **dʒ** and the **v**. And so on.

I was impressed by Rycroft's analysis of Zulu tone: a simple system of lexical tones, but complicated realization rules. His description, and the output of his rules, agreed exactly with what our native-speaker language consultant pronounced, although Mr Ngcobo, as seems often to happen with speakers of tone languages, had difficulty in identifying or analysing the tones he deployed so effortlessly. (The first consonant in his surname is a depressor nasalized click, the second a non-depressor implosive.)

For Rycroft's analysis see his 1980 monograph 'The Depression Feature in Nguni languages and its interaction with tone', Communication No. 8. Department of African Languages, Rhodes University, Grahamstown.

To bid farewell in Zulu you say *salani kahle* **salá:ni ɠaːɬé**. Literally, this means 'stay (pl.) well', and is used when saying goodbye to people who are staying where they are as the speaker leaves. Cf *hambani kahle* **hambá:ni ɠaːɬé** 'go well', used if the addressees are leaving and the speaker is staying. You should be able to work out how the pitch patterns of the two expressions differ.

13.16 Gdynia Unmasked

I was in my teens when I first became aware of places in Poland called *Gdynia* and *Gdańsk*. I remember wondering how the initial cluster **gd** could be pronounced. The nearest thing in English seemed to be the **gəd-** sequence in *Lady Godiva* **gəˈdaɪvə** and *Godolphin* (nowadays we have another example in *Gaddafi*), but I knew that that wasn't right for Polish. Yet as an initial cluster **gd-** seemed impossible to pronounce.

Then I realized that English does have the articulatory sequence **gd**, but in final position. We get it in the past tense of verbs ending in **g**, thus for example *bagged* **bægd**, *hugged* **hʌgd**. We get it medially, too, in *Ogden* **ˈɒgdən**. All I needed to do for Polish was to transfer this **gd** to syllable-initial position.

That still seemed very difficult to do. The reason (I know now) is that in English we normally pronounce these plosive sequences as overlapping articulatory gestures. You can't hear the release of the **g** in *hugged*, or for that matter in *Ogden*, because it is 'masked' by the concurrent hold phase of the **d**. What you hear is a velar approach, a long hold, and an alveolar release (if you're lucky). And we don't ever have this sort of thing at the beginning of a syllable.

It wasn't until I first visited Poland, when I was twenty, that I discovered that in Polish the initial plosives in *Gdańsk* **gdaj̃sk** and *Gdynia* **ˈgdɨɲa** are not really like the English **gd** in *hugged*. Rather, when my Polish friends demonstrated the pronunciation to me, they released the velar plosive BEFORE completing the approach for the dental. This inevitably gave rise to a tiny transitional vocoid between the two hold phases, but it was not long enough to count as a separate schwa segment, nor long enough for most speakers to be aware of its presence (compare the overt and perceived schwa in English *Godiva*).

Despite my A level in Greek, somehow I'd failed to realize that classical Greek has an exactly parallel, but voiceless, cluster in words such as κτείς *kteís* 'comb' and κτίσις *ktísis* 'foundation'. (What we did to pronounce those words in the Classical Sixth I can no longer remember.)

The stem of κτείς is κτεν- *kten-*, and from this is derived the modern zoological Latin name *Ctenophora*, the phylum of marine animals also known as 'comb jellies'. In English we abandon any attempt at the initial plosive cluster, and pronounce them simply as tɪˈnɒfərə.

Modern Greek has dissimilated the plosive sequence, making the first element fricative. The modern word for 'comb' is χτένι ˈ**xteni**.

It's an old truism of acoustic phonetics that you can't hear the hold stage of a voiceless plosive (as such). What you get in the middle of a word such as *happy* ˈ**hæpi** or *lucky* ˈlʌki is a short period of silence, as the airstream is for a moment prevented from moving through the vocal tract and out of the body. No air movement means no sound.

How, then, can we identify the place of articulation? How do we know that in the first word we have a bilabial **p** but in the second a velar **k**?

We know because of the formant transitions created as the organs of speech move into place for the complete closure (the 'approach' phase) and then again as they separate (the 'release' phase). You identify the **p** in *happy* through its effect on the end of the **æ** and on the beginning of the **i**. You identify the **k** in *lucky* by what you hear in the course of the ʌ and the **i**.

In the case of a fully voiced plosive, all you can hear during the hold phase is voicing. Again, you identify the place of articulation through the information contained in the formant transitions before and after, i.e. in the approach and the release. That's how you know that *abbey* has a **b**, *ladder* a **d**, and *lagging* a **g**.

Let's get back to the plosive cluster in *Gdynia*. In an English word such as *acting* ˈæktɪŋ we normally have the same 'masking' phenomenon we observed for the voiced plosives in *hugged* and *Ogden*. In the English **kt** or **gd** the plosives typically overlap, in that we make the approach for the second plosive before releasing the first. The sequence of events is velar approach – velar hold – alveolar approach (inaudible, because the velar hold is maintained) – double hold (velar and alveolar) – velar release (inaudible, because the alveolar hold is maintained) – alveolar hold – alveolar release. The only audible phases are the velar approach and the alveolar release. In these the formant transitions supply the clues to the places of articulation.

To identify the place of a plosive it is sufficient to hear either the approach or the release. You do not need both. That is how we can tell that the segments are ˈæktɪŋ rather than, say, ˈæptɪŋ or ˈætkɪŋ or ˈættɪŋ.

My impression from my first visit to Poland was, then, that for Polish **gd-** the two plosives did not overlap in the English way. Rather, the sequence of events was straightforwardly velar approach – velar hold – velar release – dental approach – dental hold – dental release. Rather than taking place during the velar hold, the dental approach was delayed until after the velar release. The tiny transitional nonsyllabic schwa between the plosives is created in the tiny interval of time between the two articulatory gestures, velar and dental.

We can leave the native speakers of Polish to debate whether this non-overlapping is usual, as I supposed, or only found in careful or overenunciated pronunciation, as some seem to claim. My impression is that if we compare English *actor* with Polish *aktor*, it is typical for the English plosives to overlap but for the Polish ones not to. Similarly with the name *Magda*.

In strongly Japanese-accented English, on the other hand, a word such as *actor* tends to have a greater interval between the release of the **k** and the approach of the **t**. This space might be identified as a Japanese voiceless **u̥** (thus 'アクター'). Typically, it seems to be much longer than the momentary mini-voiceless-schwa of the Polish **kt**. It reflects the Japanese mora-based timing in which equal time is allotted to each of **a, k(u), ta, a**.

13.17 Breathiness

The lead article in the August 2012 issue of the *Journal of the International Phonetic Association*, by Christina Esposito and Sameer ud Dowla Khan, concerns contrastive breathiness in consonants and vowels. Various languages have contrastive breathiness on voiced obstruents, as in the case of Hindi **bʱ**, etc; some have contrastive breathiness on semivowels or vowels, as in Zulu *yebo* **je̤ɓo** 'yes' (my example, not the authors'). A very few languages have both contrastive breathy-voiced vowels and breathy-voiced aspirated consonants, including the Gujarati and White Hmong that the authors here analyse. Since both involve breathy voicing during the vowel, the crucial question is, how is the CʰV type distinguished from the CV̤ type?

The authors studied Gujarati minimal triplets such as **ba̤ɾ** 'outside', **bʱar** 'burden', **bar** 'twelve', and White Hmong (**m̥ɔ̃ŋ**) triplets such as **da̤** 'lie, fool', **dʱa** 'separate', **da** 'yellow' (these are also tonally distinct). They found that in both languages consonantal breathiness is initially breathier than vowel breathiness. The timing of the breathiness also differs, being later for vowel breathiness than for consonant breathiness. (I summarize.)

13.18 Tap, Tap

A correspondent wrote from Mexico with what at first sight is a simple and straightforward question.

> I have been trying to figure out something about the alveolar flap or tap. I'm not sure whether the Spanish *r* as in words like *pero, cero, caro* and the like is the same as the English sound in words and phrases like *matter, Natalie, order, water, how to, about a* and the like. [...] I think they might be the same, but I'm still not sure. [...] Could you please tell me if there is any articulatory difference between the two sounds or not?

In saying 'English', my correspondent is of course referring only to AmE. In BrE (i.e. RP as taught to learners) the usual consonant in the middle of *water*

ˈwɔːtə is very different from the Spanish single **r** in *pero* ˈ**pero**. This BrE **t** is voiceless, slow, perhaps somewhat aspirated and indeed often affricated, whereas Spanish **r** is voiced, and rapid. But in AmE (as taught to learners), on the other hand. the etymological **t** in the words quoted is a voiced tap ('flap', say some) that is indeed very similar to the Spanish /r/, and is indeed sometimes transcribed identically, as **r**.

Are the two sounds merely similar, or are they 'the same'? Partly the problem is one of asking what we mean when we say that two sounds are 'the same'. Do we just mean that language learners can safely treat them as equivalent? Or is it deeper than that?

Not all Spanish **r** are identical. For example, some speakers articulate it with the tongue tip against the teeth, making it dental; but for others it may rather be alveolar. The duration of the closure is usually about 20 ms, but may on occasion be somewhat longer or shorter. The AmE sound is at least as variable, and probably more so. For example, it may not always be fully voiced (particularly for those relatively few Americans who consistently distinguish pairs such as *shutter* and *shudder*). Following the NURSE vowel, as in *dirty*, it may involve a ballistic movement, a true flap, in which the active articulator strikes the passive articulator and continues in the same trajectory, as opposed to the more usual type in which the active articulator 'bounces off' the passive, involving an up-then-down movement. In *Natalie, battle*, etc, the tap is unlike anything in Spanish, since it has lateral release. (But some speakers use a glottal stop here rather than a tap. A glottal stop is equally un-Spanish.) Because of the following ɚ, the tapped **t** in *matter* and *water* may be somewhat different from the tapped **t** in *atom* and *bottom*, where the following sound is a plain (non-r-coloured) vowel.

More importantly, perhaps, the tongue configuration before and after the consonant may differ considerably in the two languages, giving rise to different formant transitions in the on-glide and off-glide of the segment we are discussing.

The clincher comes, though, from x-ray tracings. You can see some in Ladefoged and Maddieson's *The Sounds of the World's Languages* (Blackwell 1996).

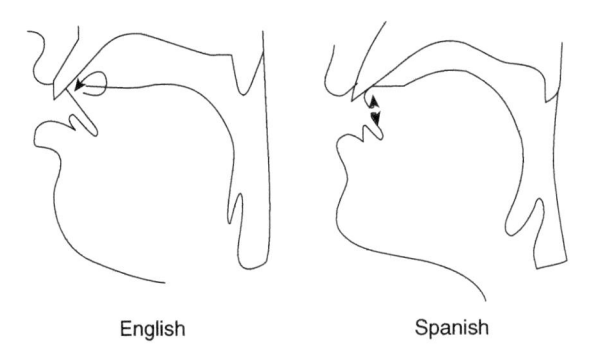

English   Spanish

The authors comment:

> The English speaker has a preparatory raising and retraction of the tongue tip during the preceding vowel [...] The tongue is then moved forward to make the contact which is captured in the frame illustrated here, after which it returns to the floor of the mouth. The Spanish tap does not involve any substantial anticipation, but instead has a quick upward and downward movement confined to the tongue tip.

It is possible that in the case of *water*, the word illustrated here, the preparatory retraction of the tongue tip may be in anticipation of the r-coloured ɚ which follows. Would we find the same retraction in a word such as *atom* ˈærəm? I do not know.

So what is my answer to my correspondent? I think we can say that the two sounds are not really exactly identical, but that for language learning purposes we can treat them as if they were.

Two further points: today's British RP does not generally use a tap for **r** as in *very, narrow*, though it was so used up to the early twentieth century and still remains in certain special styles (notably in classical singing) and in various regional accents. An American-style voiced tap for **t**, on the other hand, is fairly frequent in today's RP in certain words (e.g. *British* ˈbrɪɾɪʃ – see *Sounds Interesting*, pp. 171–172) and contexts, as well as being a regular characteristic of Northern Irish English.

13.19 Voicing Basics

Following the discussion of taps (see *Sounds Interesting*, p. 172), a correspondent ventured

> If I may ask, how would one go about making an alveolar tap voiceless as opposed to voiced?

What can I say in reply, except that you switch off the voicing as you make the tap? But for some people perhaps that is easier said than done.

One of the first things I teach any beginners' phonetics class is basic consonant classification: Voicing, Place, Manner, and how to detect and control each of these. I usually start with getting the class to hear and make the difference between voiced and voiceless sounds.

I would demonstrate each point myself, before asking everyone in the class to perform likewise. Everyone has to join in making what might seem to be silly noises.

First, make a vowel sound, for example [ɑː]. Feel the vibration of your vocal folds by putting your thumb and fingers on your Adam's apple (the outside of the larynx). Then make a voiceless sound, for example [sss], and feel the larynx again. Notice the difference.

More dramatically, cover your ears with your hands. Say [ɑː] again and notice how the buzzing fills your head. Do this again with [sss] – no buzzing.

Then alternate a pair of sounds such as **sss – zzz** or **fff – vvv**. (These pairs are fine if you're a speaker of English. If not, or if your language doesn't have these sounds, we may have to use other ones.) Do this as you cover your ears, and note the difference inside your head.

Then make **mmm**. Is it voiced or voiceless? Is there buzzing in your head as you say it? (Yes, there is, It must be voiced.) What about **lll**? and **ʃʃʃ**?

Then make the same sound **mmm**, but without the voicing. Just breathe out through the nose, with the lips firmly together. You're doing m̥m̥m̥. Alternate **mmm** – m̥m̥m̥.

Do the same with **n** – n̥n̥n̥. If you had a cleft palate you might pronounce *six* as n̥ɪʔn̥. Do it!

Try **apa apa aba aba**. It may be more difficult to detect voicing or voicelessness here, because the consonantal articulation is much quicker: we just bring the lips together for a moment, then release them. (In **m**, on the other hand, we hold the articulatory position for a longer time.) Do **aka**. Is the **k** voiced or voiceless?

You can try other experiments. Any consonant you can make voiceless you ought to be able to make voiced, and vice versa. What is the voiced counterpart of **k**? What is the voiceless counterpart of **ð**?

If you can make a voiceless velar fricative, **xxx**, then simply add voicing to get the voiced counterpart, **ɣɣɣ**.

Say ˈɣala (Modern Greek for 'milk'), and ˈlweɣo (Spanish for 'then').

Similarly for every voiced sound you can make: just switch off voicing to get the voiceless equivalent. Try a voiceless [l̥]. Do **ala – al̥a**. The only special difficulty with the voiceless tap ɾ̥ is that the sound is extremely short. As **d** is to **ɾ**, so **t** is to ɾ̥.

Making [l̥] sometimes provokes a question: how is this 'voiceless alveolar lateral' different from the Welsh *ll*-sound [ɬ]? The answer is that the former is a lateral approximant, the latter a lateral fricative: so it's a subtle difference in the manner of articulation. A voiceless approximant, if it is audible at all, must of course involve some 'cavity friction' as the air passes through the mouth cavity. A voiceless fricative, on the other hand, involves 'local friction' at the place of articulation (i.e. for [ɬ] between the side rim(s) of the tongue and the roof of the mouth).

Actually, the phonetics of Welsh involves both the approximant [l̥] and the fricative [ɬ]. Following an aspirated voiceless plosive, approximants get devoiced (i.e. the aspiration occurs during the approximant, just as in English *please* pl̥iːz). So the lateral in Welsh *pla* 'plague' pl̥aː is a voiceless approximant, which is not felt by native speakers to be the same as the voiceless fricative in a word such as *llaw* ɬau 'hand'.

I don't think you can usefully discuss phonetic classification unless you have mastered the basics of VPM (Voicing, Place, and Manner): not just intellectually, but practically.

14 EFL

14.1 Institutionalized Mispronunciations

Many non-native speakers of English believe that *comfortable* is pronounced with **-eɪbl̩** at the end, just like *table*. Native speakers, on the other hand, know that it has a weak vowel, **-əbl̩**, like other words with the *-able* suffix (*conceivable, perishable, preferable*).

This seems to be not so much a personal error of this or that EFL speaker, but an institutionalized mispronunciation passed on from teacher to learner and between learners (I've noticed it particularly among Polish EFL learners).

There are other comparable cases. I am not referring to general errors of pronunciation such as difficulties with this or that sound, but to lexically-specific errors affecting particular words in the vocabulary. (By the way, would that be **pɑː**-*ticular*? No, **pə-**.)

Many EFL learners seem to believe that *clothes* is pronounced as two syllables, **ˈkləʊðɪz** or the like. But native speakers pronounce it as one syllable, either **kləʊðz** as I think I usually say it myself, or simply **kləʊz**, i.e. as a homophone of *close* (v.).

Another institutionalized oddity, which I associate particularly with Germans, is saying *evening* (the time of day) with three syllables, **ˈiːvənɪŋ**, rather than with the two that native speakers normally use, **ˈiːvnɪŋ**. (Judging by the Old English spelling *æfnung*, this word has been disyllabic in native English for over a thousand years.)

And then there's **aɪˈdiː** for *idea*, frequently heard from people whose first language is French. But we native speakers say **aɪˈdɪə**, or in some cases **aɪˈdiːə**.

It's the spelling, stupid.

14.2 English r

An Arabic-speaking EFL learner wrote to ask about English **r**: 'Where should we pronounce **r** and where not? What are the rules?'

What advice should one give? It all depends.

- For a simple life, and if your model is American English, pronounce **r** wherever the letter *r* is written.

- However, if your model is RP or a similar form of BrE, or Australian or New Zealand English, or to fit in with those around you in Africa (for example), then you should pronounce an **r**-sound only if the sound that follows is a vowel sound. So there should be an r-sound in *red, arrive, very, tree, address, purity*, but not in *hard, firm, north, persuade, standard, modern*. At the end of a word – as in *better, far, near* – you should not pronounce **r** if the word is on its own or at the end of a sentence; but you may pronounce one if the word is followed, without a break, by another word beginning with a vowel sound.

More importantly, what is your purpose in learning English? If you just want to understand and be understood, then you can pronounce all the *r*s. If you want to fit in with native speakers in some particular place, then you must learn to do as they do. If you want to pass school examinations for which the examiners require that some particular type of pronunciation be used, then you must fit in with their requirements.

It is important to learn not just where to pronounce **r** but also how to pronounce it. If your language is Arabic, which uses a tapped r-sound (ɾ), it is worthwhile trying to acquire an English-style approximant r-sound (ɹ). A tapped ɾ sounds very odd in English if used before a vowel sound, as in *north, start, standard, murderer*.

14.3 Ask Your Favour

A very expert non-native speaker of English sent me an email beginning *I want to ask your favour*.

There's no problem in understanding the phrase: after all, it sounds like what we say in English. But it's not actually what we write. We write (and think that we say) *I want to ask you a favour*.

It's easy to see how spoken *you a* can come to be reinterpreted as *your*. From strong **juː eɪ** we derive weak **ju ə**, readily compressed to one syllable as **jʊə**. And **jʊə** is how some British people (25% of them in my preference poll) pronounce *your*.

Those who, like me and the remaining 75%, pronounce *your* as **jɔː**, or weaken it to **jə**, would leave no room for confusion with *you a*.

14.4 Buttressing?

Sometime in the 1990s I invented the term 'buttressing' to refer to the use of the strong form for an unaccented preposition with a pronoun complement, after the nucleus in sentences like:

(1) I had a <u>let</u>ter from him.

aɪ ˈhæd ə ˈletə frɒm ɪm

She sent a <u>mess</u>age to me.

ʃi ˈsent ə ˈmesɪdʒ tuː mi

I've got a <u>pres</u>ent for you.

aɪv ˈgɒt ə ˈpreznt fɔː ju

Compare

(2) I had a <u>note</u> from him.

aɪ ˈhæd ə ˈnəʊt frəm ɪm

She sent a <u>text</u> to me.

ʃi ˈsent ə ˈtekst tə mi

I've got a <u>gift</u> for you.

aɪv ˈgɒt ə ˈgɪft fə ju

The use of strong or weak form can go either way in both cases, but on the whole we tend to use a strong form in the sentences under (1), but a weak form for those under (2). The more weak syllables intervene after the nucleus, the more likely a strong form.

American colleagues tell me that this phenomenon may be British-only. Even in BrE it is admittedly only a tendency, not an iron rule.

I used this term 'buttressing' when I gave some lectures on English phonetics in Buenos Aires in 1992. Later I decided (or perhaps was persuaded by my colleagues) that it is not necessary to have a new term for this phenomenon: we can just call it 'rhythmic strong form'. It complements 'stranding' (where a word is followed by a syntactic gap, as in *What are you looking at?*): the two principles together account for strong forms in unaccented syllables.

When I returned to Buenos Aires nearly twenty years later several people approached me to say how much they liked the term 'buttressing'. Why had I abandoned it? Would I reinstate it?

I admit to a slight feeling of guilt at having invented, or at least popularized, rather a large number of new technical terms in English phonetics, and do try to keep them in check. (For instance, I decided to abandon my earlier Latinate coinage 'correption' in favour of the English 'smoothing', a term which has been widely taken up.)

But perhaps I needn't feel guilty after all. People like certain coinages. And a teacher can't set an exam question about, say, smoothing, unless the students have been familiarized not only with the phenomenon but with the name for it.

14.5   English ʒ

What keyword would you use to illustrate the English voiced palatoalveolar fricative, ʒ?

From the table of phonetic symbols for English on my website (phon.ucl.ac.uk/home/wells/phoneticsymbolsforenglish.htm) you can see that I chose *pleaṣure* and *viṣion*.

In fact there are not very many fully nativized words with this consonant, and those that do exist all tend to have the consonant in the middle of a word, between a stressed vowel and a weak vowel: *treasure, measure, leisure, usual, exposure, closure, seizure; cohesion, collision, decision, occasion, equation*. Add words which some people pronounce with ʃ, others with ʒ (*Asia, Indonesia, version, recursion, erasure, Persian*).

Only relatively recent foreign borrowings begin or end with ʒ (*gigolo, genre, jalousie, joie de vivre; beige, prestige, camouflage*, perhaps *garage* and *raj*). Those that begin or end with ʒ usually have an alternative pronunciation with dʒ. As the spellings of the everyday words with ʒ imply, this consonant came into English through the historical coalescence of z plus a palatal semivowel: zj → ʒ. There may have been an intermediate step ʒj. Indeed the New Oxford Dictionary (1907) includes a pronunciation with ʒj for *pleasure*, as does the 1914 OED for *treasure*. This possibility did not last out the century: we never have a yod after the ʒ today.

14.6 French/English Interference

Nicolas Ballier, of the University of Paris XIII, has put forward an interesting hypothesis to explain two common errors French people make in pronouncing English. They tend to mispronounce *rain* as ʁɛn on the one hand and *law* as lo (or anglicized into ləʊ) on the other.

Ballier says it's all to do with syllable structure expectations. For many French speakers their vowels e and ɛ are in complementary or nearly complementary distribution, with the higher one, e, being used in open syllables and the lower one, ɛ, being used in closed syllables. Since English *rain* is a monosyllable closed by its final consonant n, they tend to say it with their ɛ (which we perceive as our short e, the vowel of DRESS), rather than with their e (which we would accept as a version of our eɪ of FACE).

In the case of *law*, on the other hand, we have an open syllable. The French vowels o and ɔ, too, are in complementary or near-complementary distribution, with the higher o again being preferred in open syllables and the lower ɔ in closed syllables. Although English *law* would sound much better with French ɔ (particularly if phonetically modified towards English-style ɔː) than with French o, nevertheless the syllable structure makes it difficult for French people to use here.

If this is correct, we would also expect a tendency to use a DRESS-type vowel instead of FACE in *make, place, same, plate, fail*, and so on, and conversely a GOAT-type vowel instead of a mid-open vowel in *saw, draw, jaw*, etc. The letter r in the spelling acts to counteract this trend in words such as *more, four, score,* and so on, in which either a phonetic **r** of some kind (or a virtual one in the speaker's mind) causes these syllables to be felt as closed. We would also predict a tendency to use a LOT-type vowel in words where English has the GOAT vowel in a closed syllable, as in *ghost, rope, coat, home*.

Obvious, when you think about it. But for some reason I'd never thought about it before.

To the extent that some French speakers preserve the distinction between *les* **le** and *lait* **lɛ**, *paume* **pom** and *pomme* **pɔm**, this ought not to happen. But I suspect that not very many do preserve these and similar minimal pairs.

14.7 Southern Country

As I enjoyed a shore excursion while on a Mediterranean cruise, I wondered why the otherwise excellent Greek tour guide accompanying us from the port of Piraeus to the antiquities of Corinth and the Corinth Canal did not know how to pronounce the words *southern* and *country*.

These are English words she constantly uses in her spoken commentary, but despite her admirable fluency in English she has been misled by the spelling into thinking they are pronounced with **aʊ**.

But we native English speakers don't say ˈ**saʊðən** and ˈ**kaʊntri**, we say ˈ**sʌðən** and ˈ**kʌntri**. The pair *south-southern* has the same vowel alternation as *profound-profundity*, though the spelling remains unchanged. And the vowel of *country* is different from that of *count*.

Why didn't they teach our tour guide this when she was at school, or later at college when she was training to be a tourist guide?

While we're on the subject, the adjective from *mountain* is not **maʊnˈteɪniəs**. And *abroad* has a different vowel from *road*. These are other details of English pronunciation that she doesn't know.

I readily admit, dear tour guide, that all your English-speaking clients understand you with no difficulty and enjoy your informative commentaries (even if some of us know that your assertions about Greek history are sometimes a bit . . . exaggerated). I agree that your fine command of English grammar and vocabulary far exceeds my own feeble efforts to speak your language, with only my basic Modern Greek grammar and my seriously deficient vocabulary.

But at least I can pronounce your language correctly. If I want to say 'I don't know', I say **ðeŋ** ˈ**gzero** or even **ðe** ˈ**gzero**. I do not let myself be misled by your antiquated Greek spelling δεν ξέρω *dhen kséro* into imagining I ought to say **ðen** ˈ**ksero**, because I am aware that if I did that I would sound like a foreigner.

I know about the allophonic distribution of palatals and velars in your language: I know that έχω *ékho* 'I have' has a velar fricative, ˈ**exo**, while έχετε *ékhete* 'you have' has a palatal fricative, ˈ**eçete**. I can produce the appropriate sound in each case, though the spelling does not reflect the difference.

If you were to greet me with the traditional Greek words **kaˈlos ˈirθate** καλώς ήρθατε *kalós írthate* 'well have you come', I know to reply **kaˈlos saz ˈvrikame** καλώς σας βρήκαμε *kalós sas vríkame* 'well have we found you', making the voicing assimilation that Greek speakers do, but that is not shown in the spelling.

Wouldn't it be a good thing if you likewise had learnt the correct pronunciation of this handful of English words that are so essential for your profession? I'm just saying.

Actually, we English speakers got our own back (in one sense) later in the cruise. Our American cruise director, as we prepared to set sail from Mykonos, two days after our visit to what he called **kəˈrɪnθ** (i.e. *Corinth*, which I of course call **ˈkɒrɪnθ**), declared that our next port of call would be **ˈtʃeɪnɪə**, which I suppose is a reasonable guess at its pronunciation, given that it was listed in our printed itinerary as *Chania*. But unlike the cruise director, the ship's captain was Greek, so he of course pronounced Χανιά *Khaniá* correctly as **xaˈnja**.

15 Accents

15.1 Shadow of Death

As a teenager I discovered a useful trick to stave off boredom when sitting through dull sermons: mentally transcribe what was being said into shorthand, or translate it mentally into another language.

Once I learnt phonetics, I could extend this ploy by listening carefully to **how** what was said was said and perhaps transcribing it phonetically in my mind.

So when I attended a Montserratian wake for my partner's aunt, who had died at the age of 96, that is what I found myself doing. The wake is known as a *nine-night*, because it takes place nine nights after the death of the person being mourned. It is held in the house where the deceased lived, and consists of a religious part (prayers, hymn-singing, comforting the family members) followed by a party with food, drink, and increasingly animated conversation continuing into the small hours of the morning.

The religious part was led on this occasion was led by a West Indian lady, presumably a Pentecostalist, whose oral technique consisted largely of slow shouting, with a lot of repetition. (So different from my late father's quiet and thoughtful Anglican mode of public prayer.)

Tiring of the repetitive content, I started listening to her English pronunciation, and was struck by an unusual intrusive r, in the phrase which you will recognize as coming from the 23rd Psalm, *the valley of the shadow of death*. Repeatedly she said **di ˈvali ə di ˈʃadər av ˈdet**.

If you reduce the final unstressed GOAT vowel in words such as *shadow* to ə, as happens in many non-standard accents, then in non-rhotic accents intrusive **r** is likely to result.

This reduction also leads to uncertainty in spelling for the not-too-literate (since, e.g., *pillow* and *pillar* are now homophones.) A case in point was Dickens's Mr Wackford Squeers, headmaster of Dotheboys Hall in *Nicholas Nickleby*, who liked to impart the correct spelling of W-I-N-D-E-R [sic] by the practical method of getting the boys to clean them.

15.2 An Epiphany

One of my friends on the social media, an accountant from Birmingham, told me she had had what is nowadays known as an 'epiphany': a sudden realization. She mentioned that she was 'truly shocked' that so many people seem to think there's a difference between the *u* in *put* and the *u* in *cut*. Indeed, someone had explained to her that the 'Standard English' pronunciation for the vowel sounds in *put* and *cut* was the same as those in *took* and *tuck*. Her reaction was 'to me all those vowels are exactly the same and I can't even imagine a difference'.

So I said,

I could give a lecture about this, or several ... Yes, southerners, RP speakers, Americans, Australians (nearly everyone in fact except English midlanders and northerners) make a difference between the vowel of *put* and that of *cut*.

And she said,

> This week is honestly the first time I've been aware of it. Now I need to find a person who speaks properly to demonstrate for me!

Her friend from Leicester comments:

> I pronounce them the same. Mind you, we have our own *u* sound in Leicester, so I think I deserve a prize for having dropped that for something else, even if I apply it to both *cut* and *put*, *cud* and *could*;)

It's interesting that native speakers quite easily notice phonetic (realizational) differences between their own speech and other people's, implicitly or explicitly, but are very slow to become aware of phonological (systemic) differences. In my experience, Americans quite often find it hard to believe that we British distinguish the vowels of *bother* and *father*, the Scots are surprised that the rest of us don't have *good* and *food* as rhymes, as even we non-rhotic English people can find it quite difficult to get our heads round the fact that most speakers of English (but not us) distinguish *stork* from *stalk*.

15.3 Kerry, Carrie, and Carey

An American correspondent wrote to ask about sets of word such as *merry*, *marry*, and *Mary*, which he pronounces identically while being aware that people outside North America distinguish them.

> The confusion for me comes not in how the vowels sound, but how they are determined. Is there an orthographical rule that covers this effectively?

I replied that generally speaking, the *merry* words (with the DRESS vowel, i.e. RP **e**, transcribed by some as **ɛ**) are spelt with the letter *e*. The *marry* set (with the TRAP vowel, i.e. RP **æ**, alternatively transcribed **a**) are spelt with *a*, in positions where you would expect a short vowel. The *Mary* set (with the SQUARE vowel, i.e. RP **eə**, alternatively transcribed **ɛ:**) are also spelt with *a*, or *ai*, etc, in positions where you would expect a long vowel.

Merry, berry, terror, error, peril, very, bury, Jerry, Kerry have DRESS. *Marry, carry, arrow, narrow, carol, barrel, baron/barren, arid, charity* have TRAP. *Mary, vary, area, bear(er), fair(y), precarious, Pharaoh* have SQUARE.

There are one or two words where not all speakers do the same thing, e.g. *Charing Cross*. Note too the alternation in *compare* (SQUARE) – *comparison* (TRAP). Although a *baron* has TRAP, some bearers of the surname *Baron* pronounce it with the SQUARE vowel. The words *very* and *bury* have misleading spellings: they are both DRESS words, rhyming with *merry*, not with *weary* or *fury*. *Apparent* has TRAP, but *parent* has SQUARE, while speakers disagree about *transparent*. *Heritage* and *inherit* have DRESS, but *heir(ess)* has SQUARE (and no **h**).

Not all North Americans have merged all three vowels before a following **r**. There are various parts of the United States in which some or all of the distinctions are preserved. Outside North America, though, all kinds of native English preserve them, though not of course with vowel qualities identical to those of RP.

15.4 *-ing*

The sociolinguists have demonstrated that most native speakers of English fluctuate between two forms of the *-ing* ending: the 'high' (H) variant **ɪŋ**, with a velar nasal, and the 'low' (L) variant **ɪn, ən**, with an alveolar nasal.

Here I'm not discussing words that just happen to end in *-ing* (such as *king, string, wing, thing*), but those that contain the verbal suffix *-ing* (such as *rubbing, finishing, charming*). The alternation applies equally to present participials and gerunds (even though in Old English they were distinct from one another). A few other words with weak *-ing* are affected (*ceiling, pudding, morning, evening* . . .). Compounds such as *hamstring* are not affected. The *-thing* compounds (*something, anything, nothing, everything*) are special cases.

The difference is stylistic, with the H variant being used in formal situations and the L in informal/colloquial situations. Just where the line is drawn between the two possibilities varies, depending on social class and other factors.

Using the L variant is popularly known as 'dropping one's g's', although in surface phonetics it is a matter of place of articulation rather than of omitting something. It is of course shown in writing by the use of an apostrophe, putting *-in'* in place of *-ing*. People from the north of England or certain parts of the United States who retain **g** in *sing, hang, lung*, and so on also retain it in their H variant of *-ing* **ɪŋg**. For them, calling the use of the L variant 'g dropping' makes more sense than it does for the rest of us.

The L variant also has the subvariant syllabic **n̩**, used particularly after **t** (→ **ʔ**) and **d**, as in *putting* ˈpʊtɪn, ˈpʊtn̩, ˈpʊʔn̩ and *pudding* ˈpʊdn̩.

Both ɪn and n̩ are obviously also subject to possible dealveolar assimilation, producing forms with **m** and (!) **ŋ̍**. So for *running* we can have H ˈrʌnɪŋ or L ˈrʌnɪn, ˈrʌnən. Because of possible assimilation (regressive or progressive), if we are faced with ˈrʌnɪŋ ˈkwɪkli or ˈteɪkŋ̍ ˈʃɔːt the distinction between H and L is neutralized.

At the top of the social scale there is a smallish group of speakers who use H (velar) under virtually all circumstances. At the bottom there is a rather larger group who virtually always use L (alveolar). The lyrics of popular music often mandate the L variant (often shown in writing, too: *Runnin' Wild*).

Personally I have to admit membership of the first group. I don't believe I ever use the L variant except for jocular or other special effect ('linguistic slumming').

I remember when BBC English, many years ago, assigned me a producer who used the L variant extremely frequently. I was shocked at my own gut reaction, which was that he must be ignorant and uneducated, so much so that I found it difficult to take his opinions seriously.

Because it is so socially sensitive, this variable also generates hypercorrections. In *Accents of English* (p. 263) I mentioned as examples of this *a braz*[ɪŋ] *(brazen) hussy* and *Badmi*[ŋ]*ton*. The other day I heard a nice one from a railway station announcer: *Harpenden* pronounced as ˈhɑːpɪŋdən. A correspondent mentions *driving less*[ɪŋz] *(lessons)*.

15.5 Fronted GOOSE

A correspondent writes to express his worries about what he sees as recent 'unwelcome' developments in English pronunciation.

One of them is the use of a close central vowel, **ʉː** or thereabouts, rather than a fully back **uː**, in words of the GOOSE set. If you compare a typical contemporary English vowel in *ooh!* with that of German *Uhu* ˈuːhuː 'eagle owl', you will notice the difference. English learners of German nowadays find it difficult to pronounce *Uhu* or *Fuß* **fuːs** 'foot' correctly (see Section 13.8).

To varying degrees, this 'GOOSE Fronting' characterizes not only English English but also many other varieties, including some American and much southern-hemisphere English.

Long before this recent development, getting on for a century ago in fact, Daniel Jones pointed out that English **uː** is not as back as the cardinal-type quality that one hears in German. In my 1971 PhD thesis I commented on the backness of Jamaican **uː** as compared to what is usual in England. But it was Caroline Henton who first properly documented the new fronting of RP GOOSE, in her 1983 article 'Changes in the vowels of Received Pronunciation', *JPhon* 11:353–371.

Where does this development come from? As with most other sound changes, nobody really knows. But Jones pointed out in his *Outline*, again a century ago, that an 'advanced' variety of **uː** was used after **j**, as in *music* ˈmjuːzɪk. So perhaps what happened was essentially a takeover by this allophone, which became the default realization in all positions and thus displaced the backer variety used in words like *spoon* and *food* in conservative speech.

Since then things have gone further: today in England one can hear not only mid or front varieties of GOOSE, but also unrounded front vowels, risking confusion between *two* and *tea* or *goose* and *geese*.

As Jack Windsor Lewis has put it,

> Hardly anyone in the English-speaking world used a fully back version of **u**: [...] unless they wished to sound 'beautifully spoken' (or 'refained') for comic effect. But a very large proportion especially of younger speakers in England have very markedly advanced and weakly if at all rounded values, making *too true* much more like *tee tree* than it is in more conservative accents. It's possible of many younger speakers to be unsure on occasion whether they've said the word *illumination* or *elimination* or the name *Gillian* or *Julian*.

A consequence of this is that many native speakers of English have difficulty in acquiring a properly back **u** for use in foreign languages. The best advice I can give a language learner in this position is to practise whistling (which makes you round your lips). Whistle the very lowest-pitched note you can, then make a vowel sound with your tongue and lips in that position. The result should be a really back rounded **u**. Then repeat this procedure, with a higher-pitched note. That should give you a front(er) rounded **y**. Use your newly-acquired **u** for languages like Italian, Spanish, and Polish, and for the German *u* of *Buch, Uhu*, and the French *ou* of *roux*. Use your **y** for the *ü* of German *Bücher, süß* and the *u* of French *rue*.

Another technique for achieving a really back rounded **u** is to isolate the **w** of English *wall* **wɔːɫ** and then prolong it. The **ɔ**: vowel and the dark **ɫ** help to keep the articulation back rather than front (see Section 13.8).

15.6 The Quality of SQUARE

I tend to assume that my readers and correspondents have the kind of basic knowledge of linguistics that would include an understanding of how the term 'phoneme' is used (despite the fact that more sophisticated phonologists may well consider that the concept of the phoneme is unsustainable and based on ultimately untenable theoretical assumptions).

But some of the queries I receive show that this is not necessarily the case. Or at least people are not comfortable with the convention that slashes / / are used to enclose symbols for phonemes, but that symbols for speech sounds (or realizations or allophones or variants) properly go inside square brackets []. (Or you can do as I do in this book and merely embolden phonetic symbols without reference to their phonological status unless relevant.)

I was asked:

> I would like to know your point of view about /eə/ and /ɛː/. Cruttenden lists [the change from the first to the second] among the 'changes almost complete'. Also Collins and Mees, in their *Practical Phonetics and Phonology*, have already opted for the /ɛː/ symbol since 2003. The open /ɛː/ is the only one found in Upton's ODP too [...] I was wondering why both in your LPD and the EPD this alternative pronunciation is not transcribed. I might be wrong, but in my opinion, the /ɛː/ phoneme could now be considered as part of the phonetic inventory of current BrE.

This question is of course not about phonemes but about the realization and notation of one particular phoneme (the SQUARE vowel). Here's what I replied.

> I am of course well aware of the monophthongal variant of the SQUARE vowel. Please read what I wrote at www.phon.ucl.ac.uk/home/wells/ipa-english-uni.htm. In LPD I took the decision to be conservative in phonetic notation for RP, sticking for example with Gimson's EPD symbols for the TRAP and GOAT vowels. Upton has made a different decision (including a very regrettable notation for the PRICE vowel). I personally have a centring diphthong as my usual pronunciation of SQUARE in most phonetic positions. Perhaps that shows my age.
>
> I shall not be changing the transcription in any future edition of LPD, but I agree I ought to insert a note to the effect that many people use a monophthongal quality for eə. This, however, is not a new 'phoneme', as you seem to believe. It is an alternative realization of an existing phoneme. There is no possibility of words being distinguished by the choice between the monophthongal and diphthongal variants of SQUARE.

Was I being too pedantic? If so, it's what comes of a lifetime reading and commenting on students' essays.

Anyhow, the take-home message is that monophthongal SQUARE is fine. But not obligatory.

15.7 The Poet and the Phonetician

> A commentator on my blog, Ed Aveyard, wrote

> Some working-class people have the idea that a schwa [in certain unstressed syllables] is lazy and that 'posh people' don't use them [but they do, in fact]. Believe it or not, I've come across people who think that you're **supposed** to say *Garforth* with final fɔːθ and *Castleford* with final fɔːd. I wonder if some announcers have grown up with this idea of 'correct' speech and that it's coming into BBC English now.

Truly, there's nothing new under the sun. Just over a hundred years ago, in 1910, Daniel Jones, then just setting out on his career as a phonetician and not yet widely known, was forcefully attacked by Robert Bridges, the recently appointed Poet Laureate and a founder member of the Society for Pure English.

Bridges was much exercised about standards of pronunciation. As Collins and Mees put it (*The Real Professor Higgins*, Mouton 1999, Section 4.11)

> Bridges believed sincerely that the pronunciation of English was gravely threatened by declining standards, and was therefore determined to fight to restore it to what he considered to be its proper state.

In Bridges' view, its proper state was one that closely reflected the orthography. He was particularly concerned with what he termed 'the degradation of the unaccented vowels' – by which he meant the use of ə in unstressed syllables.

Quoting Jones's *Phonetic Transcriptions of English Prose* (Oxford 1907), Bridges apostrophizes the reader as follows.

> Now please observe, most gracious reader, that this is not a dream nor a joke. It shows the actual present condition of things, as formulated by an expert, promulgated by the University of Oxford, and recommended *ter* foreigners. Foreigners are really being taught that the pronunciation of *to* (tū), which is hundreds of years old, is now changed to *ter* (tə), and that in our 'careful conversation' we say *ter* and *inter* for *to* and *into*.

Mountain and *cabbage* ought, of course, in Bridges' view, to be pronounced with **eɪ** in the final syllable. *Ambulance* ought to have **-æns**. The poet continues:

> The only question can be whether Mr. Jones exaggerates the actual prevalence of degradation. Some will acquit him of any exaggeration. Others I know very well will regard him as a half-witted faddist, beneath serious notice, who should be left to perish in his vain imaginings.

'Vain imaginings' is a peculiarly inappropriate characterization of Jones's carefully observed and accurately reported descriptions of the educated pronunciation of his day.

Jones, by the way, reports that Bridges

> didn't speak with his reformed pronunciation; his pronunciation was very much like mine, except that he made rather freer use of the obscure vowel to which he took such strong objection.

In 1926 Bridges was appointed Chairman of the BBC's Advisory Committee on Spoken English. Jones, who by then was Professor of Phonetics in the University of London, was one of its members.

15.8 Fair's Fur

Walking along a street in central Liverpool one day, I was intrigued to see a hairdresser's punningly called *Ben Hair*. It took me back.

(Explanation: in Scouse, the local accent of Liverpool, the SQUARE and NURSE vowels are merged. Think chariot races.)

We had the same merger where I grew up, although our local accent was Lancashire rather than Scouse. When I was at primary school there was a girl in the class called ˈmɜːrɪ. I would clutch 5d ˈfaɪfpəns in my hand every day to pay my ˈbʊs fɜː. (That would have been a ˈθrepni ˈbɪt and two pennies.)

Those who remember Cilla Black (a Scouser) from the television programme *Blind Date* will recall that she was forever introducing girls called klɜː or ˈsɜːrə.

> In our Liverpool home,
> In our Liverpool home,
> We speak with an accent exceedingly rɜː,
> We meet under a statue exceedingly bɜː,
> If you want a cathedral we've got one to spɜː,
> In our Liverpool home.

15.9 Going on Twur

South African English seems to be moving towards twɜː for *tour* and pwɜː for *poor*. The ɜː in this environment is rounded, and could narrowly be written [ɞː].

This represents a development comparable to the change in the NEAR diphthong from ɪə to jɜː that is familiar from South Welsh English (and treated by Daniel Jones as an RP possibility in EPD, an option dropped by Gimson when he took over as editor). Both changes constitute a switch from a falling (diminuendo) diphthong to a rising (crescendo) one, and are thus a very natural kind of development. The syllabicity moves from the first, close segment to the second, mid one. A diphthong is recast as a semivowel plus strong vowel.

The putative South African change is structurally identical to the South Welsh one, but back rather than front: ʊə → wɜː reflects ɪə → jɜː.

15.10 Double Affricates

In the local pronunciation of Standard English on the island of Montserrat one striking feature is the reduction of affricate sequences. In most varieties of English spoken elsewhere, an affricate is preserved as such when followed by another affricate: we say *each chair* with -tʃtʃ- and *orange juice* with -dʒdʒ- (usually). But in Montserrat tʃ and dʒ are reduced to unexploded t and d, respectively, when followed by another affricate. Not only do we get -ttʃ- in *each chair* and -ddʒ- in *orange juice*, we also get -ttr- in *each trip*, -tdr- in *church drive*, and -ddr- in *a large drop*. (This makes *each cheese* sound identical to *eat cheese* iːttʃiːz. In these transcriptions tt, td, dt and dd stand for a single plosive articulation with a long hold phase, as in the usual pronunciation of *good dog* gʊd dɒg, and unglottalized *that dog* ðæt dɒg. The place of articulation depends on whether the affricate is palatoalveolar or postalveolar, as in simple affricates.)

For ages I had been trying to puzzle out a radio jingle played on the local radio station, Radio ZJB, to advertise the Bank of Montserrat,

> But for **iːt** transaction
> You will get swift action ...

– until suddenly I realized that they were singing *but for each transaction*.

15.11 EE RIP

David Rosewarne's great claim to fame is that in October 1984, in an article published in the *Times Educational Supplement*. he coined the expression 'Estuary English'.

In doing so he gave expression to the widespread perception that Daniel Jones-style RP was gradually losing its status as the unquestioned standard accent of educated English people. Or, putting it a different way, that RP was changing by absorbing various sound changes that previously had been restricted to Cockney or other non-prestigious varieties.

Two years earlier, in my *Accents of English*, I had written,

> Throughout [London], the working-class accent is one which shares the general characteristics of Cockney. We shall refer to this accent as **popular London** [...] Middle-class speakers typically use an accent closer to RP than popular London. *But the vast majority of such speakers nevertheless have some regional characteristics* [emphasis added]. This kind of accent might be referred to as London (or, more generally, south-eastern) Regional Standard.

I continued,

> Points of difference between it and RP might typically include greater allophonic variation in the GOOSE vowel (two compared with tool) and the GOAT vowel (go compared with goal), less Smoothing in words such as fire and power, being and doing, a certain amount of T Glottalling in prevocalic environments, and a readiness to use [i] rather than [ɪ] in happy words. So London Regional Standard might have [tʉː, tuːɫ, gɜʊ, gʌ-oɫ, fɑ+ɪə ~ fa-ɪə, pa-ʏə ~ pɑ+ʏə, ˈbɪiŋ, ˈdʊʉŋ, ðæʔˈɪz, ˈhæpi] as against RP [tuː, tuːɫ, gɜʊ, gɜʊɫ, fa-ːə, pɑ+ːə, ˈbɪŋ, ˈdʊɪŋ, ðæt ˈɪz, ˈhæpɪ].

I added the warning,

> It must be remembered that labels such as 'popular London', 'London Regional Standard' do not refer to entities we can reify but to areas along a continuum stretching from broad Cockney (itself something of an abstraction) to RP.

So Rosewarne's observations in a sense contained nothing new. He muddied the waters unhelpfully by referring to details of vocabulary and grammar (which have nothing to do with 'a new variety of pronunciation'). But the name he coined, Estuary English, was taken up quite widely, gaining resonance eventually not only with journalists but also with the general public, to such an extent that we can now expect to be readily understood if we describe someone's speech as 'estuarial'.

The estuary Rosewarne was thinking of was of course the Thames estuary, which in a geographical sense might be interpreted as extending from Teddington near Kingston upon Thames (the point where the river becomes tidal) down to Southend-on-Sea (where the Thames enters the North Sea). Rosewarne's original article says 'the heartland of this variety lies by the banks of the Thames and its estuary, but it seems to be the most influential accent in the south-east of England'; though later writers, particularly Coggle in his *Do You Speak Estuary?* (1993) implied that it covered the entire southeast of the country.

It was in response to media and academic interest in the topic that in 1998 I set up a website 'to bring together as many documents as possible that relate to Estuary English, as a convenient resource for the many interested enquirers.' As academics were able bit by bit to investigate the truth of Rosewarne's claims, I did my best to publish (or link to) their research findings.

In my view the most important of these were those by Joanna Przedlacka, incorporated in her 2002 book *Estuary English? A Sociophonetic Study of Teenage Speech in the Home Counties* (ISBN 3-631-39340-7, Bern: Peter Lang). This work, as I put it,

> demolishes the claim that EE is a single entity sweeping the southeast. Rather, we have various sound changes emanating from working-class London speech, each spreading independently.

Rosewarne's suggestion that EE 'may become the RP of the future' had already led to credulous excitement in the EFL world, particularly in central Europe and South America. Was it time to ditch RP and teach this trendy new variety?

One thing I did myself was to consider how we might agree on a phonetic transcription scheme, which would be needed for pedagogical purposes if we seriously wanted to teach this putative new accent. I suggested that we might make the following differences from RP in transcribing EE:

- for *-ing* optionally write EE **-ɪn**; for *-thing* optionally write EE **-θɪŋk**
- for RP dark l, write EE **o**
- for RP **t** when between {a vowel or sonorant} and {a consonant or word boundary}, write EE **ʔ**
- for RP **tj, dj** write EE **tʃ, dʒ**
- for RP **aɪ, aʊ** write EE **ɑɪ, æʊ**
- for RP **n̩** in various positions, write EE **ən**
- for *twenty, plenty, want(ed, ing, it, us), went* (before a vowel), in EE optionally reduce **nt** to simple **n**

But no one followed this up by criticizing my proposals or suggesting anything better.

All the excitement gradually died down. I last had cause to update the website in 2007. In the 2008 edition of LPD, my brief summary of the issue in the current was this.

> RP itself inevitably changes as the years pass. There is also a measure of diversity within it. Furthermore, the democratization undergone by English society during the second half of the twentieth century means that it is nowadays necessary to define RP in a rather broader way than was once customary. [The dictionary] includes a number of pronunciations that diverge from traditional, 'classical' RP. The 'RP' transcriptions shown in [the dictionary] in fact cover very much more than a narrowly defined RP.

EFL teachers, meanwhile, mostly know that at most we just need to update our pedagogical model of RP in the minor ways I have outlined.

In Britain media interest in the EE phenomenon has now died down, and it is many years since I have had anything to add to the website. Nevertheless, students around the world continue to write to me asking for advice or help on research they say they are carrying out on Estuary English. Unfortunately many of them are not in a position to collect actual speaker data from people in the southeast of England, so their 'research' has to be an armchair study.

> I'm interested in doing some research on Estuary English and Received Pronunciation in order to do my thesis project ... I would like to ask you if you knew or if you had any information about the percentage of usage of L-vocalization, the use of the glottal stop in final position and before consonants, and Yod-coalescence in tonic syllables. Is there any comparison between RP and EE speakers regarding the use of [these] features? ... I would very much [like to] know your opinion on the current status of RP, and whether you think EE might replace it as the accent of EFL in the short term.

What can one say? Here's what I actually said.

> Please read (or reread) Joanna Przedlacka's work. The point is that there is no real definable entity called Estuary English. You can't divide up the speakers in the southeast into those who speak EE and those who speak something else. So there can be no comparative statistics of the kind you ask for. All we can do (given money, time, and effort) is to estimate the proportions of the population of a given area who do glottalling etc in given phonetic environments and in given styles of speech.
>
> If someone uses a relatively high proportion of glottalling, you might say 'Ah! This must be a speaker of EE.' If you define EE speakers as those who use a lot of glottalling, you will indeed find that EE speakers use more glottalling than RP speakers (etc). But this argumentation is circular, therefore unscientific. A scientific approach would be to divide your speakers up by social class or some other non-linguistic criterion, then establish the possible correlation of phonetic variables such as glottalling with the nonphonetic variables.

All we have is various sound changes in progress. Many sound changes seem to spread out from London and from the working class into the middle class (and defining social class is another scientific nightmare). These sound changes all move at different rates. This kind of thing has certainly been going on in English English for at least five hundred years.

As of 2015, the leader of the Conservative party, David Cameron, is an Old Etonian and an archetypal RP speaker. But political commentators sometimes assert (with what truth I do not know) that he tries to make his speech sound more popular by using glottal stops. How does that relate to 'the current status of RP'?

For EE to be used as the sole or main pronunciation model in EFL someone would have first to define it clearly and then produce learning materials (dictionaries, textbooks, etc) using it. I don't see any likelihood of that happening. Rather, BrE-oriented ELT will continue to be based on a modernized version of RP (aka Standard Southern British English or just General British).

15.12 A Four-Letter Word

I've never been one to utter what in English are quaintly known as four-letter words. My parents never swore, my brothers don't swear, my partner doesn't swear. My colleagues at work didn't, most of my friends don't.

Not using a word oneself doesn't necessarily mean not being familiar with it in the mouths of others. In Section 6.8 I mentioned how I still remember my surprise at boarding school in the south of England when, having grown up in the north (but in an RP-speaking family), I first heard a southerner say **fʌk**. Till then I'd supposed the word to be **fʊk**, as pronounced by northerners with no FOOT-STRUT split.

Perhaps that discovery was one of the things that made me so interested in phonetics.

But I hope that we're gradually getting the message across that students will benefit from being exposed to a wide range of different varieties of English, just as native speakers are.

15.13 Bajans

One Saturday morning I was at the supermarket doing my weekly shop. I had just picked up a pack of kitchen towels and put them in my shopping trolley when my attention was caught by a woman pointing out to her husband that there was a special offer on a brand I had not chosen which made them a much better bargain than the ones I had taken. So I put mine back, picked her brand instead and briefly joined in their conversation.

They hadn't uttered more than two or three phrases, but from their speech I could tell that they were from Barbados. So I boldly said, 'You're Bajans, aren't you?'. Yes, she replied, we are: how did you know, have you been to Barbados? And we had a brief chat about the attractions of their native island.

It would be possible at this point for me to start listing the characteristics of Barbadian English that make it sound different from other Caribbean varieties: the rhoticity, the raised PRICE vowel ʌi ~ əi, the glottal stops, the unusual rhythm. But my recognizing the accent was not a matter of taking note of each of these characteristics in turn and computing the implications. Rather, it was intuitive recognition of a gestalt, a complete unanalysed pattern of sounds. I think this is how we typically recognize accents we're familiar with.

My three-volume *Accents of English* was published a third of a century ago, in 1962. You will not be surprised to know that I did not write this work by systematically starting at the beginning and working through chapter by chapter until I reached the end. Rather, I jumped around doing something here, something there, as opportunity provided. And my short section on Barbados was one of the first I drafted.

The stimulus for this was our being invited to dinner by a couple we knew in London, one of whom was Bajan, and spending the evening with them. This would have been in the early seventies. I don't think I was quite so rude as to make notes as we were talking, but as soon as I was on my own I certainly hastened to write down my phonetic impressions of his speech. The next day I wrote them up, and gave my essay to J.D. O'Connor, my supervisor for the PhD on Jamaican I had recently completed, for his comments.

At that time I had never visited Barbados. But in January 1978 I was able to spend a few days there on the way back from my first visit to Montserrat, after which I revised and extended what became Section 7.2.4, Barbados, of *Accents of English* (Cambridge University Press 1982, three volumes).

15.14 A Jamaican Allophone

When I was working on West Indian English, there were not many observations that I made that were really original. But one that was concerned the semivowel **w**. I noticed that in Jamaican (and often no doubt in other Caribbean varieties) it has a labial-palatal allophone [ɥ] before front vowels, thus *wheel* **ɥiːl**, *west* **ɥes**, *swim* **sɥɪm**, etc. As far as I know, no one had noticed this before.

As with various other features of Caribbean English, this characteristic can be explained as due to a West African substratum.

In Akan (Asante Twi) of Ghana, all consonants are palatalized before front vowels. This includes the semivowel **w**. So phonemic /**wi**/ is realized as phonetic [ɥi]. The alveolar plosives are also affricated in this environment: the name of the language, *Twi*, is accordingly pronounced **tɕɥi**.

Although the labial-palatal semivowel allophone made it across the Atlantic, the affrication did not: Jamaican *twist* is **tɥɪs**, not *****tɕɥɪs**.

15.15 He Nar Get None

This is another comment on Montserratian Creole English (see Section 6.2). It was provoked by a news report I saw on the web. Under the headline *Premier Meade Says Montserrat Is Blessed and 'He Nar Get None'* I read:

> During the statement, whilst talking about sand mining, the Premier sought to take a dig at Montserrat born calypsonian De Bear, for his 2012 hit song entitled *All Ah Dem Ah Get* by stating that contrary to insinuations in the very popular song, Meade stated, 'me nar get none.'

The point of interest here is the spelling *nar* for the Creole word pronounced **na:**. This is a function/structure/grammar word/particle used in certain Caribbean creoles (certainly in Jamaican and Montserratian, at least) but not in standard English. Its meaning is a combination of negation and progressive aspect, 'not . . . -ing'. The calypsonian's claim **a:l a dem a get** could be paraphrased in standard English as 'they are all getting', 'they're all on the take', and the premier's riposte as 'I'm not getting any'. Contrary to the calypsonian's assertion, he was not profiting from his premiership.

The Dictionary of Jamaican English DJE spells this word *naa*, in accordance with the phonemic spelling system devised by Fred Cassidy for Jamaican Creole and now recommended by the Jamaican Language Unit at the University of the West Indies as a 'standard writing system for Jamaica'. You also sometimes see the spelling *nah*. (In JC, but not MC, the progressive aspect is also used to refer to habitual action: *nah gwan a Jamaica* 'don't go on in Jamaica'.) But Jamaicans never spell it *nar* (the spelling used in the report from Montserrat that I saw), and for a very good reason: in JC this particle does not rhyme with *car, far, tar*, etc, which in JC retain their historical **r** in pronunciation (**kjaːr, faːr, taːr**).

Montserratian Creole, however, is non-rhotic. There **naː** rhymes exactly with **faː** and so on, making it common sense to spell it in the same way, with an *r*. Just as other non-rhotic speakers would if they had to.

15.16 *Bawl* and *Ball*

My American colleague Karen Chung, commenting on a picture of fractious children comforted by Santa with the caption *bawl game over*, asked,

> Are *bawl* and *ball* pronounced the same for everybody? Or differently?

I replied,

> I'm not aware of any variety of English in which they are distinct.

We know, of course, that many Americans do not distinguish the LOT and THOUGHT sets (although many other Americans do): but that's not the issue. If there are people who consistently distinguish *bawl* from *ball* (and Karen insists that she is one such), then we have to recognize a split within the THOUGHT set, with an otherwise unreported choice of vowel in *ball*.

It turns out that for Karen *ball* rhymes with *doll* and *Moll*, as well as with *tall, wall, fall, call, hall*, etc; but not with words spelled with *aul* or *awl*, e.g. *haul, maul, scrawl, trawl*.

I was interested to hear this, but I continue to find it odd that there is no mention of this possibility in Kenyon's *American Pronunciation* or as far as I can tell in any other descriptions of American English phonetics. How come that no one seems to have mentioned it before?

Karen comments further,

> For me, the *a* in *ball* is the allophone of /ɑ/ which occurs before /l/ and is slightly rounded; the *au* and *aw* are the /ɔ/ phoneme, which has more inherent rounding. I expect I'm one of a minority, but it looks like others from my part of the US (Minnesota) and in my age group do have the distinction.

She also kindly supplied a sound file in support of her description. Even if only a small number of people have this distinction, it certainly should be studied and mentioned in the literature.

We do have a comparable phenomenon in BrE, in the shape of the choice between ɔː and ɒ in words spelt *als* or *alt* – words such as *false, salt, fault, halt, also*. Since I knew about this at the time I wrote *Accents of English*, I created a special subsection (b) for THOUGHT, to cater for it (p. 146). If I'd known about Karen's type of AmE, I'd have catered for that too: but at that time I'd never come across any mention of it.

My Japanese colleague Takehiko Makino reports an American from the Midwest who merges THOUGHT and LOT with ɑ, but nevertheless has a rounded ɒ in the three words *calm, palm*, and *psalm*, though not in words such as *father*. A recording of this speaker accompanies his 2005 Japanese book on English. He also tells me of another Midwesterner, a recording of whose voice accompanies Shigeru Takebayashi's 1991 Japanese book on English phonetics: she maintains the distinction between the LOT and THOUGHT sets, but again uses her THOUGHT vowel for *calm, palm*, and *psalm*.

There's always something new to discover.

16 Lexical Stress

16.1 Prevalence

In English adjectives ending in the suffix *-ant* or *-ent* we still see the ghost of the Latin stress rule.

By this I mean that the word stress in such adjectives depends on how the stem to which the suffix is attached ends. (Obviously, we are dealing here with words of three or more syllables, i.e. with the suffix attached to a stem of two or more syllables.) If the stem ends in what Chomsky and Halle (*The Sound Pattern of English*, Harper & Row 1968) call a 'weak cluster', then the stress goes on the preceding syllable. If it ends in a 'strong cluster', then the stress goes on that syllable itself. A weak cluster consists of a short vowel followed by a maximum of one consonant. A strong cluster, on the other hand, has either a long vowel, or two or more following consonants, or both. So a weak cluster reflects a Latin single-mora ('light') syllable, while a strong cluster reflects a Latin multi-mora ('heavy') syllable.

The stress rule in Latin itself is: stress the penultimate if it is heavy (*impeˈrātōr; conˈfectus, asˈcendō*), otherwise stress the antepenultimate (*conˈfĭciō, ˈrăpĭdus*). Classicists call this the 'Penultimate Law' (W. Sidney Allen, *Vox Latina*, Cambridge University Press 1965, p. 83).

So in English we have on the one hand:

(i) ˈarrogant, belˈligerent, beˈnevolent, conˈstituent, ˈdecadent, ˈfumigant, perˈcipient, ˈpermanent, ˈreticent, sigˈnificant, ˈsubsequent

– with antepenultimate stress reflecting the Latin short vowel in *rŏgō, gĕrō, vŏlō*, etc; and on the other hand

(ii) exˈponent; abˈsorbent, aˈbundant, aˈstringent, correˈspondent, conˈvergent, inˈsistent, maˈlignant, reˈluctant

– with penultimate stress reflecting the Latin long vowel in *pōnō* and the consonant clusters in the other words.

In *acquiescent* and *abhorrent* the spellings *sc* and *rr* reflect what were consonant clusters in Latin, even though we now pronounce single consonants in English. In *apparent* the Latin vowel of *appārĕō* was long, even though we now pronounce it in BrE as short æ rather than as long eə. Conversely in *provident* Latin *-vĭd-* was short, generating antepenultimate stress, although we have a long vowel aɪ in *provide*.

It wouldn't be English if we didn't have a number of exceptions and irregularities. The vowel of Latin *plăcĕō* was short, yet we say *complacent* kəmˈpleɪsənt as if it were long. By rights *excellent* ought to be penultimate-stressed (Latin *excellens* with a double consonant), as should *protestant*. But they aren't.

All this is by way of a lead-in to an unusual pronunciation I heard the other day: *prevalent* pronounced not as the usual ˈ**prevələnt** but as **priˈveɪlənt**. Latin *vălĕō* had a short vowel, which is why most of us use antepenultimate stress not only in *prevalent* but also in *equivalent* and *ambivalent*.

I can see two factors which might lead someone to give this word penultimate stress, -ˈveɪl-. One is the verb *to prevail*, obviously related in morphology and (to some extent) in meaning. The other is chemical terminology, which has now spread to disciplines such as linguistics. In chemistry, *valency* ˈveɪlənsi (BrE) or *valence* ˈveɪləns (AmE) is a measure of the combining power of atoms of a given element. Chemists pronounce words such as *trivalent, pentavalent* and *multivalent* with penultimate stress, -ˈveɪlənt.

In LPD I do recognize the possibility of ˌæmbɪˈveɪlənt. But not yet of **priˈveɪlənt**. Ought I to?

16.2 Europeans and Shakespeareans

How do you pronounce the adjective from *Singapore*, i.e. *Singaporean*?

With most English suffixes we can be clear about their effect on word stress. Some have no effect at all, e.g. *-ing*. Some attract the main stress, e.g. *-eer, -ette*, as in *mountaiˈneer, kitcheˈnette*. Some cause the main stress to fall on the syllable before the suffix, e.g. *-ity*, as in *aˈcidity, viˈcinity*.

But with *-ean* there are two possibilities. In some cases it throws the main stress onto the preceding syllable, just like *-ity*. Thus we say *cruˈstacean, Proˈmethean* and *Shakeˈspearean*. But in other cases it attracts the main stress to itself. Thus we say *Euroˈpean, epicuˈrean, Herculean, Jacoˈbean, Pythagoˈrean*, and *Sisyˈphean*. (Not all these words may be in the average person's vocabulary, but anyhow that's what dictionaries give.)

In the case of *Caribbean* we are split. Some of us (mainly Americans) treat it like *Shakespearean* and say **kəˈrɪbiən**; others (mainly Brits) treat it like *European* and say ˌ**kærɪˈbiːən**.

Which brings us to *Singaporean*. In LPD I gave priority to ˌ**sɪŋəˈpɔːriən**, which is what Singaporeans themselves say; but I've heard one British television newsreader say ˌ**sɪŋəpɔːˈriːən**. (Irrelevantly, some speakers have **ɡ** after the **ŋ**. That's not what I'm focusing on.)

I think *Tyrolean* is equally variable.

At least with the less familiar words in *-ean* this uncertainty means that no one need worry about which stress pattern is correct.

16.3 Tautonyms

An unusual rodent pest found in a part of Hertfordshire is the edible or fat dormouse. Its scientific name is *Glis glis*. It is the only living member of the genus *Glis*. This is perhaps why, unusually for biological nomenclature, it has a specific name identical with its generic name. There are a few other such cases: the red fox, *Vulpes vulpes*, for example, and the Eurasian wren, *Troglodytes troglodytes*. We call these names tautonyms (Greek for 'same-names'). Zoologists allow them, but botanists don't.

The usual stress pattern for two-word names is double stressing (main stress on the second word), as in ˌHenry ˈSmith, ˌMerton ˈPark, ˌLyme ˈRegis. This also applies to the Latin names of plants and animals: ˌQuercus ˈrobur, Diˌcentra specˈtabilis, ˌEquus ˈzebra, ˌPasser doˈmesticus.

But in cases such as *Vulpes vulpes, Troglodytes troglodytes*, and *Glis glis* this usual pattern collides with the deep-seated Germanic principle of deaccenting repeated material. So do we keep double stressing, or do we deaccent the specific and shift the main stress onto the generic?

In the case of the edible dormouse, discussants on a television programme I happened to be watching went for the single stressing, pronouncing it furthermore as if it were a single word, a common noun, a ˈglɪsglɪs.

I have come across the spelling *Glis-glis*. Furthermore, people may treat this 'word' as invariant for number, like *sheep* ('Glis-glis are grey in colour'). – Well, you'd hardly expect them to know that the Latin plural of *glīs* is *glīrēs*. That's strictly for us classicist showoffs.

What do we do when referring to people whose forename is identical with their surname? What stress pattern do we use for someone called Morris Morris or Graham Graham? Do we find such names awkward? No, I think we cope and give them the usual double stressing. Same with New York, New York. So why should Glis glis be different for some people?

17 Connected Speech

17.1 Accenting the Unaccentable

A correspondent, a learner of EFL, asked me how I would pronounce the last word in each of the following sentences.

> I wouldn't say he was careful – in fact, I would say he was careless.
> I didn't say she was interesting, I said she was interested.

In deciding how to say these words, we are faced with conflicting rules. On the one hand, when contrasting two words or phrases like this we normally use a contrastive accent, placing it on the item under focus.

> I 'wouldn't say he was \/careful, | in 'fact I'd say he was \negligent.
> I 'didn't say she was \/interesting, | I said she was \boring.

There we've avoided my correspondent's problem by changing the wording so that it is words, rather than just morphemes, that are under contrastive focus.

But if we retain the wording he asks about, we come up against the second principle, namely that we normally place accents only on syllables that are lexically stressed. So perhaps we would have to say:

> I 'wouldn't say he was \/careful, | in 'fact I'd say he was \careless.
> I 'didn't say she was \/interesting, | I said she was \interested.

Can we override the second principle in the interests of the first? Speakers certainly sometimes do.

> I 'wouldn't say he was \/careful, | in 'fact I'd say he was 'care\less.
> I 'didn't say she was \/interesting, | I said she was 'interest\ed.

You can even accent the first half of each contrast as well as the second.

> I 'wouldn't say he was 'care\/ful, | in 'fact I'd say he was 'care\less.
> I didn't say she was 'interest\/ing, | I said she was 'interest\ed.

As for which of these options is the commonest, I have no data. If I were planning ahead as I spoke, I think I'd go for the last one I mention. And I'd pronounce the accented suffixes **fʊl, les, ɪŋ, ɪd**.

Similarly for

> We don't want \/theocracy, | we want \democracy.

– in which I'd pronounce ˈθiː- and **dem**-.

Taking matters further, how do we accent the absence of something? What if we logically need to accent zero?

Recall that when we use contrastive focus we do it by nuclear-accenting the contrasted item(s).

- It wasn't blue, | it was green.
- They weren't wicked, | they were just badly behaved.
- I don't want to interrogate you, | I'd just like to have a brief word or two with you.
- Was it your arm that got bitten?
- – No, it was my leg!

This may involve deaccenting a repeated item.

- It wasn't any old shade of green, | it was pea-green.
- Not only did I injure my hand, | it was my right hand.

Sometimes the contrastive element is not a complete word. We can place the nuclear accent on a contrastive morpheme.

- It wasn't lunchtime, | it was teatime.

But what if that morpheme is not lexically stressed? Can we still place a nuclear accent on it? Yes, we can.

- I didn't ask for a teapot, | I asked for a teacup.
- It wasn't really blue, | just bluish.

How do we treat cases like these?

- I'm not thin, | just thinner. (Can we accent *-er*?)
- I didn't say 'approach', | I said 'reproach'. (Can we accent *ap-* and *re-*?)
- They didn't accede, | they seceded. (Can we accent *ac-* and *se-*?)
- She wasn't attacking, | she was being attacked. (Can we accent *-ing*? What about *-ed*, phonetically just [t]?)

I don't think we really have any hard and fast rules about this. The speaker has to weigh up, as he goes along, the pressure to avoid accenting a repeated item and the contrary pressure not to accent a normally unstressed syllable.

These musings were provoked (not invoked!) by hearing a reading from the Bible during a church service. The relevant verse (Romans 12:2) ran

> And be not conformed to this world: but be ye transformed by the renewing of your mind, that ye may prove what is that good, and acceptable, and perfect, will of God.

I think I would have been tempted to pronounce

- And be not conformed | to this world: | but be ye transformed ...

But the person reading on this occasion gave us

- ... conformed | ... transformed ...

with **kən-** and **trɑːns-**.

During a broadcast political debate in the House of Commons, I heard a politician wanting to contrast *unemployment* and *employment*.

> Instead of harping on about unemployment, why doesn't he congratulate the Government on the increase in employment?

This politician duly put the first nuclear accent on *un-*, but was then faced with the problem of how to accent the antonym. And what he did was to shift the last nuclear accent not onto zero (the absence of *un-*), where it logically belonged, but onto the nearest available syllable.

- … about u̲nemployment, | … increase in employ̲ment?

And, interestingly, he didn't switch the vowel of *em-* to **e**, but kept it as **ɪ**.

- … əbaʊt ˈʌnɪmplɔɪmənt, | … ɪŋkriːs ɪn ɪmplɔɪmənt

17.2 Irritating Hamburgers

A correspondent from Spain wrote to ask about the rhythmic patterns of words such as *irritating*.

> If Spanish speakers are asked to place the primary stress in the correct place …, they will invariably make the last syllable 'pulsed'. If they are asked to pulse lightly on any vowel between the primary stress and the last syllable, they will turn this light pulse into the primary stress of the word, i.e. they will say either ˈɪrɪteɪˌtɪŋ or ɪrɪˈteɪtɪŋ but not ˈɪrɪˌteɪtɪŋ.

This question relates to possible posttonic secondary stress, which is bound up with the important distinction in English between strong and weak vowels.

To recap, the weak vowels in English are **i, u**, and **ə**. The strong vowels are all the rest. (Exceptionally, ɪ and ʊ can be either strong or weak. Under **ə** we include all the syllabic consonants, including AmE ɚ.) In *irritating* ˈɪrɪteɪtɪŋ the vowels are strong, weak, strong, weak respectively.

Because of this, native speakers tend to perceive the penultimate syllable, teɪt, as being more strongly 'stressed' than the final syllable ɪŋ. But what they want to call 'stress' is arguably no more than a way of saying that the vowel is strong (= not reduced).

Actual rhythmic beats following the main word stress accent are all pretty optional, which is why the British tradition is not to show any secondary stress in words like this. We transcribe *irritating* as ˈɪrɪteɪtɪŋ. The alternative tradition, usually followed in the States and (for example) Japan, is to recognize a secondary stress on the penultimate, thus ˈɪrɪˌteɪtɪŋ *irritàting*.

My correspondent asked particularly about the words *worshiper* and *worshipful*: do they rhythmically resemble *hamburger*, or perhaps *educate*? Which are the strongest (potentially 'pulsed') vowels in the words *qualificative, prejudices, accompanying*? What is the rhythmic pattern of the word *participle*, when it has initial primary stress?

Introspectively, *worship(p)er* (ˈwɜːʃɪpə, strong-weak-weak) is rhythmically different from *hamburger* (ˈhæm(ˌ)bɜːɡə, strong-strong-weak). In *hamburger* the penultimate vowel is long; in *worship(p)er* it is short. Both are also different from *educate* (ˈedjukeɪt or ˈedʒəkeɪt, strong-weak-strong). The last vowel of *worshipful* can be pronounced strong or weak, so this one can go either way, like *worshipper* or like *educate*.

Qualificative is a pretty rare word. I would pronounce it ˈkwɒlɪfɪkətɪv (strong-weak-weak-weak-weak). Such a long string of weak vowels is unusual, and some people avoid it by saying ˈkwɒlɪfɪkeɪtɪv (strong-weak-weak-strong-weak). *Prejudices* is ˈpredʒudɪsɪz (s-w-w-w). *Accompanying* is əˈkʌmpəniɪŋ (w-s-w-w-w).

People are divided about *participle*. I give it initial stress and say ˈpɑːt(ɪ)sɪpl̩ (s-(w-)w-w).

However... despite all this apparent hair-splitting, my advice to Spanish-speaking EFL learners is not to attempt any degree of stress after the main stress in a word. Ignore all posttonic stresses. This applies even in compounds like *washing machine* ˈwɒʃɪŋ məˌʃiːn. Attempts at a conscious secondary stress are likely to lead only to mispronunciations of the type ˌwɒʃɪŋ məˈʃiːn.

17.3 Impressed?

In my book *English Intonation: an Introduction* (Cambridge University Press 2006) I decided to treat the rise-fall tone (p. 217) as a subvariety of the Fall. In my view this makes sense. Likewise, I treat the mid-level nuclear tone as a subvariety of the (low) Rise (p. 224).

What are the grounds for treating the English rise-fall nuclear tone as a subvariety of the Fall tone rather than as an independent tone?. My approach is different from that of Halliday, for example, who treats it as separate, while uniting high and low falls as the same basic tone. For me, the fall tone covers O'Connor and Arnold's High Fall, Low Fall and Rise-fall. All have in common the physical characteristic of a nuclear pitch movement that either falls throughout or ends in a fall, ending always on a lowish pitch, with the tail (if present) having a low level terminal tendency. (Nowadays, people would say they all incorporate a Low boundary tone.) In terms of pragmatic meaning, all share the general characteristic of being what Brazil calls 'proclaiming', typically implying definitiveness, finality, or assertion.

Any sentence type may have a Fall, but with exclamations it is obligatory: they are always said with a Fall of some kind (including the possibility of a rise-fall).

What a re'markable \hat! (*excited, enthusiastic*)
What a re'markable \hat! (*deadpan, unimpressed*)
What a re'markable ^hat! (*impressed, perhaps gossipy*)
* What a re'markable /hat! (*ungrammatical except as an echo question*)

As anyone who has taught intonation analysis to native speakers of English will have noticed, the typical response to demonstrating the rise-fall is that the class breaks out into giggles.

Pedagogically speaking, I have no evidence that treating the rise-fall as a variety of fall helps EFL students understand what is going on. But it seems a reasonable thing to do. Learners should only tackle it after the basic tones (rise, fall, fall-rise) have been thoroughly learnt and understood. Otherwise there's a serious danger of students confusing the rise-fall with the fall-rise. (For native speakers who might confuse them, just ask whether or not it makes you giggle.)

That's why I relegated discussion of the rise-fall to the back of the book, in the section devoted to Beyond the Three Ts: Finer Distinctions of Tone.

17.4   You Would Say That!

Being a function word, *would* is usually unaccented (and often reduced to *'d*).

They 'said they would 'meet us at the 'airport.
'What would you 'do | if you 'won a 'million 'dollars?
In 'those days | they would 'sit out in the 'garden.
If 'I were 'you,| I'd 'go and ask at re'ception.

In clause-initial position, though, it is optionally accented (see my book *English Intonation*, p. 238: "In yes-no questions, accentuation of an initial auxiliary or modal verb is optional").

(')Would you 'like some 'coffee?
(')Would you be 'interested in 'joining us?
(')Would they a'gree, do you think?

However I have noticed one usage in which *would* seems to be obligatorily accented. An example is in this complaint about a sudden change in the weather, which I found myself saying the other day.

It \would start raining | 'just as we went out∨side!

In spoken English, *would* is sometimes used disapprovingly "to say that an action is typical or expected" (LDOCE).

The following examples don't sound right unless you accent *would*.

You 'would go and ∨spoil it, | \wouldn't you?
She 'would say ∨that, | \wouldn't she?

(?) You'd go and ⱽspoil it, | \wouldn't you?
(?) She'd 'say ⱽthat, | \wouldn't she?

17.5 Open Wide, Please

As I lay in the dentist's chair with my mouth wide open and stuffed with dental instruments, the dentist asked,

Is 'everything O/K?

Given those circumstances, the range of possible places and manners of articulation I could deploy was severely restricted, and I answered

/ŋŋ̊ŋ

– which means 'yes'. Under normal circumstances I would have said

/mm̥m

or

/m͡ŋm̥ŋ̊m͡ŋ

or

/ə̃hə̃

or even possibly

/Yup.

But it occurs to me that with any other form of words (if that's what they were) I would not have used this rising tone. (By the way, it's a mid rise, and ends higher than a grudging low rise.) Other ways of saying 'yes' would have not a rising but a falling tone.

*/Sure.
 \Sure.
 \Yes, | I'm \fine.

Even *yes* in its normal pronunciation **jes** feels odd with this mid rise. Only **jʌp̚** or **jep̚**, final plosive unreleased, will do.

I have no idea why.

And how would I have answered 'no'? If I were American I'd've said

ˀʔŋʔ\ʔŋʔ

But since I'm not, I would have had to say just

\ŋ::

or something of the sort. Ouch!

17.5 Open Wide, Please

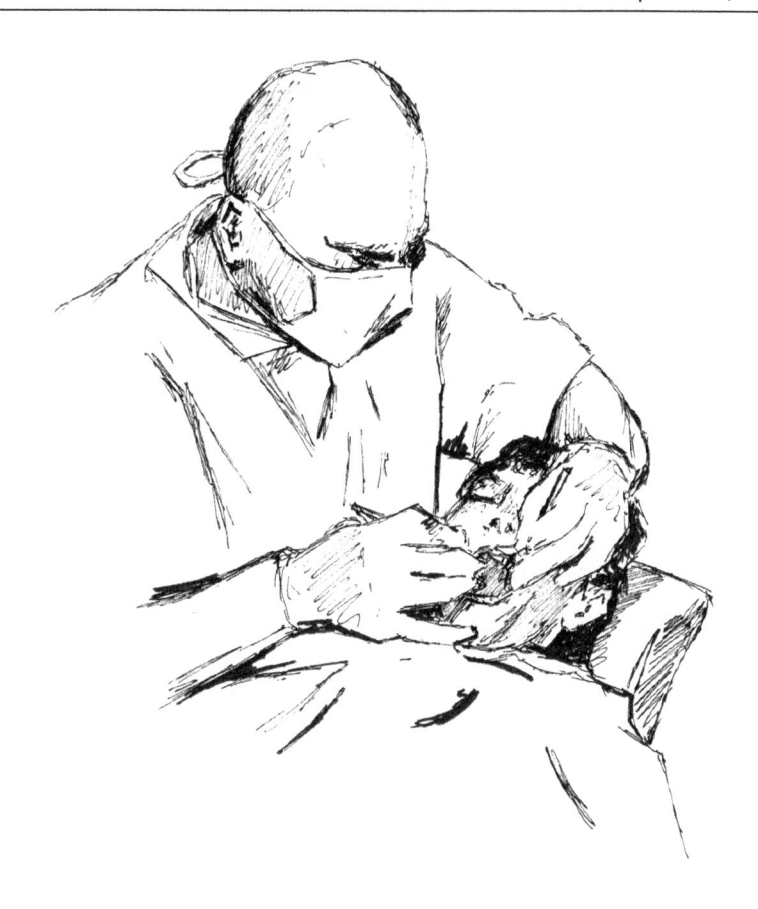

18 Texts in Transcription

18.1 ə bɔːltɪk kruːz

A few years ago I went on a Baltic cruise. Here's my report, written in phonetic transcription. It gives every reader the opportunity (i) to see how I usually pronounce, and (ii) to object to this or that detail of my transcription scheme.

fə ðə lɑːs tuː wiːks aɪv biːn kʌt ɒf frəm ɪntənet kɒntækt. ðə riːzn ɪz ðət aɪv biːn ɒn hɒlɪdeɪ, ɪn fækt ɒn ə kruːz tə ðə bɔːltɪk.

kruːzɪŋ meɪks fər ə veri rɪlæksɪŋ hɒlɪdeɪ. ɪts laɪk steɪɪŋ ɪn ə lʌkʃəri həʊtel wɪð ɔːl miːlz ən entəteɪnmənts ɪŋkluːdɪd. ən əz wel əz ðæt, məʊs mɔːnɪŋz ju weɪk ʌp ɪn ə njuː pleɪs. wɒt kʊd bi naɪsə?

ɑː ʃɪp wəz ðə dʒuːəl əv ðə siːz (*Jewel of the Seas*), əv ðə rɔɪəl kærɪbiːən laɪn. wiː stɑːtɪd frəm hærɪdʒ (*Harwich*), ə siːpɔːt wɪtʃ aɪ hædnt vɪzɪtɪd sɪns ðə deɪz wen ðə prɪnsɪpl weɪ frəm lʌndən tə nɔːðn jʊərəp wəz baɪ reɪl ən siː feri.

ɑː fɜːs pɔːt əv kɔːl wəz kəʊpənheɪɡən, əz tʃɑːmɪŋ əz evə. rɑːðə ðən teɪk ə peɪd ʃɔːr ɪkskɜːʃn wi meɪd ɑːr əʊn. wi wɔːkt ɪntə taʊn pɑːs ðə stætʃuː əv ðə lɪtl mɜːmeɪd ən ðə rɔɪəl pæləs, ðen əlɒŋ ðə pɪdestriənaɪzd strɔɪət (*Strøget*).

neks keɪm stɒkhəʊm. ə swiːdɪʃ frend həd kaɪndli əɡriːd tə miːt əs ðeər ət ðə kiːsaɪd, ən wi went təɡeðə baɪ bʌs ən træm tə vɪzɪt ði əʊpən eə mjuːziːəm kʌm zuː, skænsən (*Skansen*).

ɪn helsɪŋki ɪt wəz reɪnɪŋ. wi steɪd ɒn ðə ʃɪp.

ðə fɜːðɪs pɔɪnt əv ɑː dʒɜːni wəz snt piːtəzbɜːɡ (*St Petersburg, Санкт-Петербург*). ə vɪzɪt tə ðə feɪməs eəmɪtɑːʒ (*Hermitage, Эрмитаж*) pæləs ən ɑːt ɡæləri wəz ʌnmɪsəbl, əv kɔːs, ən wiː ɔːlsəʊ tʊk ən ɪkskɜːʃn tə ðə rɔɪəl pæləs əv piːtəhɒf (*Peterhof, Петергоф*), wɪð ɡɑːdnz fʊl əv ðə məʊs mɑːvləs faʊntɪnz.

ɒn ðen tə tælɪn (*Tallinn*), wɪtʃ pruːvd tə bi ðə haɪ pɔɪnt əv ðə həʊl kruːz. ɪts laɪk ə feəriteɪl taʊn wɪð pɪktʃəresk tʃɜːtʃɪz ən kɑːslz, naʊ wʌns əɡen ðə kæpɪtl əv ən ɪndɪpendənt estəʊniə.

ɑː lɑːs stɒp wəz ɡɒθnbɜːɡ (*Gothenburg, Göteborg*), weər ɪt wəz reɪnɪŋ əɡen.

ðə wəz wʌn mɔː deɪ ət siː, ən wi wə bæk ɪn hærɪdʒ, rɪlækst ən rɪfreʃt.

18.2 ædɪŋ ˈstres

One reader was enthusiastic about seeing a passage entirely in transcription, but asked

184

wɒt ɪz ən əprəʊprɪət stres maːkɪŋ wen wi trænskraɪb ə kənektɪd tekst?

So I replied as follows.

wɪə diːlɪŋ hɪə wɪð kənektɪd spiːtʃ, nɒt wɪð wɜːdz ɪn aɪsəleɪʃn. ðə stres ʃəʊn ɪn dɪkʃnrɪz rɪleɪts tə ðə lætə, nɒt ðə fɔːmə.

1. ɪf wi dʒʌst ˌrɪprəˈdjuːs wɜːd stres əz ʃəʊn ɪn ˈdɪkʃnrɪz, wi ˈsɪərɪəsli ˌmɪsrepriˈzent ðə ˈneɪtʃər əv kənˈtɪnjuəs spiːtʃ. ɪn pəˈtɪkjələ, ˈmɒnəˌsɪləblz rɪˈsiːv nəʊ stres maːks. ði ˈəʊnli wɜːdz ðət duː get stres ˈmaːkɪŋ aː ˈpɒlɪˌsɪləblz.

    səʊ lets æd stres maːks tə ðə mɒnəsɪləblz. bət nɒt tu ɔːl əv ðəm – dʒʌst tə ðə kɒntent wɜːdz, nɒt ðə fʌŋkʃn wɜːdz. wiːl hæv tə meɪk ə sensɪbl dɪsɪʒn əbaʊt wɜːdz ðət ər ɒn ðə bɔːdəlaɪn bɪtwiːn ðə tuː – wɜːdz laɪk ˈdʒʌst'.

2. ɪf wi ˈdʒʌst ˌrɪprəˈdjuːs ˈwɜːd ˈstres əz ˈʃəʊn ɪn ˈdɪkʃnrɪz, wi ˈsɪərɪəsli ˌmɪsrepriˈzent ðə ˈneɪtʃər əv kənˈtɪnjuəs ˈspiːtʃ. ɪn pəˈtɪkjələ, ˈmɒnəˌsɪləblz rɪˈsiːv ˈnəʊ ˈstres ˈmaːks. ði ˈəʊnli ˈwɜːdz ðət duː ˈget ˈstres ˈmaːkɪŋ aː ˈpɒlɪˌsɪləblz.

    bət ðɪs ɪz stɪl nɒt gʊd. wi niːd tə rɪmuːv ðəʊz stres maːks ðət duː nɒt get trænzfɔːmd ɪntu æksnts, ðæt ɪz wɪtʃ duː nɒt rɪsiːv pɪtʃ prɒmɪnəns ɪn kənektɪd spiːtʃ.

    - sʌm əv ðɪs ɪz leksɪkl. wi məs rɪmuːv ðə stres maːk ɒn ðə sekənd elɪmənt əv kɒmpaʊndz.
    - sʌm ɪz prægmætɪk. wi kən rɪmuːv ðə stres maːks ɒn rɪpiːtɪd wɜːdz, nɒnkəntraːstɪv wɜːdz et setrə. bət wi niːd tu æd ðəm tə fʌŋkʃn wɜːdz juːzd kəntraːstɪvli.
    - sʌm ɪz ruːl gʌvnd. wi kæn (tu ə dɪgriː ɒpʃnəli) ʃɪft stres maːks ɪn əkɔːdns wɪð ðə prɪnsɪpl əv 'stres ʃɪft' əfektɪŋ wɜːdz wɪð mɔː ɒn wʌn leksɪkl stres.

3. ɪf wi ˈdʒʌst ˈrɪprədjuːs ˈwɜːd stres əz ˈʃəʊn ɪn ˈdɪkʃnrɪz, wi ˈsɪərɪəsli ˈmɪsrepriˈzent ðə ˈneɪtʃər əv kənˈtɪnjuəs ˈspiːtʃ. ɪn pəˈtɪkjələ, ˈmɒnəsɪləblz rɪˈsiːv ˈnəʊ stres maːks. ði ˈəʊnli wɜːdz ðət ˈduː get stres maːkɪŋ aː ˈpɒlɪsɪləblz.

    jul nəʊtɪs ðət aɪv nɒt əʊnli ʃəʊn stres (æksnt) ɒn əprəʊprɪət mɒnəsɪləblz, bət aɪv ɔːlsəʊ teɪkən əkaʊnt əv stres ʃɪft.

    wiv naʊ riːtʃt ə steɪdʒ kɒrəspɒndɪŋ tə wɒt wi aːsk stjuːdnts tə duː wen ðeɪ trænskraɪb ə pæsɪdʒ əv kəntɪnjuəs ɪŋglɪʃ.

    haʊevə ðɪs ɪz stɪl əʊnli haːf ðə stɔːri. nɒt ɔːl æksnts ər iːkwəl. kənektɪd spiːtʃ ɪz kærɪktəraɪzd baɪ ɪntəneɪʃn. lets maːk ðæt tuː.

    fɜːst steɪdʒ – dɪvaɪd ɪntu aɪ piːz (ɪntəneɪʃn freɪzɪz). ðɪs miːnz wi kən get rɪd əv pʌŋktʃueɪʃn maːks.

4. ɪf wi ˈdʒʌst ˈrɪprədjuːs ˈwɜːd stres | əz ˈʃəʊn ɪn ˈdɪkʃnrɪz | wi ˈsɪərɪəsli ˈmɪsrepriˈzent | ðə ˈneɪtʃər əv kənˈtɪnjuəs ˈspiːtʃ ‖ ɪn pəˈtɪkjələ |

ˈmɒnəsɪləblz | riːsiːv ˈnəʊ stres mɑːks ‖ ði ˈəʊnli wɜːdz | ðət ˈduː get stres mɑːkɪŋ | ɑː ˈpɒlisɪləblz ‖
    ˈsekənd steɪdʒ | ˈʌndəlaɪn ðə ˈnjuːkliə təʊnz ‖

5. ɪf wi ˈdʒʌst ˈriprədjuːs <u>ˈwɜːd</u> stres | əz ˈʃəʊn ɪn <u>ˈdɪkʃnriz</u> | wi ˈsɪərɪəsli ˈmɪsrepriˈ<u>zent</u> | ðə ˈneɪtʃər əv kənˈtɪnjuəs <u>ˈspiːtʃ</u> ‖ ɪn pəˈtɪkjələ <u>ˈmɒnəsɪləblz</u> | riːsiːv <u>ˈnəʊ</u> stres mɑːks ‖ ði <u>ˈəʊn</u>li wɜːdz | ðət <u>ˈdu</u> get stres mɑːkɪŋ | ɑː <u>ˈpɒ</u>lisɪləblz ‖
    ˈθɜːd steɪdʒ | kənvɜːt ˈnjuːkliər ˈæksnt mɑːks | ɪntə ˈtəʊn mɑːks ‖

6. ɪf wi ˈdʒʌst ˈriprədjuːs \/<u>ˈwɜːd</u> stres | əz ˈʃəʊn ɪn \/<u>ˈdɪkʃnriz</u> | wi ˈsɪərɪəsli ˈmɪsrepri/<u>zent</u> | ðə ˈneɪtʃər əv kənˈtɪnjuəs <u>spiːtʃ</u> ‖ ɪn pə\/ˈtɪkjələ \/<u>ˈmɒnəsɪləblz</u> | riːsiːv <u>nəʊ</u> stres mɑːks ‖ ði <u>əʊn</u>li wɜːdz | ðət /<u>ˈduː</u> get stres mɑːkɪŋ | ɑː <u>ˈpɒ</u>lisɪləblz ‖

ðæts maɪ aɪdɪər əv ə riːznəbli fʊl prəsɒdɪk trænskrɪpʃn̩. ðər ə wʌn ə tuː ɪmpɔːtnt pɔɪnts tə bi meɪd.

- ðər ə mʌltɪpl pɒsəbl æksnt ən ɪntəneɪʃn pætnz tə tʃuːz frɒm. ðə mɑːkɪŋ aɪ həv tʃəʊzn ɪz əʊnli wʌn əmʌŋ sevrəl pɒsəbl plɔːzəbl vɜːʃnz.
- ɪn səplaɪɪŋ ə fʊl ɪntəneɪʃn mɑːkʌp aɪ əm ɔːlsəʊ tʃuːzɪŋ tə **pəfɔːm** ðə tekst ɪn ə pətɪkjələ weɪ.
- ə tekst wɪðaʊt stres ~ æksnt ~ ɪntəneɪʃn mɑːkʌp ɪz mɔː laɪk ən ɔːθəɡræfɪk tekst – ɪt liːvz ðə riːdə friː tə tʃuːz ən əprəʊprɪət prəsɒdɪk pætn.

fɔːtʃənətli ɪŋglɪʃ hæz veri fjuː mɪnɪml peəz dɪfərɪŋ ɪn leksɪkl stres ələʊn. səʊ fər ɔːdnri pɜːpəsɪz (laɪk ðɪs) wi rɪəli dəʊnt niːd tə juːz stres mɑːks wen trænskraɪbɪŋ ə kəntɪnjuəs tekst – ənles wɪə pətɪkjələli ɪntrəstɪd ɪn ðə prɒsədi.

18.3 ɪn ðə pʌb

hɪəz ənʌðər entri rɪtn̩ həʊlli ɪn fənetɪk trænskrɪpʃn̩.

lɑːs naɪt aɪ pleɪd maɪ mələʊdɪən ət ə seʃn̩ ɪn ə pʌb ɒn wɪmbl̩dən kɒmən, nɒt veri fɑː frəm weər aɪ lɪv. ðiːz seʃn̩z ə held wʌns ə mʌnθ ən ɔːɡənaɪzd baɪ ə ləʊkl̩ mɒrɪs saɪd.

dʒʌst ʌndə twenti piːpl̩ tɜːnd ʌp fə ðə seʃn̩. ðeɪ ɪŋkluːdɪd θriː ʌðə mələʊdɪən pleɪəz. ɪts ɔːlwɪz ɪntrəstɪŋ tə kəmpeə nəʊts. bɪfɔː wi stɑːtɪd, wʌn əv ðəm kaɪndli əlaʊd mi tə traɪ aʊt hɪz ɪnstrəmənt (mʌtʃ mɔːr ɪkspensɪv ðəm maɪn).

evrɪwʌn wəz siːtɪd əraʊnd teɪblz ɪn ə smɔːl rʊm ɪn ðə pʌb (ðə snʌg). wʌns ðə seʃn̩ prɒpə wəz ʌndə weɪ, ðə fɔːmən (tʃeəmən) kɔːld ɒn iːtʃ pɑːtɪsɪpənt ɪn tɜːn tə liːd ə tjuːn ɔːr ə sɒŋ. ðə prəʊɡræm wəz ə mɪkstʃər əv ɪnstrəmentl̩ stʌf (fɪdl̩z, kɒnsətiːnə, maʊθ ɔːɡən, mələʊdɪənz) ənd ʌnəkʌmpənɪd sɪŋɪŋ. tuː ruːlz əplaɪd, əz ɪz juːʒuəl ɪn pʌb seʃn̩z – nəʊ æmplɪfɪkeɪʃn̩ ən nəʊ pleɪɪŋ ɔː sɪŋɪŋ frəm ə rɪtn̩ skɔː.

ðə sıŋəz sæŋ veəriəs fəʊk sɒŋz ən fəʊk-staɪl sɒŋz. wiː ɪnstrəmentl̩ɪss pleɪd ɪŋglɪʃ (ənd ʌðə) dɑːns tjuːnz. ðiːz ə tɪpɪkli θɜːti tuː bɑː riːlz, dʒɪgz, hɔːnpaɪps ɔː wɔːltsɪz, wɪð ðə strʌktʃər AABB. ðə kənvenʃn̩ ɪz ðət ju pleɪ iːtʃ tjuːn θriː taɪmz θruː, gɪvɪŋ ʌðə pleɪəz taɪm tə pɪk ʌp ðə melədi ən dʒɔɪn ɪn ɪf ðeɪ kæn.

maɪ əʊn fɜːs kɒntrɪbjuːʃn̩ wəz ə raʊdi riːl kɔːld tʃaɪniːz breɪkdaʊn (*Chinese Breakdown*), wɪtʃ tə maɪ səpraɪz ði ʌðə pleɪəz dɪdn̩t nəʊ – ɪt wəz wʌn əv ðə steɪplz əv ðə bænd aɪ juːs tə pleɪ ɪn fɔːti jɪəz əgəʊ – fɒləʊb baɪ ðə krʊkɪd stəʊvpaɪp (*Crooked Stovepipe*). leɪtə, wem maɪ tɜːn keɪm raʊnd əgen, aɪ pleɪd dʒesɪz hɔːnpaɪp (*Jessie's Hornpipe*), segweɪŋ ɪntə səʊldʒəz dʒɔɪ (*Soldier's Joy*), wɪtʃ **evriwʌn** nəʊz.

18.4 kænədər ən əlæskə

wʌn ə ðə prɪvəlɪdʒɪz əv biːɪŋ rɪtaɪəd ɪz ðət aɪ kən gəʊ ɒn hɒlədeɪ wenevr aɪ fiːl laɪk ɪt, wɪðaʊʔ wʌriɪŋ əbaʊʔ tɜːm deɪts ən ðə laɪk. ən ðæts wɒt aɪv dʒʌs dʌn.

ɑː hɒlədeɪ wəz ən ɪskɔːtɪd tʊə ɪn ðə kəneɪdiən rɒkɪz plʌs ə kruːz tu əlæskə. ðə fɜːs wiːk wəz ɪn ðə rɒki maʊntɪnz. wi fluː tə kælgəri, ən frəm ðeə hæd ə θriː deɪ kəʊtʃ trɪp steɪŋ əʊvənaɪt ɪn bænf, leɪk luːiːz ən dʒæspə, fɒləʊd baɪ ə tuːdeɪ treɪn raɪd daʊn θruː kæmluːps, fɪnɪʃɪŋ ɪn væŋkuːvə.

ðə həʊl θɪŋ wəz mɑːvləs, bəʔ kɒntrəri tə maɪ ekspekteɪʃn aɪ faʊnd ðə rəʊd pɑːt iːvn betə ðən ðə reɪl pɑːt. wi hæd ə veri nɒlɪdʒəbl draɪvə ənd wər eɪbl tə stɒp evri aʊər ɔː səʊ tə stretʃ ɑː legz ən ədmaə ðə siːnəri.

ðə haɪ pɔɪnts fə mi: wə ðə gɒndələ raɪd tə ðə tɒp əv sʌlfə maʊntɪn əʊvəlʊkɪŋ bæmf, ðə grɪzli beə wi sɔː əʔ ðə saɪd əv ðə rəʊd əz wi wə draɪvɪŋ əlɒŋ ði aɪsfiːld pɑːkweɪ – siː ðə fəʊtəʊ aɪ tʊk – ən draɪvɪŋ raɪt ʌp ɒntu ə glæsɪə ən wɔːkɪŋ əbaʊt ɒn ɪt ɪn ə blɪzəd. ən əv kɔːs evriweə ðə maʊntɪn siːnəri wəz breθteɪkɪŋ.

fə ðə treɪn dʒɜːni wi sæt ɪn ə glɑːs tɒpt ɒbzəveɪʃn kɑː əz wi sneɪkt əlɒŋ θruː maʊntɪn gɔːdʒɪz ən dens fɒrɪss. ðɪs wəz nɒt laɪk ə jʊərəpiːən ɔː dʒæpəniːz treɪn, rʌʃɪŋ pɑːst evrɪθɪŋ ət tuː hʌndrəd kɪləmiːtəz ən aə. rɑːðə, wi trʌndld veri dʒentli əlɒŋ, wɪð friːkwənt stɒps əʔ pɑːsɪŋ pleɪsɪz səʊ əz tu əlaʊ ə treɪn kʌmɪŋ ɪn ði ɒpəzɪʔ dərekʃn tə pɑːs əs ɒn wɒt wəz məʊsli ə sɪŋgl træk laɪn.

ðə sekəm wiːk wəz ðə kruːz. ɑːftr ə tuːdeɪ steɪ ɪn væŋkuːvə wi ɪmbɑːkt ɒn ɑː ʃɪp wɪð tuː θaʊznd ʌðə pæsɪndʒəz ən set seɪl təwɔːdz əlæskə. ɑː fɜːs stɒp wəz ət ə fɔːmə sæmən kænəri ɒn tlɪŋgɪt lænd, weə wi frəʊz ɒn ə draɪv θruː ðə fɒrɪst ən əlɒŋ ðə ʃɔːr ɪn ən əʊpənsaɪdɪd viːɪkl. bət aɪ dɪd hɪə sm spəʊkən tlɪŋgɪt.

frəm ðeə wi kəntɪnjuːd nɔːθwədz tə riːtʃ ðə vɑːst hʌndrəd kɪləmiːtə waɪd hʌbəd glæsɪə, weə wiː hæd səm eksələnt fəʊtəʊ ɒpətjuːnətiz. ðə bluː kʌləreɪʃn əv pɑːt əv ðə glæsjər ɪz səpəʊzɪdli djuː tə ðə fækt ðəʔ ðæʔ pɑːt əv ði aɪs həz biːn kəmprest baɪ ðə weɪt əv ði aɪs əbʌv ɪt fə θaʊznz əv jɪəz, pʊʃɪŋ aʊt eni rɪzɪdjʊəl bʌblz əv eər ən səʊ ɔːltərɪŋ ðə rɪfræktɪv ɪndeks əv ði aɪs.

æz wi rɪtɜːnd təwɔːdz kænədə wi kɔːld ɪn ət dʒuːnəʊ ən ketʃɪkæn, bəʊθ veri smɔːl taʊnz wɪð nəʊ rəʊd kənekʃnz – ju kən əʊnli get ðeə baɪ siː ɔː baɪ eə. frəm dʒuːnəʊ wi tʊk ən ɪkskɜːʃn ɪn ə fləʊt pleɪn, wɪtʃ ɡeɪv əs wʌndəfl vjuːz əʊvə ði ʌntʌtʃt aɪs əv maʊntɪn sləʊps əŋ ɡlæsɪəz.

18.5 strəʊk

I wrote the following on 28–29 June 2012, one week after had I suffered a stroke. I wanted to check that my mental powers were not affected, even if my left hand was.

ɒn wenzdi mɔːnɪŋ lɑːs wiːk aɪ drəʊv maɪ pɑːtnə tə ɡætwɪk eəpɔːt. hiː wəz ɒf tə mɒntsəræt fə hɪz ʌŋklz hʌndrədθ bɜːθdeɪ selɪbreɪʃnz. ɪn ði iːvnɪŋ aɪ hæd dɪnə wɪð frenz ət ə restərɒnt ɪn krɔɪdn. æz aɪ went tə kætʃ ðə træm həʊm aɪ faʊnd ðət maɪ left hænd dɪdnt siːm tə bi wɜːkɪŋ prɒpli, ən ðen maɪ left leɡ kəlæpst ʌndə mi ən aɪ fel daʊn. pɑːsəzbaɪ keɪm tə maɪ help ən kɔːld ən æmbjʊləns, wɪtʃ tʊk mi tu eɪ ən iː (æksɪdnt ən ɪmɜːdʒənsi) ət sn dʒɔːdʒɪz hɒspɪtl tuːtɪŋ. θæŋks tu ɔːl ðə frendz kɒliːɡz ən fæmli hu əv vɪzɪtɪd mi ɪn hɒspɪtl. aɪ həv naʊ biːn muːvd tə snt helɪə hɒspɪtl ɪn sʌtn.

θriː tʃɪəz fə ði en eɪtʃ es. ɪts ət taɪmz laɪk ðɪs ðət ju rɪəlaɪz haʊ lʌki wi ɑːr ɪn ðə juː keɪ tə hæv ɪt. ɪn sʌm ʌðə kʌntrɪz aɪ wʊd bi tʃɑːdʒd fər evri skæn, evri test, evri drɪp, evri kæθɪtər, evri ɪntəvenʃn. hɪə ðər ə nəʊ tʃɑːdʒɪz, evrɪθɪŋ ɪz friː ət ðə pɔɪnt əv juːs. aɪ əm hæpi tə peɪ maɪ tæksɪz ɪn ɪkstʃeɪndʒ fə ðɪs piːs əv maɪnd.

Less obvious proper names: **tuːtɪŋ** *Tooting*, **snt helɪə** *St Helier*, **sʌtn** *Sutton*, **en eɪtʃ es** *National Health Service*.

PART IV

Roundup

19   Rhetoric

19.1   Presentation Techniques

I generally enjoy attending academic conferences and lecturers by visiting speakers at my own university. Some talks, however, are not so good. It's not that what the lecturer says isn't interesting or important: it's that their presentation technique leaves much to be desired.

- Sometimes a speaker starts "Good morning – um – " and the whole talk is punctuated with distracting hesitation noises.
- Some speakers do not know how to use a microphone properly, with the result that they are largely inaudible.
- Some struggle with their PowerPoint or other displays, crowding too much material onto a single slide or displaying a slide for such a short time that the audience cannot take it in.
- Some conference speakers have problems with pacing, so that by the time the chair warns them that time is nearly up they have still not got to their main point.
- Some make no eye contact with the audience, and are thus unable to react to body-language feedback.
- The key failure is usually that many people just ***read out a prepared text***. This is almost never a good idea. If you are following a verbatim written script you can't easily speed up or slow down to fit the allotted time, you don't get eye contact with the audience, and you usually read too fast. You may emphasize the wrong words. You stumble and can recover only by going back to the beginning of the sentence. (It is true that actors, broadcasters and the clergy do often speak from a prepared script and may do it very well. But it's clearly a skill that many people lack unless explicitly taught.)

I really wonder how some conference speakers can function as professional lecturers and teachers.

I think that we phoneticians can in general congratulate ourselves on being good public speakers. If only that were true of everyone who speaks in public!

19.2 I Can't Help It: It's Just the Way I Am

Are phoneticians born or made? Is phonetic skill innate, or must it be acquired by training?

At UCL the cognitive neuroscientist Sophie Scott has carried out research comparing the brain function of a group of trained phoneticians with that of a matched control group of non-phoneticians.

Looking at the left Heschl's gyrus (the first part of the cortex to process incoming auditory information), she says that she finds more 'structure' there in the phoneticians than in the non-phoneticians. She suggests this is probably so even in utero, though how you could detect the difference between foetuses destined to be phoneticians from those not so destined I have no idea. Anyhow, this implies that phonetic ability is an innate predisposition. People born with this genetic quality are going to be drawn to working with sound: not necessarily as phoneticians, but perhaps alternatively as sound engineers, musicians, etc.

On the other hand she also claims that there is a specific training effect. Phonetic training causes another part of the brain, the pars opercularis, to grow larger. This is not a genetic predisposition, but is acquired through phonetic training.

Her claim that potential phonetic ability is innate fits in with my personal life experience: when I discovered phonetics it was like falling in love. I had found my métier! Phonetics was what I wanted to do. Probably if I had chosen to study modern languages or science at school instead of the classics I actually chose I would still have ended up in the same place.

Perhaps the same applies to you. It's like predestination.

19.3 Sound Advice

I suspect that most university phoneticians have been approached at one time or another to testify as expert witnesses in court cases. I know of at least two who have resigned from university posts in phonetics in order to go freelance as forensic voice experts. My late colleague John Baldwin used to do a great amount of this kind of work, and unlike most forensic phoneticians relied on his listening skills rather than on instrumental laboratory evidence. (He was the subject of a leading judicial decision that the non-instrumental evidence of a trained phonetician is admissible as 'expert testimony' in British courts.)

Personally, I do not generally accept invitations to act in such cases. The only one in which I did become involved, many years ago, actually involved syntax rather than phonetics. It concerned a Trinidadian defendant who was contesting part of a written police statement reporting his words when being interrogated about some crime. The statement was ten pages long, and he agreed that the first eight and a half pages were accurate. He said that the last page and a half, where the damaging admissions were located, was not: he had never said the words alleged.

At the request of his lawyers, I examined the written statement. Then I asked him to come and see me. Without explaining what I was looking for, I set a tape recorder going and fed him with questions for an hour, just to keep him talking – about anything and everything.

I had noticed that in the transcribed sentences which he had denied uttering there were three instances of a passive construction with an agent phrase (of the type *he was seen by the woman, I was asked by my friend, the window was broken by the children*). I knew that for West Indians with the level of education of the accused such constructions are unusual. And so it proved: in the hour's material I recorded – despite my covert attempts to elicit passive sentences with *by-* phrases – he uttered not a single one. It was a reasonable inference that the police had fabricated the parts of the written statement containing the passive sentences. (These sentences might have meant much the same as what he had actually said, but they could not be accepted as a verbatim record, which is what they purported to be.)

When his lawyers reported my finding to the prosecution, the latter decided to drop the main charge and proceed only with a minor one, which the accused admitted. So I never had my day in court.

20 Language Mosaic

20.1 Ndjuka

Most of the speakers of Ndjuka (also known as Ndyuka, Djuka, or Aukan) live in Suriname. Like Saramaccan, Ndjuka is an English-lexicon Creole spoken by Maroons (aka Bush Negroes) whose ancestors were shipped as slaves over three hundred years ago to work on English colonial plantations. Those who managed to escape fled deep into the rain forest, where they established communities along rivers in eastern Suriname and parts of neighbouring French Guiana.

Unlike the English-lexicon Caribbean creoles such as Jamaican and Trinidadian, spoken in what were until less than sixty years ago British colonies, Ndjuka and Saramaccan have been entirely out of contact with standard English for centuries. So whereas Jamaican Creole is spoken in a diglossic continuum extending from basilectal deep Creole to acrolectal Jamaican Standard English, Ndjuka is a free-standing language exhibiting approximately zero mutual intelligibility with English.

As with many sub-Saharan African languages, but not English, Ndjuka syllable structure allows for initial clusters of nasal plus plosive, as in the name of the language **ndjuká** and the word for 'snail', **ŋkólá**. The clusters **kw** and **gw** are alternatively pronounced as double-articulated **k͡p**, **g͡b**, as in **gwé** or **gbé** from English *go away*. Double articulation of plosives is a familiar feature of West African languages, as in the language name Igbo (Ibo).

Ndjuka is a tone language. There is a minimal pair **na** 'is' vs **ná** 'isn't'. Vowel length is also distinctive. While **báká** means 'back', **bákáa** means 'white man' (compare Jamaican *backra*), and **baáká** means 'black'.

Words of obviously English origin include **fátú** 'fat', **bígí** 'big', **mófó** 'mouth', **tífí** 'tooth', **tápú** 'stop', **sinékí** 'snake'.

20.2 As We Were

Once upon a time, my children, before we had computers for word processing, we used primitive machines called typewriters.

I learnt to type almost at the same time as I learnt to write, because my father had a typewriter on which I spent many happy hours even before I was old enough to go to school. (I entered primary school in 1944.)

That was a mechanical typewriter, as was my own first typewriter, which I bought when a student, in 1959. (Electric typewriters were much too expensive for the likes of us. As for word processors, it wasn't until the mid-eighties that ordinary people started to use computers for word processing: my first word-processed published work, photoset from an electronic file, was my Welsh-Esperanto dictionary in 1985.)

In order to write phonetic symbols in the days of typewriters, the machines had to be expensively customized, one or more of the standard characters (each a physical metal stamp carrying the outline of the letter) replaced by a phonetic character. The number of keys on a typewriter was somewhat smaller than the number we are now accustomed to: so no square brackets, curly brackets or angle brackets, no backslash or vertical bar, and in the United Kingdom, no $ or #. You made an exclamation mark (!) by doing dot-backspace-apostrophe. On the other hand, to cope with our pre-decimal currency we did need fraction signs: not only ½ but also ¼ and ¾. (For an ordinary inland letter during my childhood you needed a 2½d stamp, pronounced ˌtʌpniˈheɪpni – that is, the price of postage was 2½d, ˌtʌpənsˈheɪpni.)

Apart from these fraction keys, there were not many keys that could be made available for phonetic symbols. That is why at that time symbol economy was so important in phonetic transcription. On my first typewriter I had ə θ ð ŋ ʃ ʒ ɑ. Together with an apostrophe serving as a stress mark and the colon as a length mark, this was enough to type Jones's 'simplified' transcription of English, which used **o** for LOT and **a** for TRAP. I was the envy of my fellow-students, who had to write all phonetic symbols in by hand. But I could not use it to type our modern Gimson-style transcription, nor a phonetic transcription of French or German.

Specialist institutions such as university departments of phonetics were able to afford specialist typewriters. At UCL we had several. Our most elaborate machine, known familiarly as the Mighty Wurlitzer, had two full-size keyboards yoked together, and a sturdy lever to move the platen assembly physically across along a shaft from one to the other. On the left keyboard were the standard typewriter characters, on the right keyboard were the phonetic ones. Many of my early lecture handouts were created on it (using wax stencils for a Gestetner duplicator – we didn't have xerox machines in those days, either).

The next stage in the development of machine writing involved electric typewriters, which were like manual ones except that they were powered by electricity. From them developed various mechanical devices capable in principle of being driven by electronic input from a computer. But you could also operate them manually, and that's how most of us used them.

The first invention was the 'golfball' typewriter, in which the physical metal stamps for each character were arranged around the surface of a small metal sphere. (The sphere was officially called a 'typeball', though generally people called them golfballs.) The electrical mechanism of the typewriter rotated and tilted the golfball for each letter required, causing it to strike the ribbon against the platen, leaving a visible mark on the paper beneath. Differently from ordinary typewriters, the platen assembly remained fixed while the golfball assembly moved across the page as typing progressed. The IBM Selectric golfball typewriter came on the market in the early sixties. To begin with they were very expensive; the first time I saw one in operation was in 1971.

The user was limited to the set of 96 characters represented physically on the golfball. However, the golfball could be detached and replaced by a different one, which meant that for the first time we had a choice of fonts (type faces and type sizes, each on a separate golfball) on the same machine, e.g. Elite, Letter Gothic, Courier or Pica, and 10-pt or 12-pt. A golfball could also bear special characters, e.g. accented letters for particular languages. And phonetic symbols? To begin with, phoneticians could at great expense have golfballs customized, involving the replacement of spare characters by phonetic ones – an operation involving casting metal type and soldering it into place. (I remember that the University of Leeds had such a customized golfball in the early seventies.) Then a company called Camwil, based in Hawaii, produced and marketed a specialist golfball full of IPA symbols, which most phoneticians bought and used.

The other possibility in the seventies and eighties was the 'daisywheel' printer. A daisywheel was a metal or plastic wheel with 96 spokes or petals, each of which bore a different character. Typing a character caused the wheel to rotate and present the desired metal stamp to the ribbon and platen, where a hammer would strike it to print the character. As far as I am aware, no phonetic daisywheels were ever produced.

Used as a computer printer, daisywheel printers were about three times faster than golfballs. Both were very noisy in use.

These technologies could produce an emulation of bold text by striking several times rather than once. They could not produce italic text unless the user took off one golfball/daisywheel and replaced it by a special italic one.

After golfballs and daisywheels, the next important development in our ability to print phonetic symbols was the dot-matrix printer. This had a printhead with nine pins arranged in a vertical line. The head ran backwards and forwards across the platen while the pins struck an ink ribbon. This was controlled by a computer.

The resolution for the printers we used in the eighties was 9 × 5 for each character (or for wide ones 9 × 6). This produced readable text, although the characters were very crude.

Without special software, the printer could only print the 96 characters of the ASCII set, plain or italic. However, in order to accommodate languages other than English, a few of the ASCII characters had alternatives that could be accessed via special code sequences. So æ and ø, for example, were available not because they were IPA symbols but because they were needed for Danish and Norwegian:

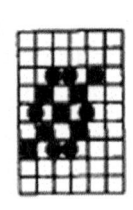

The man who made the full set of IPA symbols available for phoneticians was my colleague Mark Huckvale, then working as a research assistant at UCL. He created his *Phonetic Script Formatter* (PSF) software in 1983 or 1984.

He writes:

> We had BBC microcomputers equiped with the Torch Z-80 add-on that ran the 'CPN' operating system, which was a modified version of CP/M. This setup allowed us to run Wordstar, and we were able to print to Epson dot-matrix printers.
>
> PSF took Wordstar document files embedded with special codes to indicate a switch into the phonetic font. The program would then print the document, using a graphics mode of the Epson printer for the phonetic symbols.

Here is a sample of the resulting ouput. It is from a research report I wrote in 1987, using WordStar with PSF.

Here, enlarged, are one or two symbols.

Actually, quite a few of us must have been experimenting with dot-matrix phonetic symbols during the eighties. These were the heroic days of home computing, when we were all teaching ourselves how to do simple Basic programming. I know that I found out how to modify the character set on a Sinclair ZX Spectrum that I had. The result could be displayed on screen (which was a television screen in those days), but the only way to print it out was on special aluminium-coated paper.

Martin Barry has sent me a specimen of the printout of his own efforts. He says he has been

> ... dredging up forgotten memories. I produced something a bit like the system Mark Huckvale describes, only for Sinclair QL, which means that only about three people in the world ever used it. I'm racking my brains to

remember how it was done – if I remember correctly, I hacked the subscript and superscript fonts on the word processing package bundled with the computer, so that subscript was replaced by IPA and superscript by Cyrillic. It was about 1985 or 1986, so around the time of NLQ printers (and before I took possession of my first Macintosh in 1987). Here is a scan of a mouldering handout – look, symbols for transcribing intonation too!

jɔː \pærəts ded ‖ ðə bɔɪ

ðə ⋁relɪʃ wɪtʃ ɪz ·klɑːs f

↓maɪ ↑⋁pærət ded | sed

\aɪp | sed ðə bɔɪ briːfliː ‖

Then came (Near Letter Quality) dot-matrix printers, which had 24 pins instead of nine. But I don't think we ever had a way of printing phonetic symbols with them. Then we moved on to WYSIWYG and eventually the inkjet and laser printers that we use today To begin with we had custom single-byte phonetic fonts – at first proprietary, then free from SIL (sil.org). Nowadays we have Truetype and Opentype Unicode fonts routinely bundled with all new computers, and the whole world has access to IPA symbols, just as it has to Cyrillic, Hebrew, Arabic, Devanagari, and Chinese/Japanese/Korean charsets.

20.3 Miscellanea

Here are some points from conference papers I have listened to.

- In the Berber language Tashlhiyt many words are vowelless, for example **kk** 'cross'. Geminate consonants contrast with single ones even in word-initial (and utterance-initial) position, e.g. **ttut** 'forget him' vs **tut** 'she hit'. (One correspondent points out that you also get initial geminates in various forms of spoken Arabic, through the assimilation of the definite article, with minimal pairs such as **ʃæms** 'sun' vs **ʃːæms** 'the sun'. Another draws attention to Luganda, with pairs such as *gwa* 'fall', *ggwa* 'end', both pronounced as spelt.)
- In Iraqi Arabic the voiceless 'pharyngeal fricative' **ħ** and its voiced counterpart the *'ayn* **ʕ** can actually be aryepiglottic trills, according to John Esling – who proposes to write them **ʜ** and **ʢ** respectively. If I understood him correctly, he also claims that the 'glottal' stop is actually epilaryngeal. My knowledge of anatomy is not sufficient to enable me to judge these claims.

- In the Wu Chinese of Qingtian there is a tonal depression feature reminiscent of that of Zulu. The triggering consonants were presumably once voiced; but now, however, they are voiceless.
- In the Chinese of Qiyang there are complex contour tones that don't fit the usual tone templates. They are high- and low fall-rise-fall tones. On a five-point scale, where 5 is the highest, their pitch patterns are 4232 and 2142.
- The Swedish accent 2 (tone 2) is the marked one: it takes longer to process perceptually than does accent 1.
- Everyone now seems to call the intonation nucleus or tonic the 'focus'. Well yes: but as I see it the nuclear syllable actually marks only the word at the *end* of the whole focus domain. Among laboratory phoneticians the trendy term for the low, more or less level, pitch of the tail in intonation is now 'post-focus compression'.
- In some Australian English **el** has become **æl**, making *celery* a homophone of *salary* and *hell* a homophone of *Hal*.

The 2015 International Congress of Phonetic Sciences was held in Glasgow, Scotland. At the formal opening ceremony it was particularly nice to be welcomed in Scottish Gaelic as well as in English and Scots. The Gaelic greeting was displayed on the screen, followed by its IPA transcription: *Fàilte oirbh uile gu Baile Ghlaschu* **faːlʲtʲə ɣrʲev ulʲə kə palʲə ɣl̪asəxɔ**. As with Russian and Irish, to pronounce Scottish Gaelic accurately you need to be able to control secondary articulation ('broad', i.e. plain or velarized, vs 'slender', i.e. palatal or palatalized). As with Hindi, you also need to be able to control aspiration and the difference between dental and alveolar places of primary articulation, though in Scottish Gaelic the latter is relevant only in nasals and liquids.

20.4 Vowel Colour

What colour would you say ɛ was? And ɒ?

For many of us those questions may seem pretty fatuous. We're used to the metaphorical use of the term 'vowel colour' as a synonym of 'vowel quality': something to be described in terms of front/back, close/open (or high/low), and rounded/unrounded. But actual hues? Is this vowel pink, that one green? Meaningless questions, surely.

Not for everyone. Some people exhibit a neurological condition known as synaesthesia. For them, numbers or letters or days of the week are characterized by different hues. (It's not the same as phonaesthesia, which is to do with sound symbolism. Though I suppose the two are related.)

If there are synaesthetes who think that particular letters have particular colours (and apparently there are), what about speech sounds? Are they coloured, too? That's the subject of a piece of research carried out by Rob Drummond of Manchester Metropolitan University.

He conducted an online survey involving nearly 1,500 respondents and recordings of twelve English vowel sounds. Just 189 of the respondents were 'more than 50% sure' of their judgments of the colours of the sounds. Simplifying greatly, we can say that in general they judged close front vowels (those of English FLEECE and KIT) to be in the yellow-beige-green area, relatively open vowels (TRAP, BATH, STRUT, LOT, commA, NURSE) to be brownish, and non-open back vowels (THOUGHT, FOOT GOOSE) to be dark blue. Or thereabouts.

These judgements correspond to the traditional use of 'dark' to characterize a velarized ɫ and 'light' (or 'clear') a non-velarized l.

You can read the details at www.robdrummond.co.uk/wp-content/uploads/2011/06/baap2012.pdf.

20.5 False Friends

It must have been getting on for twenty years since I last visited Cardiff, and as you would imagine there had been various changes. One of them was linguistic: not only was the public signage now much more systematically bilingual than the half-hearted attempts I remembered from earlier visits, but all the announcements over the public address system at Cardiff Central station (that's Caerdydd Canolog) are now given first in Welsh, then in English.

As I was waiting on the station for my train back to London, there was a problem. Because of cows on the line at Sain Ffagan/St Fagans, trains coming from the west had to be diverted and my return journey was delayed by over half an hour. So I got to listen to a lot of bilingual announcements.

And I discovered a new Welsh-English false friend. *Mae'r trên hwn wedi'i ddileu*, said the announcer, or words to that effect. The Welsh word *dileu* is pronounced **dɪˈleɪ**, as near as dammit identically with the English word *delay*. Unthinkingly, I mentally translated 'this train has been delayed'.

But my mental translation was wrong. The meaning of *dileu* is not 'delay' but 'cancel' (in this context, that is – it can also mean 'get rid of, abolish, delete'). The announcement duly continued, in English, *This service has been cancelled*.

I would never have confused Welsh *dileu* and English *delay* in writing, only in speech. So this pair are what we might call 'phonetic false friends'.

All of us who have studied foreign languages are familiar with the notion of a false friend. For most of the 'faux amis' I remember from school French lessons, it was the written form on which we concentrated: *actuel* doesn't mean 'actual' (but rather 'present, current, topical'), though if you heard **aktɥɛl** you'd hardly think the speaker had said ˈæktʃuəl.

German *Gift*, on the other hand, is not only a written false friend of English *gift* but also a phonetic one, since both are pronounced **gɪft**. (The German word means 'poison'.)

I suppose you could say that French *choix* 'choice' is a phonetic false friend of English *schwa*, since both are pronounced ʃwɑ (with perhaps some leeway in the precise quality and length of the vowel). But no one would ever confuse them in writing.

Likewise, for us non-rhotic speakers German *Bahn* 'path, track, railway' is a phonetic false friend of English *barn*. But no one literate is going to confuse them. The word for 'hedgehog', *Igel* ˈiːɡl̩, is a similar item. It sound much like English 'eagle', which is a quite different animal. But on a nature walk you might easily catch sight of both of them.

What are the conditions under which we need to be on the lookout for phonetic-only false friends?

20.6 Polish Spoken Here

Excited about newly released data from the 2011 census showing that Polish is spoken by over half a million people in the United Kingdom, making it now our third most widely spoken language after English and Welsh, The Guardian newspaper launched into an editorial that started off full of phonetic technical terms ...

> With its mind-bending plosives, tongue-twisting fricatives and terrifying affricates, Polish is not the easiest of languages to master. Try saying Szczebrzeszyn (sounds a bit like shtebdeshin) for the merest hint of the challenges involved.

... before degenerating into ignorant silliness.

> To non-Polish speakers, just saying hello sounds more like a polite sneeze than a greeting, while the combination of z with almost every other consonant creates a palette of snuffles that can be distinguished only with the most diligent study.

Why Polish plosives should be 'mind-bending' when English ones are presumably not is far from clear. For many NNSs I suspect that the English fricative system, with its unfamiliar θ and ð, is at least as 'tongue-twisting' as the Polish system with its unfamiliar **x, ɕ** and **ʑ**.

But I cannot help suspecting that is not the sounds of Polish that seem full of 'terrifying' 'challenges' so much as the unfamiliar orthographic conventions. The spellings *cz, rz, sz*, far from 'creating' a palette of snuffles, are merely unfamiliar ways of spelling sounds very similar to those we spell in English inconsistently with *ch* or *tch* (as in *chop* and *catch*) for the first, with *s, z,* or *g* (as in *vision, seizure*, and *beige*) for the second, and with *sh, ti, ssi* or various other possibilities (as in *shop, position, passion, ocean, sugar*, etc) for the third. OK, the Polish **tʂ, ʐ, ʂ** sound a bit 'darker' than English **tʃ, ʒ, ʃ**, being somewhat more retroflex and less palatal; but that needn't worry us.

The town of Szczebrzeszyn **ʂtʂɛˈbʐɛʂin** features in the longer version of a famous tongue-twister that Poles always try to get foreigners to perform: *chrząszcz brzmi w trzcinie* 'a beetle is buzzing in the reed(s)', **xʂɔ̃wʂtʂ bʐmi ftʂtɕiɲɛ**, sometimes extended with *w Szczebrzeszynie* 'in Szczebrzeszyn' **fʂtʂɛbʐɛˈʂiɲɛ**.

I leave it to you to decide whether or not the Polish for 'hello', *cześć* **tʂɛɕtɕ**, 'sounds like a polite sneeze'.

21 Postscript

21.1 Skills Now Useless

Time marches on, and some of the skills I learnt as a small child are now useless. I am thinking in particular of those relating to the pounds-shillings-and-pence currency we had in Britain before decimalization in 1971.

Adding, subtracting, multiplying, and dividing sums of money was quite complicated in those days. And there were no calculators to help us.

There were twelve pence in a shilling, twenty shillings to a pound. Fivepence was written *5d* and pronounced ˈfaɪfpəns (note the irregular voicing assimilation and the weakening of *-pence*). Multiplying it by two was straightforward: 10d ˈtenpəns (or usually ˈtempəns). Multiplying it by three, however, gave you one shilling and threepence, written 1s 3d or more usually 1/3 ˈwʌn ən ˈθriː. Threepence on its own, however, was pronounced ˈθrepəns or ˈθrʌpəns.

The coins I would have in my pocket as a boy would probably include a halfpenny ˈheɪpni (½d), a penny, a threepenny bit ˈθrepni ˈbɪt (3d), a sixpenny ˈsɪkspəni piece or sixpence ˈsɪkspəns (6d), also known as a tanner, a shilling piece (1/-), a florin ˈflɒrɪn worth 2/-, sometimes called a two bob bit, and a half-crown ˈhɑːf ˈkraʊn, worth 2s 6d, 2/6 ˈhɑːf ə ˈkraʊn or ˈtuː ən ˈsɪks,. By the time I moved on from primary school, the farthing ˈfɑːðɪŋ (¼d) had disappeared from general use, though before I even started school I can remember my mother sending me to the shop for a small loaf that cost fourpence three-farthings (4¾d).

Two half-crowns made five bob (5/-), and eight half-crowns made a pound. Elevenpence times three made 2s 9d. 'Come on, boy', my prep school maths master might say, 'how much is £1 divided by three? And by eight?' (Answers: 6s 8d and 2s 6d.). What's 3d divided by two? (1½d, that is a penny halfpenny ˈheɪpni or three halfpence ˈheɪpəns.)

My grandfather would send a gift of a ten-shilling note (or a postal order for ten shillings), with an instruction that I should divide it with my brothers proportionately to our respective ages in years. In my thank-you letter of reply I had to set out my calculations.

Postage for an ordinary letter was 2½d ˈtʌpəns ˈheɪpni, so for it you needed a 2½d stamp (or you could use some combination of 2d ˈtʌp(ə)ni, 1d ˈpeni and ½d ˈheɪpni stamps). Postage for a dozen letters would come to 2/6, obviously.

These feats of everyday arithmetic that I and my contemporaries learnt are no longer of any practical use.

The surname *Halfpenny*, despite having probably originated as a nickname for someone of little worth or short stature, is nevertheless pronounced (in the United Kingdom, at least) ˈhɑːfpəni.

After 1971, the short-lived decimal ½p was a half **piː** or half a **piː**. And while pre-decimal 2d was ˈtʌpəns, modern decimal 2p is two **pens** or, more usually, two **piː**.

21.2 Memory

One of the things I most regret about growing older is the decline in my ability to memorize things. Not to boast, but between the ages of 10 and 18 I somehow committed to memory great swathes of Latin and Greek morphology (or Accidence, as it was then known – declensions and conjugations, regular and irregular), not to mention mathematical formulae, geometrical proofs, historical dates, French verbs and vocabulary, how to read music, and I suppose well over ten thousand additional English words with their spellings and meanings. That was mainly through formal lessons in school. On my own I taught myself a limited amount of Italian, the Cyrillic alphabet, thousands of Gregg shorthand outlines, and to play the melodeon. To add to school-generated conversational fluency in French, I acquired rather better privately-acquired fluency in German and Esperanto.

You want to know the value of pi? No problem. What the sine of an angle is? How to calculate the area of a circle? Solving quadratic equations? The lyrics of every pop song from the early fifties? Of course. Once learnt, always remembered. And scores of square dances, country dances, and Scottish dances.

Not any more. Now I struggle just to try and memorize a paltry hundred kana symbols or a few lines of song for the choir. Learnt today, gone tomorrow. What makes it especially galling is that so much of this memorizing in my youth was effortless and unplanned. No one <u>made</u> me learn the words of Doris Day's *The Deadwood Stage*. I didn't even <u>try</u> to learn them. They just came.

I suppose the period of effortless learning extended to my undergraduate and postgraduate years. I do not recall having to make any particular effort to memorize a hundred-plus phonetic symbols. My teacher or my book told me about them: I listened and read, and from then on I knew them. (However I do have to admit that as an undergraduate I failed to acquire anything more than a superficial acquaintance with Sanskrit morphology and the Devanāgarī to write it with. So by then motivation must have been a factor: Sanskrit wasn't part of the examination.)

Now I can't even remember the Hebrew and Arabic alphabets without checking. That's because I didn't attempt to learn them till later in life. I even struggle with Japanese kana, not to mention Chinese characters. I will never be able to read Georgian or Armenian, Bengali or Thai.

21.3 Letter to My 16-Year-Old Self

I have been reading *Dear Me: a Letter to My Sixteen-Year-Old Self*, edited by Joseph Galliano (Simon & Schuster 2009). In this book various well-known public figures offer advice to their teenage selves.

Inspired by these examples, here is my own letter to myself as a sixteen-year-old.

Dear John,

I know you are still a bit worried about whether you did the right thing in choosing to specialize in Greek two years ago rather than in Spanish or in Science. Your best subjects at age 14 were French and maths; but you couldn't combine these after that, so you have now entered the Classical Sixth. Don't worry: your destiny is to become a phonetician. As it is, you will reach this destination through a degree in classics, but you could equally well have got there via modern languages and linguistics or via physics, mathematics and signal processing.

One thing: twenty years or so from now you will be gradually losing your present remarkable skill at language learning – your ability to master enormous amounts of foreign-language grammar and vocabulary with ease and enjoyment. (I won't add 'effortlessly', because I know you work hard at it.) Make the most of this ability while you still have it. This is the year you take A levels in Latin and Greek, and you have just become intrigued with Esperanto. Stick with these (you will), but try and find a way to master some or all of Old English, Spanish, Arabic, Russian, Chinese and Japanese before you reach thirty-five (unfortunately, you won't, though you will manage to learn Welsh to a decent standard). Keep up your French and learn some more Italian and some modern Greek (you won't really do this as well as you might). Seize the marvellous opportunity your parents will shortly offer you to learn German by living for a time with a German family (you will). Seize every opportunity to travel that comes your way (you will, starting with when you return from Germany: from then on you'll travel abroad every year of your life).

You're already full of adolescent fervour about equal rights for people of every race and of indignation about racial discrimination. Stick with it. You may not know any black people now, but soon they'll be an important part of your life. Before you die, not only the South Africans but also the Americans will elect a black president!

I don't have to tell you never to take up smoking, because it's something that already disgusts you.

Don't be conceited, and try not to be smug.

Don't worry about being no good at sports. Years from now, when many of the First XI have grown fat and lost their hair, you will discover an ability to do distance running. The first time you cross the finishing line of the London

Marathon you will feel a surge of pride even greater than you did on getting your PhD. As you know, it's yourself you have to beat, not other people.

Don't worry about sex. Most of the other boys at school are interested in girls, but you know you aren't. Have fun while you are young (even though at the moment it's still illegal for you to do what comes naturally to you in this connection). When you are twenty-nine you will meet a man whom you will love and who will love you, and the two of you will spend the rest of your lives together. Decades later, when the UK no longer condemns such relationships but on the contrary makes it possible for people to celebrate them publicly, you and he will become Civil Partners, with the same legal rights as a married couple. Before you die, you will even have the option of converting your civil partnership into a marriage. You may find this difficult to believe now, in 1955, but it's going to happen. Lucky you.

Yes, do realize how very lucky in life you are. You come from a close and happy family. You have talented parents who love each other and love you and encourage you. You take all this for granted. It is only later that you find that not all families are like that.

You are lucky in that you are attending an excellent school and that you find school work easy and can generally sail through exams. Continue to channel your excess intellectual energy into reading widely and learning new things (but I don't have to tell you that).

You are lucky to live in a country which despite the wartime (and post-war) austerity you grew up with is relatively prosperous and becoming more so, a country where no one starves, and where our National Health Service means that no one has to worry about finding the money to pay for health care.

You are also lucky in being a native speaker of English, a language which a lot of people around the world want to learn. This will make your ability to talk and write knowledgeably about its pronunciation very useful (even if teaching English is not the main thing that interests you).

Don't worry so much. It doesn't matter if your fellow pupils think you're a swot and if you're not very popular among them. It's all going to work out OK.

Love
John, sixty years on.

Index of Words

Acre, 50
Acrefair, 51
adhere, 77
aged, 21
agrément, 55
alleged, 22
anemone, 18
antimony, 19, 25, 26
Arnos Grove, 46
Ashtabula, 48
awry, 88

bedroom, 68
Beguildy, 51
Bessacarr, 45
Billerica, 49
bombardier, 32
Breughel, 40

canine, 27
Caol, 46
Castleford, 48
choisya, 3
Claughton, 45
clothes, 151
Coetzee, 40
Cologne, 54
comfortable, 151
conch, 11
Corinth, 156
country, 155

deteriorate, 83
diamond, 24

epergne, 25
epitome, 87
Eugenie, 38
evening, 151
exist, 65

fuchsia, 3

Gabriel, 36
Gateacre, 51
ginkgo, 56
Glaswegian, 35
Glis glis, 175
Grasmere, 48
gypsophila, 3

ha'p'orth, 23
Harrovian, 34
Hull, 47

idea, 151
Israel, 31

jewellery, 17

keirin, 9
Kim Jong-un, 40
Kittitian, 34
Kraków, 53
kumquat, 12

L'Aquila, 52
Laocoön, 32
Liebestod, 57
lychee, 14

Machynlleth, 50
Maghull, 43
mandragora, 20
mayor, 8
McElderry, 37
metamorphosis, 28
Munich, 54

naïve, 31
netsuke, 5
Newcastle, 48
nth, 18

obstruent, 16

particular, 151
Peabody, 49
Penge, 49
physalis, 15
Piccadilly, 50
pinot grigio, 55
Pontcysyllte, 44
Poznań, 53
prevalent, 174

quasi-, 20
Quincy, 49

reboant, 16
Redcar, 45
remuneration, 18
rowlock, 16

saint, 29
sandwich, 73
seismic, 19
Sentamu, 38
Sharapova, 58

Singaporean, 174
Slaugham, 45
sojourn, 19
southern, 155
speleothem, 4
stalactite, 4
stalagmite, 4
synod, 17
Szechuan, 52

Talacre, 51
than, 22

Ulysses, 33
Upholland, 47

Voldemort, 41

Wadeford, 49
wardrobe, 68
weigela, 3
Wigan, 47
Wrocław, 53

General Index

Afrikaans, 40
approximant, 52, 57, 75, 86, 111, 112, 114, 116, 121, 125, 126, 141, 150, 152
Arabic, 26, 50, 91, 99, 107, 118, 125, 133, 137, 151, 152, 199, 205, 206
aspiration, 68, 69, 108, 115, 126, 127, 141, 150, 200
assimilation, 30, 76, 82, 143, 156, 160, 199, 204

Barbados, 4, 168
Berber, 199
Boris Johnson, 36

Cantonese, 12, 14, 66, 70, 139
cardinal vowel, 119, 135, 136
Catalan, 140
Chinese, 14, 35, 52, 56, 57, 71, 75, 85, 86, 94, 105, 114, 118, 142, 187, 199, 200, 205, 206
Classical Greek, 91
click, 66, 107, 121, 140, 145
contrastive focus, 178

daisywheel, 196
Daniel Jones, 14, 17, 19, 26, 28, 38, 67, 70, 71, 77, 113, 119, 129, 132, 135, 136, 142, 160, 162, 164, 165
David Rosewarne, 165
depressor, 133, 143, 144
digraph, 19, 90, 91, 93, 94, 102, 140
Dinka, 138
dot-matrix, 197
Dutch, 39, 40, 102, 111, 133, 137

ejective, 120, 121, 132, 133
elision, 30, 75, 80, 81, 82
Esperanto, 61, 195, 205, 206
Estuary English, 165, 166, 167

Farsi, 112
Flemish, 39, 40
Fred Cassidy, 170

geminate, 70
German, 3, 7, 14, 20, 32, 36, 40, 53, 54, 57, 58, 59, 60, 61, 62, 91, 101, 102, 106, 111, 115, 118, 119, 133, 135, 136, 137, 139, 160, 161, 195, 202, 205, 206
glottal stop, 66, 108, 129, 130, 137, 138, 148, 167
golfball, 196
Greek, 4, 11, 15, 17, 20, 24, 26, 28, 32, 33, 38, 50, 61, 62, 80, 81, 82, 83, 87, 88, 89, 91, 92, 101, 114, 119, 145, 150, 155, 156, 175, 205, 206
Gujarati, 147

Hebrew, 31, 50, 91, 125, 133, 138, 199, 205
Heschl's gyrus, 192
hiatus, 80
Hmong, 147
hymns, 28, 29
hypercorrection, 160

implosive, 120, 130, 131, 132, 144
intrusive r, 31, 157
Italian, 32, 37, 41, 52, 53, 55, 56, 57, 70, 81, 84, 95, 96, 119, 134, 139, 140, 161, 205, 206

Jamaican, 24, 160, 169, 170, 194
Japanese, 5, 6, 9, 14, 15, 56, 59, 66, 73, 88, 99, 105, 106, 109, 119, 147, 172, 199, 205, 206
Joanna Przedlacka, 166
juncture, 67

Korean, 41, 105, 106, 115, 199

lateral fricative, 11, 118, 121, 140, 141, 142, 150
Latin, 11, 17, 19, 20, 21, 24, 26, 27, 28, 31, 32, 33, 34, 38, 44, 53, 56, 60, 61, 62, 77, 80, 81, 88, 89, 91, 92, 96, 99, 101, 103, 106, 107, 112, 140, 146, 173, 175, 205, 206
Luganda, 138

Modern Greek, 20, 82, 146, 155
Montserrat, 37, 43, 164, 165, 169, 170, 171

Ndjuka, 194
Nivkh, 138

O'Connor, 120

210

palatoalveolar, 90, 91, 93, 153, 165
phonetic alphabet, 105
Plosives, 69
Polari, 4
Polish, 40, 52, 53, 57, 59, 61, 62, 83, 91, 119, 142, 143, 145, 146, 151, 161, 202, 203
Portuguese, 139, 140

release, 9, 66, 69, 70, 71, 72, 87, 126, 127, 128, 129, 130, 132, 141, 145, 146, 148, 150
respelling, 85, 96, 105, 114
Robert Bridges, 162
Russian, 17, 58, 61, 62, 88, 90, 93, 99, 111, 137, 142, 143, 200, 206

Scottish Gaelic, 200
Scouse, 49, 163, 164
Sindhi, 131
siSwati, 133
slumming, 160
Spanish, 32, 34, 57, 60, 61, 62, 86, 87, 94, 102, 112, 114, 119, 126, 127, 134, 139, 140, 147, 148, 149, 150, 161, 179, 180, 206
spelling pronunciation, 7, 11, 13, 14, 16, 53, 77, 81, 88, 95, 96
stranding, 23, 153

stress shift, 50
strong form, 23, 29, 67, 73, 152, 153
Swedish, 3, 40, 100, 111, 113, 137, 200
syllabic consonant, 30, 77, 109

transcription, xi, 6, 65, 80, 93, 99, 108, 112, 114, 116, 142, 162, 166, 184, 195, 200
trill, 111, 112, 113, 128, 134, 135
Twi, 169
typewriter, 195

Unicode, 116, 117, 118, 129, 199
unreleased, 66, 70, 71, 72, 109, 128, 129, 130, 182

Vietnamese, 138
VOT, 126, 127

weak form, 22, 23, 30, 67, 73, 153
Welsh, 11, 44, 49, 50, 51, 101, 102, 133, 139, 140, 141, 150, 164, 195, 201, 202, 206

Xhosa, 91, 131, 138, 140

Zulu, 11, 88, 91, 104, 131, 133, 138, 140, 142, 143, 144, 147, 200